Edited by

WILLIAM MILLER &
D. STEPHEN ROCKWOOD

The Scarecrow Press, Inc.
Metuchen, N.J., & London
1981

COLLEGE LIBRARIANSHIP

14400

Library of Congress Cataloging in Publication Data
Main entry under title:

College librarianship.

   1. Libraries, University and college--United States--
Addresses, essays, lectures. 2. Library education--
United States--Addresses, essays, lectures. I. Miller,
William, 1947-   II. Rockwood, D. Stephen.
Z675.U5C6455   027.7'0973   80-25546
ISBN 0-8108-1383-1

ACKNOWLEDGMENTS

"Collection Development from a College Perspective," by William Miller and D. Stephen Rockwood, and "Collection Development from a College Perspective: A Comment and a Response," by William Miller and Evan L Farber, are reprinted, slightly revised, from College & Research Libraries 40 (July 1979): 318-28, by permission of the authors and the American Library Association, copyright © 1979.

CONTENTS

iv

v

INTRODUCTION

As a group college libraries are an important part of the American academic scene, but little is known about them or about how they are run. For some reason the journals that cover academic librarianship concentrate most heavily on universities, relegating college libraries to the background. This volume represents an attempt both to broaden our knowledge of smaller academic libraries and to aid all of those librarians who are struggling to provide the best possible service in today's colleges.

Originally we intended this volume to be simply a "how-to" guide for the college librarian. As we researched the topic, however, we found that something more was needed. So little is known about college libraries that we felt the necessity to broaden our scope and to include comparative and theoretical articles that would provide a sense of where the college library now stands and where it is going. The combination of theory and practice makes this an appropriate volume for both the beginning and the experienced college librarian.

In soliciting and selecting contributions for this collection we operated on the assumption that the college library is much more than a small version of the university library. We believe, along with Jacques Barzun, that

> the subjects of learning underlies [sic] the subjects of information. You can forget the details of history or chemistry and have gained immense profit from learning them, because by learning them you

1

have become a different being, but forget the details of real-estate management or ice-cream making and you have nothing [The American University
(Harper & Row, 1978), p. 217].

The college library, physically and financially unable to gather and store all of the information that students could use,
must concentrate on furthering the educational process by
teaching research skills and making students aware of the
universe of informational resources available. This is not to
say that the college library should not attempt to gather
stores of information, but rather that it must selectively
gather the informational materials that best facilitate the educational process. Since the college library can never acquire
everything, it should then aspire to the acquisition of the most
useful things. This idea, perhaps more than any other, uni-
fies the essays in this collection.

The articles themselves are varied in subject and
methodology. Taken together, they provide a good picture of
today's American college library, and of current methodologies
used to study these institutions. "A Survey of Libraries in
American Four-Year Colleges," by Dennis Reynolds, will
enable librarians to gain some knowledge of how their libraries stack up against a representative sampling of college
libraries, but it also underscores the diversity among small
college libraries. A knowledge of what one's peer institutions
are doing can be invaluable; this survey provides a quick
tabular overview of and introduction to the American college
library today.

Peter Dollard's introductory overview is, by contrast,
highly theoretical. In "A Paradigm for College Libraries"
Dollard attempts to delineate the philosophical distinctions
between the college and other kinds of libraries--school, university, state, and public--in order to arrive at a better notion of what the college library is. Finally, Dollard considers the college library in terms of goals, access, patrons
served, laboratory function, and corporate identity.

George C. Newman's "Budgetary Trends in Small Private Liberal Arts College Libraries" is another survey that
contains much potentially valuable information. Newman examines the budgets of thirty-two Ohio college libraries for
the years between 1966-67 and 1977-78 and reaches some interesting conclusions about both the decline in real-dollar
purchasing power of the libraries and the ways that the decline will affect college libraries in the future.

Perhaps the most difficult problem facing the college librarian today is administration. As financial resources shrink under inflationary pressure, librarians must direct more and more attention toward maximizing the effect of every dollar spent. Susan Lee's "A Modest Management Approach" presents a planning strategy designed to improve the return on the college library's resources by concentrating on the things that a small college library can do best.

Librarians not only manage money, they manage people, and H. Palmer Hall addresses himself to "Personnel Administration in the College Library. " Noting that personnel relations are actually human relations, Hall argues that "good human relations" are essential to college library administration. He advocates a warm, hands-on approach to personnel for the college librarian as the only system effective in the small-college environment.

Another aspect of personnel management in the college library consists of conforming to what sometimes seems a bewildering array of laws dealing with hiring, promotion, and other employment practices. Jeniece Guy of the ALA's Office for Library Personnel Resources explains employment laws as they apply to college libraries in "Equal Employment Opportunity and the College Library Administrator. " Guy also discusses how librarians can ensure that their institutions avoid running afoul of these laws, and their impact upon libraries. As librarians who have witnessed at firsthand the traumatic and divisive effects a discrimination complaint can have on a library staff, we believe that familiarity with the material in Guy's article may enable librarians to avoid not only legal trouble, but unnecessary staff problems.

As Charles Maurer points out in "Close Encounters of Diverse Kinds: A Management Panorama for the Director of the Smaller College Library, " the job of the library director is one of the most difficult on campus. Maurer examines the director's job in a light-hearted, but certainly not light-headed, manner. This article, more than anything that we have ever read, illuminates the condition of the college library director.

Management of the college archives is a difficult task, one for which few college librarians are trained. Sister Martha Counihan's "The Establishment of an Archives in a Small College Library" discusses the role of the college archives and is an extensive guide to any librarian faced with establishing, maintaining, or revamping an archives collection.

Faculty status for college librarians has been a major issue for many years. Unfortunately, as William Miller demonstrates in "Faculty Status in the College Library," librarians disagree not only on the need for faculty status but also on what it actually is. Miller clarifies the murky state of affairs and raises questions about the need for, and desirability of, universal faculty status.

Sound collection-development practices are essential if a college library is to fulfill its function of serving the academic community. William Miller and D. Stephen Rockwood's article on "Collection Development from a College Perspective" provides guidance to the college librarian who must of necessity collect very carefully in today's tight fiscal environment. Miller and Rockwood define the student as the primary user for whom colleges should collect, and base their decisions on this assumption. A lively interchange between Miller and Evan L. Farber, which follows this piece, clarifies such issues as whether college libraries should subscribe to foreign-language periodicals.

In addition to selecting material, the acquisitions librarian can help to shape the collection through decisions regarding original ordering, replacement, format, and gifts. Walter Hogan compares "Acquisitions in College and University Libraries" and demonstrates that the college acquisitions librarian's ability to participate in the full range of library activities represents both a great opportunity and a great responsibility. What the college librarian makes of this opportunity, Hogan concludes, determines whether the job is exciting and stimulating or boring and mechanical.

Marian Bishop looks at "The Challenge of Cataloging in the College Environment," and she draws many of the same conclusions about the job as Hogan drew in regard to acquisitions. Bishop notes that the college cataloger is close to both the collection and its users and thus has a chance to tailor the work to ensure maximum access to the collection. Although networking has increased standardization of cataloging among college libraries, Bishop believes that there is still a need for individuality in cataloging in college librarianship; she persuasively argues that the college cataloger, forced to balance the needs of local library patrons against the demands for standardization made by the network, has perhaps the hardest task of any academic cataloger.

Library instruction is becoming particularly important to college libraries, and Frances L. Hopkins has contributed a thoughtful article on the subject. As its title suggests, "User Instruction in the College Library: Origins, Prospects, and a Practical Program" is much more than a brief survey of the subject. Hopkins looks at the philosophy, history, and methods of user instruction; she also proposes an instructional program that is tailored to the college library.

Like user instruction, the development of media resources is changing the face of college librarianship. Dana Smith discusses "Media Resources in College Libraries as Facilitators of Higher Learning" and proposes that college libraries follow the lead of junior colleges in making nonprint materials an integral part of their collections. While Smith recognizes that nonprint materials are difficult to handle given traditional library organization, he contends that the problems are certainly surmountable and that the rewards of a sound media program far outweigh the effort necessary to overcome the difficulties.

Government Documents represent another insufficiently used resource in the college library, and Kathleen Heim and Marilyn Moody have examined a number of institutions to determine why this is so. Their article, "Government Documents in the College Library: The State of the Art," provides some important insights into how documents are used in colleges and draws some conclusions about how they should be handled and used. Heim and Moody's work should provide impetus to librarians to add these low-cost and potentially invaluable resources to their collections, and to make them an integral part of the working collection to which students have access.

The concluding article is an unusually long, and unusually brilliant, piece by Frazer G. Poole on planning the new library building or addition. We have heard numerous horror stories about new library buildings that were inappropriate, inefficient, or expensive to staff and operate. "Planning the College Library Building--Process and Problems" will guide the college librarian through the entire process of library planning to ensure that the new building is a boon instead of a bane to the college. However popular "no growth" theories become, some colleges will always be adding space, and librarians facing such additions will benefit greatly from Poole's advice.

6 • College Librarianship

We do not pretend that this book is either a complete guide to college librarianship or a complete examination of every aspect of the college library. We hope, however, that it will serve as a useful repository of information and as a spur to further research and study on a subject that has been ignored for too long.

A SURVEY OF LIBRARIES
IN AMERICAN FOUR-YEAR COLLEGES

Dennis Reynolds

Background

A theme that will be brought out in many of the essays in
this book is the lack of attention given to the college library
in the American library literature.   The steady flow of books,
articles, and even specialized journals devoted to the academic library maintains a strong focus on larger, research-
oriented university facilities.   Although there are characteristics common to all academic libraries regardless of their
size, there are important differences between the libraries
of a large university, a smaller four-year liberal arts institution, and a community college.   From personnel and staffing patterns through reference and technical services, the
operation and characteristics of college and community college libraries simply cannot always be described in terms
appropriate to the multimillion-volume university library that
is the focus of much of the literature.

Librarians who have worked at colleges are aware that
their libraries differ not only from their university counterparts but also from one another, in operation, organization,
and use.   The present paper is a report of a survey sent to
300 college libraries in the United States in late 1978 that attempted to gather data on characteristics of and issues pertinent to college libraries.   Rather than studying a particular
characteristic in great detail, the survey was designed to provide a broad base of general information.   In the end, it is

the more narrowly defined projects that will be the most beneficial to our understanding of the similarities and differences among college libraries; the present study was designed to provide a broader overview that might help to suggest areas for more detailed attention in the future.

Introduction

The survey was sent to 300 college libraries in the United States. This included virtually all libraries listed in the thirtieth edition of the American Library Directory that met all three of the following criteria:

(1) Located at an institution in which the highest degree conferred is the bachelor's.

(2) Located at an institution in which between 500 and 2,000 students are enrolled.

(3) Holdings of between 65,000 and 250,000 volumes, or between 55,000 and 225,000 titles in the event that the number of volumes was not specified.

Of the 300 questionnaires sent out, 178 were returned, for a response rate of 59.3 percent. Six surveys were returned unanswered with an explanation in most cases that the library had been absorbed by another library or that the information in the American Library Directory was inaccurate and the library did not fit the criteria outlined above. There were thus 172 usable responses. Because inclusion was defined on the basis of information three years old, enrollment in 1978 had exceeded 2,000 or fallen below 500 in a few cases, and in a few other instances limited graduate programs in a single discipline or two had been instituted since 1975. Because of the recency of these changes, responses from such libraries were still included in the tabulations.

Most of the information gathered in the survey may be broken down into three categories: (1) level of use; (2) extent of automation; and (3) characteristics of professional personnel. The results appear below in twenty-five tables, most of which are broken down for each of five different groups of libraries, according to size: (1) fewer than 80,000 volumes; (2) 80,000-99,000 volumes; (3) 100,000-124,000; (4) 125,000-174,000; and (5) 175,000 or more. For purposes of grouping libraries that reported their size by number of titles rather than by volumes, the number of titles reported was multiplied by 1. 2 to arrive at an estimated number of volumes.

All data appearing in the tables below are current as of Autumn 1978. For tables that indicate "Most Recent Year," data reported by libraries were from the most recent twelve-month period for which figures were available. In nearly all cases this twelve-month period was either July 1, 1977--June 30, 1978, or January 1, 1977--December 31, 1977.

1. RESPONDING LIBRARIES BY SIZE OF LIBRARY AND STUDENT ENROLLMENT

Size of Library (Vols.)	Number of Students at Institution						
	Less than 600	600-799	800-999	1000-1399	1400-1799	1800 & Over	Total
60,000-- 79,000	5	8	4	8	1	0	26
80,000-- 99,000	7	9	7	13	3	1	40
100,000--124,000	1	11	15	14	12	4	57
125,000--174,000	1	3	9	10	4	6	33
175,000 & Over	0	0	2	9	1	4	16
ALL LIBRARIES	14	31	37	54	21	15	172

2. PERIODICAL SUBSCRIPTIONS

Size of Library (Vols.)	# of Libraries Reporting	# of Periodical Subscriptions					Avg.	Median
		Less than 400	400-599	600-799	800-999	1000 & Over		
60,000-- 79,000	25	5	16	3	1	0	479	465
80,000-- 99,000	38	3	21	10	2	2	577	549
100,000--124,000	55	3	23	19	6	4	635	607
125,000--174,000	32	1	8	15	5	3	700	634
175,000 & Over	16	1	1	2	3	9	1076	1079
ALL LIBRARIES	166	13	69	49	17	18	630	600

3. STUDENT LOAN-PERIOD

Size of Library (Vols.)	# of Libraries Reporting	Loan Period					
		2 Wks.	3 Wks.	4 Wks. - 1 Mo.	Term	Other	
60,000-- 79,000	26	13	4	4	1	4	
80,000-- 99,000	40	18	10	5	2	5	
100,000--124,000	56	17	17	15	2	5	
125,000--174,000	33	9	8	5	6	5	
175,000 & Over	16	5	2	6	1	2	
ALL LIBRARIES	171	62	41	35	12	21	

4. FACULTY LOAN-PERIOD

Size of Library (Vols.)	# of Libraries Reporting	Loan Period			
		Less than Term	Term	Academic Year/ Year/Indefinite	Other
60,000-- 79,000	26	3	14	8	1
80,000-- 99,000	37	3	18	15	1
100,000--124,000	53	5	26	22	0
125,000--174,000	30	3	7	20	0
175,000 & Over	16	0	7	8	1
ALL LIBRARIES	162	14	72	73	3

5. HOME-USE CIRCULATION (Most Recent Year)

Size of Library (Vols.)	# of Libraries Reporting	# of Home-Use Circulations (in thousands)					Avg.	Median
		Less than 10	10-19	20-29	30-49	50 and Over		
60,000-- 79,000	24	7	14	1	0	2	17.0	13.7
80,000-- 99,000	36	5	19	9	1	2	18.3	14.6
100,000--124,000	50	5	25	14	5	1	20.8	18.0
125,000--174,000	32	0	9	16	4	3	26.5	23.0
175,000 & Over	16	0	4	2	6	4	39.0	37.0
ALL LIBRARIES	158	17	71	42	16	12	22.6	18.7

6. RESERVE-USE CIRCULATION (Most Recent Year)

Size of Library (Vols.)	# of Libraries Reporting	# of Reserve-Use Circulations (in thousands)					Avg.	Median
		Less than 5	5-9	10-19	20-29	30 and Over		
60,000-- 79,000	18	13	4	1	0	0	4.1	3.1
80,000-- 99,000	27	14	7	5	1	0	6.8	4.5
100,000--124,000	44	16	16	8	4	0	7.8	6.1
125,000--174,000	30	14	5	9	1	1	9.3	5.4
175,000 & Over	15	2	2	4	3	4	19.8	15.5
ALL LIBRARIES	134	59	34	27	9	5	8.8	5.5

7. INTERLIBRARY LOAN REQUESTS SUBMITTED (Most Recent Year)

Size of Library (Vols.)	# of Libraries Reporting	# of I.L.L. Requests Submitted				Avg.	Median
		0-99	100-299	300-999	1000 & Over		
60,000-- 79,000	22	5	9	5	3	362	219
80,000-- 99,000	37	16	14	7	0	183	112
100,000--124,000	56	18	18	14	6	453	157
125,000--174,000	33	6	11	9	7	693	251
175,000 & Over	15	0	1	6	8	1413	1100
ALL LIBRARIES	163	45	53	41	24	510	214

8. AVERAGE HOME-USE CIRCULATION PER STUDENT (Most Recent Year)
(total home-use circulation divided by # of students enrolled)

Size of Library (Vols.)	# of Libraries	Average # of Home-Use Circulations per Student					Avg.	Median
		Less than 10	10-19	20-29	30-39	50 and Over		
60,000-- 79,000	24	6	9	6	1	2	20.1	13.9
80,000-- 99,000	36	3	17	10	3	3	20.8	19.0
100,000--124,000	50	6	27	12	2	3	20.0	17.2
125,000--174,000	32	0	16	12	3	1	23.6	20.1
175,000 & Over	16	0	5	5	3	3	28.4	25.5
ALL LIBRARIES	158	15	74	45	12	12	21.8	18.7

9. AVERAGE RESERVE-USE CIRCULATION PER STUDENT (Most Recent Year)
(total reserve-use circulation divided by # of students enrolled)

Size of Library (Vols.)	# of Libraries	Average # of Reserve-Use Circulations per Student					Avg.	Median
		Less than 2.0	2.0-4.9	5.0-9.9	10.0-14.9	15.0 & Over		
60,000-- 79,000	18	5	5	6	1	1	5.0	4.5
80,000-- 99,000	27	3	10	4	7	3	8.3	5.1
100,000--124,000	44	7	10	16	6	5	7.4	5.7
125,000--174,000	30	2	12	9	5	2	7.2	5.1
175,000 & Over	15	1	2	5	2	5	12.5	9.3
ALL LIBRARIES	134	18	39	40	21	16	7.8	5.8

10. AVERAGE # OF INTERLIBRARY LOAN REQUESTS PER STUDENT (Most Recent Year)
(total # of I.L.L. requests divided by # of students enrolled)

Size of Library (Vols.)	# of Libraries Reporting	Average # of I.L.L. Requests per Student				Avg.	Median
		0.00-0.09	0.10-0.49	0.50-0.99	1.00 & Over		
60,000-- 79,000	22	4	9	6	3	0.47	0.25
80,000-- 99,000	37	15	19	2	1	0.23	0.11
100,000--124,000	56	16	28	5	7	0.40	0.18
125,000--174,000	33	8	16	3	6	0.58	0.27
175,000 & Over	15	0	6	3	6	1.05	0.69
ALL LIBRARIES	163	43	78	19	23	0.46	0.22

11. LIBRARIES ON OCLC

Size of Library (Vols.)	# of Libraries Reporting	# of Libraries on OCLC	# of Libraries not on OCLC	% of Libraries on OCLC
60,000-- 79,000	26	13	13	50.0%
80,000-- 99,000	40	23	17	57.5%
100,000--124,000	57	38	19	66.7%
125,000--174,000	33	23	10	69.7%
175,000 & Over	16	14	2	87.5%
ALL LIBRARIES	172	111	61	64.5%

12. % OF HOLDINGS ENTERED INTO OCLC

Size of Library (Vols.)	# of Libraries Reporting	% of Holdings Entered into OCLC				
		1%-9%	10%-24%	25%-49%	50%-74%	75%-100%
60,000-- 79,000	11	6	2	3	0	0
80,000-- 99,000	17	7	3	5	1	1
100,000--124,000	30	16	4	7	3	0
125,000--174,000	16	12	3	0	1	0
175,000 & Over	9	3	3	2	1	0
ALL LIBRARIES	83	44	15	17	6	1

13. AUTOMATED CIRCULATION SYSTEM

All 172 libraries answered the question as to whether or not it had an automated circulation system. 169 libraries did not have an automated system for circulation. Of the 3 libraries which did have an automated system, 2 were in-house and the other was a commercially available system.

14. AUTOMATED ACQUISITIONS SYSTEM

All 172 libraries also answered this question, and again 169 libraries reported not having an automated system, while 3 libraries did have an automated acquisitions system. These 3 libraries were all different libraries from those which had an automated circulation system.

15. ON-LINE BIBLIOGRAPHIC DATA BASES

Libraries Offering On-Line Bibliographic Data-Base Service

Size of Library (Vols.)	# of Libraries Reporting	Yes	No	% Yes
60,000-- 79,000	26	2	24	7.7%
80,000-- 99,000	40	2	38	5.0%
100,000--124,000	57	8	49	14.0%
125,000--174,000	33	3	30	9.1%
175,000 & Over	16	2	14	12.5%
ALL LIBRARIES	172	17	155*	9.9%

*Of these, 10 reported having arrangements with other libraries to provide this service for them.

Of the 17 libraries which responded yes, 7 reported that they charged patrons for the service, while the other 10 reported that they did not charge.

16. UNDERGRADUATE MAJORS

	% of Individuals in Each Position Who Have an Undergraduate Major in Corresponding Subject			
	Director	R.S./Ref.	T.S./Cat.	Total
Number of Individuals	153	130	118	401
Majors:				
LIBRARY SCIENCE	3.9%	2.3%	10.2%	5.2%
EDUCATION	15.7%	16.2%	18.6%	16.7%
HUMANITIES:				
English	30.1%	33.8%	26.3%	30.2%
Classics	4.6%	3.8%	1.7%	3.5%
French	2.0%	1.5%	0.8%	1.5%
Spanish	1.3%	0.8%	--	0.7%
German	--	0.8%	0.8%	0.5%
Russian	--	0.8%	0.8%	0.5%
General & Comparative Literature	0.7%	0.8%	4.2%	1.7%
Linguistics	1.3%	--	0.8%	0.7%
Philosophy	1.3%	2.3%	1.7%	1.7%
Religion, Theology	2.6%	2.3%	0.8%	2.0%
General Humanities	1.3%	1.5%	--	1.0%
TOTAL HUMANITIES	45.2%	48.6%	37.9%	44.0%

17. DEGREES IN LIBRARY SCIENCE

Position	# of Individuals for Whom Data Was Reported	Highest Degree in Library Science				
		None	B.A.	M.A.	6th Year	Ph.D.
Director	167	3.6%	1.8%	85.0%	1.8%	7.7%
Reader Services/Reference	150	6.7%	0.7%	90.6%	2.0%	0.0%
Technical Services/Catalog	149	12.8%	2.7%	83.8%	0.7%	0.0%

18. ADVANCED SUBJECT DEGREES: MASTER'S DEGREES

DIRECTORS

Number Reporting: 154
Number with Subject M.A.'s: 64 (41.6% of total)

Subject:	# with M.A.'s:
History	26
English	15
Religion, Theology	8
Education	3
Political Science	3

READER SERVICES/REFERENCE AND TECHNICAL SERVICES/CATALOGER POSITIONS (COMBINED)

Number Reporting: 248 (combined)
Number with Subject M.A.'s: 59 (23.8% of total)

Subject:	# with M.A.'s:
English	13
History	11
Religion, Theology	9
Education	6
Music	4

Classics   2
Educational Media   2

1 each for: Biology, French, International Relations, Music, Philosophy, Psychology, Theatre & Drama

Comparative Literature 3
American Studies   2
Sociology   2

1 each for: Asian Studies, Business, Economics, Educational Media, French, International Relations, Journalism, Linguistics, Home Economics

19. ADVANCED SUBJECT DEGREES: DOCTORATES

DIRECTORS

Number Reporting: 154
Number with Subject PhD's: 20 (13.0%)

Subjects: History, 7; English, 5; Education, 5; Relgion, Theology, 2; Public Administration, 1; Psychology, 1.

READER SERVICES/REFERENCE AND TECHNICAL SERVICES/CATALOGER POSITIONS (COMBINED)

Number Reporting: 238 (combined)
Number with Subject PhD's: 12 (4.8%)

Subjects: English, 5; History, 2; Education, 1; Classics, 1; Linguistics, 1; Music, 1; Religion, Theology, 1.

20. FACULTY STATUS: DIRECTORS

Size of Library (Vols.)	# of Libraries Reporting	Faculty Status: Directors		
		Yes	No	% Yes
60,000-- 79,000	25	20	5	80.0%
80,000-- 99,000	40	36	4	90.0%
100,000--124,000	52	46	6	88.5%
125,000--174,000	31	30	1	96.8%
175,000 & Over	16	15	1	93.8%
ALL LIBRARIES	164	147	17	89.6%

21. FACULTY STATUS: READER SERVICES/REFERENCE LIBRARIANS

Size of Library (Vols.)	# of Libraries Reporting	Faculty Status: R.S./Ref. Librns.		
		Yes	No	% Yes
60,000-- 79,000	20	15	5	75.0%
80,000-- 99,000	34	29	5	85.3%
100,000--124,000	44	33	11	75.0%
125,000--174,000	29	24	5	82.8%
175,000 & Over	16	8	8	50.0%
ALL LIBRARIES	143	109	34	76.2%

22. FACULTY STATUS: HEAD OF TECHNICAL SERVICES CATALOGERS

Size of Library (Vols.)	# of Libraries Reporting	Faculty Status: T.S./Cat. Librns.		
		Yes	No	% Yes
60,000-- 79,000	18	13	5	72.2%
80,000-- 99,000	30	24	6	80.0%
100,000--124,000	45	33	12	73.3%
125,000--174,000	29	23	6	79.3%
175,000 & Over	14	6	8	42.9%
ALL LIBRARIES	136	99	37	72.8%

23. NUMBER OF YEARS IN PRESENT LIBRARY: DIRECTORS

Size of Library (Vols.)	# of Libraries Reporting	Number of Years in Present Library						
		0-3	3-7	7-15	15-25	25 & Over	Avg.	Median
60,000-- 79,000	25	8	6	9	2	0	7.0	5.0
80,000-- 99,000	38	10	3	18	2	5	10.3	10.0
100,000--124,000	54	11	12	16	7	8	11.1	8.3
125,000--174,000	31	8	6	10	4	3	9.7	9.0
175,000 & Over	16	2	4	6	2	2	11.6	10.0
ALL LIBRARIES	164	39	31	59	17	18	10.1	9.0

24. NUMBER OF YEARS IN PRESENT LIBRARY: READER SERVICES/REFERENCE LIBRARIAN

Size of Library (Vols.)	# of Libraries Reporting	Number of Years in Present Library					Avg.	Median
		0-3	3-7	7-15	15-25	25 & Over		
60,000-- 79,000	18	7	5	4	1	1	6.2	4.0
80,000-- 99,000	34	13	10	7	4	0	5.8	4.0
100,000--124,000	51	9	15	21	6	0	7.4	7.0
125,000--174,000	30	8	8	10	3	1	7.4	6.5
175,000 & Over	19*	7	6	4	1	1	7.0	5.0
ALL LIBRARIES	152	44	44	46	15	3	6.9	5.0

*Some libraries in this size group reported data for more than one individual in this position.

25. NUMBER OF YEARS IN PRESENT LIBRARY: TECHNICAL SERVICES LIBRARIAN/CATALOGER

Size of Library (Vols.)	# of Libraries Reporting	Number of Years in Present Library					Avg.	Median
		0-3	3-7	7-15	15-25	25 & Over		
60,000-- 79,000	18	6	4	6	2	0	7.2	5.0
80,000-- 99,000	32	7	9	14	2	0	7.3	7.0
100,000--124,000	47	12	9	20	4	2	7.7	7.0
125,000--174,000	31	4	6	14	4	3	10.2	9.0
175,000 & Over	17*	4	3	8	2	0	7.9	8.0
ALL LIBRARIES	145	33	31	62	14	5	8.1	8.0

*One of the libraries in this size group reported data for more than one individual in this position.

Discussion

Tables 1 through 4 present figures for some features that do not fit conveniently into any of the three categories described in later sections. Table 1 is a profile of responding libraries by size of library and student enrollment. A perusal of this table immediately suggests that while the criteria for inclusion of libraries in this study were fairly narrowly defined, the criteria were broad enough to merit the use of several size categories in the presentation of results.

Table 2 presents data concerning the number of periodical subscriptions in the 166 libraries that provided this information. The overall average was 630 subscriptions, with a median of 600. Expectedly, libraries in the larger-size categories tended to subscribe to more titles than did libraries in the smaller-size categories. However, it is also evident that there was considerable variation within each size category. At the extremes, two libraries with fewer than 100,000 volumes subscribed to more than 1,000 periodical titles, while one library with more than 175,000 volumes subscribed to only 200. The overall average and general trend suggest that college libraries still place an emphasis on purchasing books and other media, with a core of periodicals geared largely to the undergraduate educational, as opposed to research, role of the college library.

One of the questions on the survey asked for information on loan periods for books for both students and faculty, and these results are presented in Tables 3 and 4, respectively. The most common student loan period was two weeks, which was in practice in more than one-third of the responding libraries, and another one-fourth of the libraries had a three-week student loan period. Only twelve responding libraries reported a full-term loan period of a quarter or semester, and six of these were in libraries of between 125,000 and 174,000 volumes.

As shown in Table 4, the picture for faculty loan periods is quite different. Only fourteen of the 162 libraries that responded to this question indicated a faculty loan period of less than a full term. The remaining libraries were split about evenly between full-term loans and loans for a full academic year or longer. While it appears that shorter loan periods for students have taken hold in the college library, the same certainly cannot be said for faculty loan periods.

Library Use. Tables 5 through 10 present reports of three types of library use: home-use circulation, reserve-use circulation, and interlibrary loan. It should be noted that Tables 5, 6, and 7 present results in absolute numbers for these three types of library use. These can be misleading in that they do not take account of the size of the "user population" in each library. An attempt to account for this feature is made in Tables 8, 9, and 10. A "per student" calculation was made for home-use circulation, reserve-use circulation, and interlibrary loan requests at each institution, and these values form the basis for categorizing the results in Tables 8, 9, and 10. Though student enrollment cannot be strictly equated with user population, this measure does provide a more equitable means of presenting the results. A second point concerning the library-use tables is the matter of average values. Because a small number of extreme values can greatly affect the average number for a larger group, the more important measure in examining the tables on library use in this study is the median, which represents the "middle value," with half the libraries in a group exceeding that value and the other half falling under it.

There was an enormous range of responses to the questions concerning each of these three types of library use. Two libraries had less than three home-use circulations per student per year, while at the other end of the spectrum three libraries had a per-student average exceeding eighty per year. The majority of libraries in all size categories had an average per-student figure falling between ten and thirty, with an overall median figure of just under nineteen. The overall median for reserve-use circulation was slightly less than six per student per year, but here again there was tremendous variety among the responses: a number of libraries had less than one reserve-use circulation per student per year, but there were also several libraries that had more than twenty per student per year. Perhaps the greatest variability in library-use statistics was in the realm of interlibrary loan requests submitted. There were fifteen libraries that reported a total of fewer than twenty-five interlibrary loan requests submitted by students and faculty during an entire year. On the other hand, there were also fifteen libraries that reported more than 1,500 requests submitted. In terms of requests submitted per student, the figures ranged from virtually zero to more than four per student per year.

Tables 5 through 10 suggest a very general trend for library-use figures per student to be larger in the larger-library groups, but this is only a general trend, with considerable variation. The tables in the Appendix do not address the question of the interrelationships among the three types of library-use statistics. In order to examine this, a test of correlation was made between two sets of data: home-use circulation per student with reserve-use circulation per student, and home-use circulation per student with interlibrary loan requests per student. In neither case were the results entirely convincing toward a strong positive relationship. The correlation coefficient between home-use and reserve-use circulation per student was $r = .33$; while this is significant at the .01 level, it is not an extremely strong relationship. The libraries in this study that had a comparatively high home-use circulation per student did not necessarily also have a comparatively high reserve-use circulation per student, and vice versa. The correlation coefficient between home-use circulations per student and interlibrary loan requests per student was $r = .05$, a figure that is statistically insignificant and that suggests that no strong positive relationship exists between these two types of library use.

The wide variability of the figures reported above and the low correlations support the contention of college librarians that even within fairly narrow categories of "library type" there is a great deal of variation in library-use patterns. The level of integration of the library with the college classroom, the policies toward open and closed reserve, and the attitude toward interlibrary loan at the undergraduate level all contribute to this variation, and the figures for the three types of library use reported in this survey should be examined only with these other factors strongly in mind.

Library Automation. Another major part of the survey focused on several aspects of automation in college libraries. The results appear in Tables 11 through 15. Specifically, information was sought concerning the use of OCLC, automated circulation systems, automated acquisitions systems, and access to on-line bibliographic data-bases, such as Lockheed DIALOG, SDC ORBIT, BRS, and the New York Times Information Bank.

Of the 172 responding libraries, 111 (nearly 65 percent) were members of OCLC. The percentage of libraries belonging to OCLC definitely increased from the smaller- to

larger-library categories, but even in the smallest-size category of fewer than 80,000 volumes, OCLC membership was well represented (50 percent). Another question concerning OCLC was the extent to which libraries had entered their collection, including both by inputting new records into the data-base and by updating on already-existing OCLC master records. Eighty-three libraries provided an estimate of the items in their collection for which they had entered their holdings symbol into OCLC, and in forty-four cases the figure was less than 10 percent, while in only seven cases was it above 50 percent. It was not asked of each library whether it was actively engaged in a retrospective conversion project, but these figures strongly suggest that in most of the reporting libraries such projects are still in an incipient stage.

As for automated circulation and acquisition systems, only six libraries had one or the other, with three having a circulation system and three others having an acquisitions system. Considering the high percentage of responding libraries belonging to OCLC, it will be interesting to see the impact of the OCLC acquisitions subsystem on the latter figure, and the question of OCLC's future policy toward developing a circulation capability was still under consideration in 1980.

Only about 10 percent of the responding libraries had on-site access to bibliographic data-bases, such as Lockheed, SDC, and others, at the time this survey was taken in 1978. It is extremely probable that this figure has increased since that date. Several libraries indicated on the survey that they did not yet offer this service, but that they would begin to do so during calendar year 1979.

With the exception of OCLC, the level of automation in college libraries appears to have been relatively low in 1978. Probably the two factors most greatly contributing to this have been capitalization costs and the role of research in the college library. The introduction of OCLC simply would not have been possible in many libraries without the availability of Kellogg grants. Of the other three types of automation investigated, the one requiring the least capitalization is access to vendor data-bases, such as Lockheed, SDC, and BRS. However, for many college libraries the connect-hour expense is still cause for hesitation, especially given the undergraduate-education rather than long-term-research orientation of the college. For faculty and honors research many college libraries have found that arrangements can be made with larger institutions to conduct searches of the on-line systems. Nevertheless, more and more college libraries appear to be setting themselves up for on-site searching.

Professional Personnel. Several questions on the survey dealt with characteristics of professional personnel in college libraries: library degrees, faculty status, length of employment at the present institution, undergraduate majors, and advanced degrees in addition to or in fields other than library science. The results to these questions are presented in Tables 16 through 25.

As for the educational background of college librarians, Table 16 shows that the three largest disciplines of concentration at the undergraduate level were clearly English, history, and education. Nearly 70 percent of all directors, reader services/reference librarians, and technical services librarians/catalogers have an undergraduate background in at least one of these three areas. At the other end of the spectrum, only about 5 percent of those surveyed had an undergraduate major in any of the biological or physical sciences.

A very high percentage of people in each of the three positions have earned a degree in library science, as shown in Table 17. Of college library directors, only 3.6 percent did not have at least a Bachelor's degree in Library Science, and nearly 95 percent had a Master's degree or higher in Library Science. The figure pertaining to M.L.S. degrees for reader services/reference librarians was nearly as high, with nearly 93 percent having a library degree at the Master's or sixth-year levels. The position of technical services librarian/cataloger had a slightly smaller percentage, with about 84 percent having a Master's or sixth-year degree.

A somewhat surprising result was the level to which college librarians had received advanced degrees in addition to their library degree. As outlined in Tables 18 and 19, more than 40 percent of college library directors had Master's degrees in other fields, with 13 percent having doctorates in other fields. The equivalent figures for reader services/reference librarians and technical services librarians/catalogers were about 20 percent with a Master's and 5 percent with a doctorate. Once again, English, history, and education were among the strongest fields of concentration.

The question of faculty status seems to pervade all academic libraries, small or large. In the libraries surveyed here librarians in professional positions appear to have faculty status more often than not (Tables 20 through 22). Nearly 90 percent of the directors had been awarded faculty status, while the figures for the other two positions were in the vicinity of 75 percent. While the percentages are relatively stable across the library-size categories within this survey, it is interesting to note an exception to this for both reader services/reference librarians and technical services librarians/catalogers in college libraries of 175,000 or more volumes. In these settings only 50 percent of those in the former position and only about 43 percent in the latter had faculty status.

Tables 23 through 25 address the question of longevity of professional personnel in college libraries. At the time the survey was taken nearly 25 percent of the directors had been in their present library less than three years, while on the other hand more than 20 percent had been in their present library for at least fifteen years. The equivalent percentages for reader services/reference librarians were slightly under 30 percent and about 12 percent, and for technical services librarians/catalogers 23 percent and 13 percent. While there do appear to be some differences in longevity between the three positions, they are not large ones. That a combined percentage of about 25 percent in all three positions have been in their present library for less than three years does suggest a rather high degree of mobility, but it is also worth noting that nearly one-half of the individuals for whom figures were reported have been in their present library at least seven years.

Though there is certainly variability in the results presented in Tables 16 through 25, the results do suggest a few generalizations. Perhaps the most decisive of these are the importance of an advanced degree in Library Science for securing a professional position in the college library and the clear trend toward faculty status in all but the larger college libraries. The significant percentage of individuals having advanced degrees in fields in addition to the M. L. S. is also interesting. Though a question on teaching loads of college librarians was not asked in this survey, it is quite probable that many of those librarians with additional advanced degrees are teaching courses in academic disciplines in the college.

Conclusion

The results of this survey lend support to the idea that there is a great deal of diversity among college libraries in the United States.   The reasons behind the diversity are numerous and complex, and ultimately the best analyses of them will be qualitative, rather than quantitative.   One hopes that the results presented here will suggest areas of comparative inquiry and comment, and that they will better enable us to understand the processes at work in the American college library.

A PARADIGM FOR COLLEGE LIBRARIES

Peter Dollard

During a time of increasing fragmentation in the library profession it is important to reiterate at the outset that libraries of various types have enough commonalities that one may
discuss all libraries as though their essential activities were
the same. Differences exist among them because the stress
placed on a particular aspect of service varies from one kind
of library to another. One library might place most stress
on the quality of its collection, another on the rapidity with
which it can provide information to a user.

This article attempts to present a new paradigm for
the college library in the hope that a new approach will stimulate thinking about libraries generally. I intend to rework
some truisms and to combine those truisms with several new
elements. Part one will identify five features that distinguish
college libraries from other kinds of libraries. The second
part will then describe the working consequences of those
five characteristics. And last, both the paradigm and its
consequences will be related to the temperamental and intellectual characteristics that make some individuals more suited
to the profession than others.

Five Characteristics of the College Library

My paradigm includes five components: corporate status,
clientele, collection goals, bibliographic function, and laboratory role. We can begin by showing how this set of charac-

teristics enables us to describe college libraries as a distinct subset of libraries.

Corporate Status. Though it is conceivable for libraries to exist independently, normally they are established to meet the needs of some larger corporate entity, such as a city, government agency, corporation, society, or school. Libraries are one of several mechanisms for meeting those larger corporate ends. Some of these libraries belong to for-profit corporate bodies, which establish libraries because such facilities help maximize profits (directly or indirectly-- for example, by drawing in researchers), or set an appropriate tone, or assist from the public-relations point of view.

Academic libraries clearly are not required to justify themselves in terms of maximizing profits. Indeed, many college business managers regard with chagrin the seeming indifference to matters of expenditures/income they believe to be so characteristics of librarians. We can reduce considerably the number of libraries we must consider, then, simply by excluding the libraries of for-profit corporate bodies.

Clientele. Who uses the library and why?[1] We would all prefer those patrons who are driven by a thirst for knowledge and wisdom. Many library users are so driven, and one might argue that they are the bedrock upon which libraries stand. The fact is, however, that some people choose to enter libraries while others are required to do so. A reader might make frequent trips to a local public library to satisfy a heavy reading habit, or to "encourage" his or her children to read, or to gain status; a businessperson might find it helpful professionally to consult a public library's resources.

Such users are "inner-directed," in that they have chosen to go to a library as a means of meeting a personal need. They are quite distinct from, for example, the high school student who is sent by a teacher to a library to do a "library research paper." There are laws requiring that students attend high school, and the grading/diploma mechanism helps ensure that students meet classroom expectations. We can regard this latter group of library users as "other-directed," in that some other person is responsible for their presence in the library. Students who are required to use libraries are captive to a force outside themselves: academic librarians must deal routinely with such patrons.

Academic/school libraries clearly serve an other-directed captive clientele. At the same time, there are not-for-profit libraries whose clientele is inner-directed: government-agency libraries, state libraries, association libraries. Our classifying process, however, has enabled us to narrow our field of vision to that subset of libraries (1) which are parts of not-for-profit corporate entities, and (2) whose other-directed clientele is in some sense captive to that institution. These libraries are the school/academic libraries, which serve young people from kindergarten on through college.

There is a large degree of difference, of course, between the first grader and the post-orals Ph. D. candidate. Even the typical college student writing a freshman term paper is quite a different person to deal with from the Ph. D. candidate. After all, it's the rare Ph. D. candidate who would change a dissertation topic after ten minutes of fruitless fumbling in the Readers' Guide.

At some point in the spectrum of school/academic libraries these "captive" users simply cease to be other-directed. They internalize a set of values that makes their expectations of the library quite different from the experience they had in their earlier schooling. That change in the attitude of the clientele is accounted for more easily, however, by switching our focus to a review of collection goals.

Collection Goals. The "Alexandrian"[2] research library strives for comprehensiveness, aiming to acquire all materials pertinent to the most advanced levels of study in a wide range of disciplines. It does so in order to attract and to serve scholars. In fact, the university research library is almost an end in itself; it is a mechanism for the preservation and transmission of recorded knowledge. It is a vital social resource that is designed to be used by "inner-directed" scholars and researchers. In the real academic world scholars are captive to "publish or perish" values, but, at least to some extent, most university professors regard themselves as participants in the ongoing process of defining and refining our cultural and intellectual heritage. The research library is meant to meet the needs of these disinterested scholars and scholars-to-be, all of whom are devoted to increasing human knowlege. Its service to an other-directed undergraduate clientele should not obscure that primary mission. The research library is different from other academic/school libraries because its most important clientele is not captive.

Contrary to our initial feeling, then, the college library is to be grouped with the grade school library--both
belonging to not-for-profit institutions serving a captive
clientele--rather than with the research library. The college library, like the school library, makes no effort to develop comprehensive collections to serve leading scholars,
and while there have been attempts to do so, of course, it
is rarely a major mission of a college library. In sheer
size, college libraries of 150,000 volumes are far more akin
to high school libraries than to the multimillion-volume collections found in research institutions.

Bibliographic Access. Our feeling that grade school
libraries differ so much from college libraries is due to the
different roles the two play in relation to the provision of
bibliographic access. At the most elementary level, schools
do not presume that bibliographic access is required: picture
books for prereaders are simply made available. At the next
step there may be a card catalog, but there is also an assumption that most students will find what they want either by
browsing or by asking. At some level the card catalog becomes more important, encyclopedias are consulted, and even
an abridged Readers' Guide is brought into use. Few school
libraries ever go beyond such bibliographic aids. High school
seniors may be required to use more, but there is usually an
assumption that the school library is not obliged to stack its
shelves to meet such needs. Again, there is a spectrum on
which college libraries must be placed in relationship to university and school libraries. This time, however, the demarcation line is most clearly drawn at the school-library
end, since college libraries are more easily distinguished
from school libraries by their philosophy of good bibliographic access than by their collection goals.

At one end of this combined spectrum the school library provides a small collection of materials. As we move
along the line the size and depth of the collection grows and,
at the point that bibliographic access becomes important, we
have left behind school libraries and entered the range of
two-year, four-year, and small-university libraries. As we
move further along this spectrum the two-year colleges drop
off first, and then, as we move toward the point where the
collection becomes an end in itself, the four-year colleges
and small universities drop off. There is gradual change
from one end to the other with two clear points of demarcation: collection goals and bibliographic access.

The College Library's Role as Laboratory. There is

34 • College Librarianship

an even more basic assumption underlying these ideas about collection goals and bibliographic access. Those ideas, after all, derive from a concept of the proper role to be played by each kind of library. The school library's function is to serve as a "laboratory" in the learning process. It is a means of teaching proper use of libraries rather than an end in itself. Children should be taught to read, write, cipher, and use the library. A "research paper" is at this level not usually expected to be a contribution to the corpus of knowledge: there is rarely a rigid requirement that such papers display evidence of thorough library research. The intention is usually the fairly straightforward one of having students experience in a small way what the real research experience is all about. The point is often just to use indexing services or encyclopedias or card catalogs as a kind of parallel to what both teacher and student would agree is the more important task: getting a good grade on a paper.

As the student moves through the school system this laboratory experience becomes more and more intensive, culminating at last in the real research process at an upper level or graduate program. On the spectrum described earlier we have, at one end, the library serving as a place where the appreciation of books is taught. At a point on the spectrum the concern for orienting people toward books is overshadowed by the concern for teaching people how the mechanism works, and that is our "laboratory" area. At last, on the other end of the spectrum, we emerge into that area where the laboratory concept is overshadowed by the concept that the library contains a corpus of knowledge that is in itself a valuable social resource.

Summary. Our paradigm describes college libraries as institutions that function as laboratories for an other-directed, captive clientele within the organizational structure of a larger not-for-profit corporate body. Such libraries are characterized by de facto rigid limitations on their collection goals as well as by a concern for providing good bibliographic access to the scholarly record.

Consequences of the Paradigm

Collection Goals. What consequences for the day-to-day operations of the college library follow from this paradigm? College librarians see consequences most clearly when dealing with that complex set of interactions related to collection development. At its worse extreme, professors (commonly referring to their college as a "university")[3] will submit requests for books clearly too esoteric for the college library, in obedience to a reflex to order anything in their special field, since that is one of the many lessons learned in their Ph. D. programs. The same sort of problem surfaces in any college library that attempts to conduct a vigorous deacquisitions policy. Even those classroom instructors who will concede that it may be unnecessary to add esoteric materials to their college's library often have difficulty comprehending why librarians would possibly want to pull a book out of a collection. Most of these people will certainly accept the reasoning, once it is explained to them, but, for the most part, a year later they will have forgotten that reasoning and bounced right back to their research-library conviction that all books deserve to be preserved in all libraries. Many classroom instructors presume that one of the jobs of their librarians is to provide ever-larger numbers of shelves for ever-larger numbers of books.

There is, then, a significant negative consequence of this failure to determine clearly a college library's collection goals: a regular need to educate and re-educate classroom instructors in what at times becomes almost a running battle, pitting the philistines against the book lovers. The real quarrel is between those who want to address their college's laboratory need and those who want to address the needs of the research libraries they came to know when they were graduate students. Another negative consequence is that classroom instructors sometimes deduce from this debate that librarians are mere administrators of rules and not, like themselves, book lovers. The librarian's credibility can be weakened considerably if this research/laboratory distinction is not clearly drawn.

Another negative consequence is that teachers, role models for their students, will, naturally enough, promote their views of libraries as part of their instruction. They can denigrate their college's library and librarians, or send their students to larger libraries, or raise unreasonable expectations in the minds of their students about what should be found in the "proper" kind of library. There is even the opposite problem of instructors who know full well the limitations of their colleges' libraries and who therefore discourage library research altogether.

Such beliefs and attitudes are reflected in the views

students have of their college library. Most freshmen have
previously worked in libraries a tenth the size of their college library, if they've used libraries at all. Turned loose
in what many of them regard as an enormous edifice, they
are given the message by one and all that this "massive"
collection is actually quite small. There is proof of that
when the student discovers that one cited item after another
is not in the library. The more a college library's collection goals diverge from the goals appropriate to a college,
the greater the likelihood that students will be baffled by
their library's resources.

Bibliographic Access. The second element in the
paradigm, provision of bibliographic access, relates quite
closely both to collection development and to the concept of the
"laboratory" function of the college library.

For example, if I accept the idea that the college library is a laboratory, then it makes a great deal of sense
to relate very specifically the titles covered by my indexing
services to my subscription list. Such a practice helps define my collection goals quite overtly and measurably. That
practice also helps make the library a much more useful
laboratory, since it increases the likelihood that students
learning the research process will be able to unearth useful
materials.

As an element in itself, however, bibliographic access has other consequences. College is where most students learn to use libraries. [4] They must usually learn to
read and construct citations; they have trouble distinguishing
the word "biography" from the word "bibliography"; few understand what an abstract is; even fewer understand the ways
in which various bibliographical aids can be identified and
used. One consequence of the commitment to the provision
of bibliographic access is the obligation to teach students
how to manipulate bibliographic tools, whether they are indexes, abstracts, monographic bibliographies, or automated
data-bases. Instruction in the use of such tools should be
routine in any college library, both informally and formally,
both in classes offered by librarians and in classes taught
by librarians at the request of a teacher. It is not sufficient
to presume that classroom instructors do so, since a high
percentage of such instructors simply are not aware of the
wealth of their library's resources.

The Library as Laboratory. In the area of collection

development, some rather drastic revisions of current practice might be considered. Essay Index, for example, or even the festschriften listed in the MLA Bibliography, might well be regarded as acquisitions guides. Garfield[5] has gone another step. Why not cancel journal subscriptions altogether and subscribe instead to a looseleaf service that provides the most commonly cited articles in a discipline? We might also be more conscious of the need to identify those courses in which library research skills are taught by teachers rather than librarians. McGrath[6] suggests that it is desirable to classify the courses in one's college catalog for acquisitions purposes. Can we push even farther and see if that procedure might generate LC subject headings that would in turn take us back to the Subject Guide to Books in Print for selection purposes? At Earlham College up-to-date bibliographies are maintained for most courses offered. Such possibilities abound, though most current selection processes do not at all function in such a way. We read reviews, do our best to guess at what might be needed, depend on faculty requests-- and many of our choices go entirely unread.

If we took the laboratory notion seriously, we'd undoubtedly increase the percentage of our books that are read. For example, what if we actually acted upon our awareness that students often rely on the bibliographies in their textbooks and built our selection policy accordingly? What if we persuaded our classroom colleagues to cooperate quite explicitly by making assignments derive directly from materials the library actually has?

Because we do not apply this laboratory model, we and our students and teachers are frequently frustrated in our search for materials. We are left with vague selection policies and we find that the ambitious search strategies we describe to our students lead to dead ends.

Corporate Status. The last two elements in our paradigm are twined together in the same kinds of ways the first three were. But let us back off for a moment and weigh dispassionately the function of colleges.

Colleges commonly include in their catalogs language to the general effect that they are "concerned with the individual." Furthermore, colleges commonly serve a fairly narrow spectrum in American society, usually people between the ages of 17 and 23. Some schools go even farther and actually take a formal position that, for example, their mission is to serve young people in a residential, day, full-time capacity. Note also that colleges ignore data that indi-cate low correlation between college grades and "success" in later life, or the lack of convincing evidence that one's "ma-jor" in college bears any necessary relation to one's choice of lifework.

Such considerations have led many social commenta-tors to the belief that college is best seen as a rite of pas-sage, or as a means of maintaining the status quo in class structure, or as a mechanism for withholding labor from an already-glutted marketplace, or as a means of delaying the entry into full adult status, or even as a means of subject-ing the "student as nigger" to an enforced round of repetitive and ritualistic hazing whose aim is not to educate but to pro-duce docile and predictable middle-management employees. The old phrase for such ideas, of course, was in loco par-entis.

Whether any or all of those perceptions have validity is not the point here. The point is merely to suggest that it is not always helpful to confine our thoughts to the overt features of event. Higher education, for example, with its claims to disinterested scholarship, is a major lobbyist in Washington and pulls in a high percentage of personal, state, and federal funds. Anyone with experience in a college knows full well that most academic people are terribly concerned with the protection and expansion of their own academic "turf" and are perfectly willing to go to court if, in the face of re-trenchment, a judgment is made that their institution would be better off without their particular major.

One might argue that society continues to support academia, both public and private, because academic insti-tutions and their libraries are involved in a parallel enter-prise that is altogether different from the educational purpose that is at the fore. That broader social purpose is reflected, for example, by the way in which the school library is housed securely within the single building that holds all of a school's classrooms and offices. The college library, typically, is an altogether separate building. Their environment protects children both from weather and from the hazards of moving through a city. Adults are expected to deal with such ele-ments. The college library is a building for adults in that it is separate; it is a transitional building in that it is small and rather warm in appearance.

Few school libraries are open on weekends or evenings, yet college libraries almost always are. The school library's hours are a clear signal to the children that their playtime is more important than additional schoolwork; the college library's extended hours are a clear message that those who wish to win at the college game must keep at the game for many hours outside the class.

A college library's interior design may also be seen as a means of helping to facilitate this transition. College libraries are rarely designed as though their major function is to provide a repository for materials. Instead, their interior organization relates to several important social functions of the college.

Much space ostensibly devoted to reading areas, with clusters of tables and chairs, in fact facilitates interaction with peers. Colleges provide many kinds of occasions and facilities in which young people can learn to play adult roles. If such role learning makes study difficult, it is typically the case that study loses. Librarians say they don't want to be stereotyped hushers, and the young people themselves are quite unwilling for the most part to enforce quiet rules. Here is, in other words, tacit recognition that the social activity is of more consequence than the study activity that is ostensibly what the "study area" is for.

Clientele. What clientele do college libraries serve? Off-campus users are common, as are nonacademic staff members, such as secretaries, admissions officers, and fundraisers. We need not consider those people here since they are not the college library's major clientele.

The teaching faculty role is more complex. On the one hand, they select books, serve on library committees, and often can exert significant pressure on library services. However, as library users, they normally account for only a small percentage of total use. As indicated earlier, teachers do not relate to the college library in the same way that students do. Students, unlike any other portion of a college library's clientele, are required to use their college's library.

The consequences (and frustrations!) of dealing on a day-to-day basis with this "captive" clientele are well known to academic librarians. There are the procrastinators who delay major research papers, the fence jumpers ready to change topics at the blink of an eye, the fatalists perfectly willing to accept the failure to provide an answer to a question so long as they can report back to their profs that a librarian told them there was no answer, the book hogs skilled at checking out all books on a topic in order to decrease competition from their peers, the misshelvers skilled at hiding books in the stacks in order to have their own convenience of access, the mutilators who decide to wreak their anger over a course on books they had to read for that course, and so on. When students are driven to the library they can react like driven animals, finding many negative ways of expressing the anxiety induced by the experience.

By the same token, it can be a delight to work with undergraduates, helping them come to terms with assigned topics, helping them reason their way through the research process, and even, on occasion, working with students who have crossed the threshold and want to dig deeply on their own into a subject.

A Summary of Consequences. Contributing to the larger corporate purpose of the college of which they are a part, college libraries help provide one social mechanism that helps some young people move from childhood to full adult status. Many library policies, as well as much of the physical appearance of college libraries, can be seen to reflect that larger social goal, rather than a pedagogical or even repository role. That larger social goal is seen in the laboratory need met by the materials housed in a college library as well as by the ways in which those materials are accessed. Furthermore, the "laboratory" concept relates very directly to the training to be provided to young people being prepared for the middle range of white-collar employment.

Work Tenor in College Libraries

This paradigm should help define the intellectual and temperamental characteristics that make some people more suited than others for the library profession. Librarianship is well known as a "second choice" profession, so much so that 0.1 percent[7] of freshmen entering college identify it as a career goal. It is also true that many librarians leave the profession, in many cases extremely dissatisfied with what they found in the field.

It is obvious that librarians must have a strong sense of service. The not-for-profit status of colleges directly reinforces that particular ethic. Unlike other service professions, however, there is no direct quid pro quo in librarianship. Physicians or lawyers send a bill for their services. Teachers do not bill for their services regularly, but the grading mechanism puts the student very much "in debt" to the teacher in terms of the satisfaction of career goals. Librarianship is a service profession in a purer sense than many others, since it lacks direct exchange value. One cannot be assured of better grades[8] or a better job merely because one knows how to use a library.

The idea of the college library's "captive" clientele relates to the service ethic in a different way. In the preceding paragraph we concentrated on responsive service. The second kind of service is outreach service. Legal-aid societies look for deserving cases to defend. Medical researchers find antidotes and take them to the sick. Missionaries trudge through remote regions seeking out "clients" to whom truth can be delivered.

Missionaries, of course, sometimes find their clients are disinclined to be saved. Teachers can find themselves providing their service in the midst of a violence-ridden blackboard jungle. Likewise, librarians must be able, temperamentally, to deal with clients who can be indifferent to the service provided. The indifferent, hostile, or scheming student cannot be ignored any more than the student who uses the college library with interest and enthusiasm. The college librarian must have the sense that all students who use the library are potential candidates for instruction in library use. And so, college reference librarians frequently find themselves teaching a methodology when all the user wants is any three articles on Shakespeare so that a professor's "bib" requirements can be met.

But the corporate-status element of the paradigm has a managerial as well as a service component. The managerial may in fact conflict with the service ideal. For example, one must normally order fewer books than one has requests for because of budgetary constraints imposed from outside the library. What is more, management requirements often take one away from situations in which one can interact directly with users. Some librarians become so beset by the managerial requirements of their work that they retreat from public areas to hidden nooks whenever they want to get their "work" done without interruption.

The college teacher is hired to provide a service that is not directly managerial (whatever the meaning of the Yeshiva case), 9 but the college librarian is usually given a job description that spells out managerial tasks that fill out a good part of the day. Establishment, evaluation, and implementation of policy and procedure have traditionally been ongoing tasks in a library. One aspect of this managerial role that has not been sufficiently reviewed is that particular bifocal trait of mind that is able to perceive the microscopic at the same time as the macroscopic. Who has not seen a librarian walking next to a range of shelves, discussing some problem with a colleague or patron, and, hardly pausing in either speech or step, pull down a misshelved book? Experienced librarians find that such books practically leap out at them. A librarian might spend thirty minutes checking every last variation of a garbled citation before finding the tiny detail that was far enough wrong to make the work unlocatable. Librarians can frequently find books even though given the wrong author and/or title and/or subject, precisely because they are aware of the way details can become fouled up. But a librarian must at the same time be able to deal with much more general issues: are patrons well served by microfiche catalogs? How well does a selection policy support a college's curriculum? What are the best means of integrating one's library into a regional document delivery system?

These managerial problems must be recognized, especially by college librarians, as a means, not an end. Wright has pointed out the extent to which management ideas have confused librarians' notions of their proper function. 10 One might well argue that a librarian in a research setting has a major responsibility to manage instead of serve users directly. It may prove difficult, for example, to justify lessening the value of a century-old uncut novel in French merely because a person wants to read it. A librarian in a corporate library might also be sorely tempted to manage in a narrowly perceived cost-effective way. But the college librarian should keep the managerial function clearly subordinated to the major goal of maximizing the laboratory potential of the library.

That leads directly to another quality academic librarians must have: they must to a large extent see their role as that of a teacher. You do not answer reference questions, you demonstrate a research methodology. Bibliographic guides are designed to teach as well as list pertinent resources. Technical services librarians in college libraries are commonly scheduled at the reference desk and are commonly waylayed by users who need reference help. A librarian supervising student assistants often teaches more than simply how to get a specific job done. It is not that teaching is a major activity of all college librarians, but that college librarians must enjoy teaching when the occasion arises.

Related to the service ethic, but also very much related to a particular mind-set, is the way college librarians relate to all the parts of the collection they are developing. You must have enough general knowledge and curiosity and be sincerely interested in a wide enough variety of subjects in order to pursue collection development with some vigor. It is not enough to admire only Will Durant. You must also appreciate the scholars, the cliometricians as well as the traditionalists. Furthermore, you must be able to move almost in an instant from the interpretation of a law to the address of a corporation to the interpretation of a literary text to the finding of a set of chemical properties. And you must be able to ride at the surface of these intellectual quests, resisting the natural desire to proceed with the patron until the question is fully answered. You must have a real conviction that knowledge and learning in all their variety are valuable ends in themselves to be able to develop your collection with zest.

Last in the list of desiderata is a healthy dose of skepticism toward bibliographic access. In order to teach bibliographic access well librarians must understand at least intuitively what epistemology is all about. Our crisp and tidy subject headings do not describe articles and books very well, [11] and, since those same articles and books are only attempts to describe reality, we find ourselves far removed from the essence of things. Not only are there questions of epistemology, but questions of etymology, since the very terms we select to pinpoint our subjects have the delightful habit of evolving in their own peculiar ways. [12] Perhaps one of the most valuable things to be taught by a librarian is this skepticism toward all the terminology we depend on to access the materials housed in a library. Librarians should at least be well aware of, for example, the possibility that librarianship, in Wright's phrase, involves the "management of human intellection"; it is "a metaphysical technology of knowing based on philosophy." [13]

The paradigm developed here can be related to the

temperamental and intellectual characteristics that describe
the work performed by college librarians. The sedate image
of the librarian is not accurate, nor is that of the iron-
fisted keeper of the books.   Such individuals do not last in
the college library profession or, if they do, they find remote corners of their libraries in which to hide.   Yet, an
unbalanced mixture of the attributes I have described could
make a person unhappy in a college library.   A person
strongly interested in management per se becomes impatient
with the service or teaching or epistemological aspects of
college library work.   A person devoted to scholarship per
se may be frustrated by the limitations imposed by collection-
development policies or managerial chores.

One of the fascinating experiences of the college library is the gear-shifting[14] done all day long as one attempts to perform all the roles suggested here.   As I am
"managing," I am interrupted with an urgent reference question that leads me not only to instruction in the use of a
particular index, but on to a concern for the terminological
ambiguities of a subject area I have never before explored,
only to be interrupted once more by a faculty member who
wants to discuss an in-class presentation, etc., etc.   I find
that I am constantly moving between roles and, within each
role, I am dealing with a wide range of concerns from the
smallest detail--shall I bring my class at 9 on Tuesday?--
to the largest--how can I teach my students to use the library?

A college librarian, then, should have a strong service orientation, a missionary zeal, managerial abilities, a
mind flexible and imaginative enough to deal with the full
range of procedural and policy issues, an interest in teaching, a genuine conviction that learning is a valuable end in
itself, and an awareness of the ambiguities and mysteries
beneath the apparently serene face of the library's bibliographic tools.

Those characteristics relate quite clearly to the five
elements in the paradigm used in this paper.   They are not
necessarily the impossible dream they might at first seem.
Many college librarians adapt quite readily to these needs as
they come to the fore.   Others never do; they move on to
other kinds of libraries or out of the profession altogether.

Notes

¹Michael Madden, Lifestyles of Library Users and Non-users, University of Illinois Graduate School of Library Science Occasional Papers, no. 137 (Champaign: University of Illinois, 1969).

²Daniel Gore, "Farewell to Alexandria: The Theory of the No-Growth, High-Performance Library," in his Farewell to Alexandria: Solutions to Space, Growth, and Performance Problems of Libraries (Westport, Conn.: Greenwood, 1976), p. 166.

³Evan I. Farber, "College Librarians and the University-Library Syndrome," in The Academic Library: Essays in Honor Of Guy R. Lyle, ed. Evan I. Farber and Ruth Walling (Metuchen, N.J.: Scarecrow, 1974), pp. 12-23.

⁴At Alma College, for example, a selective liberal arts college, 98 percent of entering freshmen in Fall 1978 could not record correctly the full LC call number of a book when shown a reproduction of a catalog card; 76 percent could not identify from tracings subject headings to use to find books on similar subjects; 57 percent could not identify correctly the word under which the title card they were shown would be filed.

⁵Eugene Garfield, "No-Growth Libraries and Citation Analysis; or, Pulling Weeds with ISI's Journal Citation Reports," in his Essays of an Information Scientist (Philadelphia: ISI, 1977), vol. 2, pp. 300-03.

⁶William E. McGrath and Norma Durand, "Classifying Courses in the University Catalog," College & Research Libraries 30 (November 1969): 533-39.

⁷"Characteristics and Attitudes of 1978-79 College Freshmen," Chronicle of Higher Education, January 22, 1979, pp. 14-15.

⁸Larry Hardesty, "The Academic Library: Unused and Unneeded?" The Library Scene 4 (December 1975/March 1976): 14-16.

⁹Beverly T. Watkins, "High Court Calls Yeshiva Faculty Managers, Not Subject to National Labor Relations Act," Chronicle of Higher Education, February 25, 1980, p. 1.

¹⁰Curtis H. Wright, "Inquiry in Science and Librarianship," Journal of Library History 13 (Summer 1978): 250-64.

¹¹Don R. Swanson, "Information Retrieval as a Trial-and-Error Process," Library Quarterly 47 (April 1977): 128-48.

¹²Sanford Berman, Prejudices and Antipathies: A Tract on the LC List of Subject Heads Concerning People (Metuchen, N.J.: Scarecrow, 1971).

[13]Wright, "Inquiry," p. 261.

[14]Richard De Gennaro, "Library Administration and New Management Systems," Library Journal 103 (December 15, 1978): 2477-82.

BUDGETARY TRENDS IN SMALL PRIVATE LIBERAL ARTS COLLEGE LIBRARIES

George Charles Newman

While the procedure for budgeting remains essentially the same from year to year and from college to college, budgets themselves change depending upon the fortunes of the college, the economy, and even the mood of the times. The 1960s was a period of expansion in higher education. The number of newly enrolled college students increased, money for education was given priority at both the federal and state levels, new curricular offerings were developed, and new buildings were erected on campuses. These changes affected all segments of higher education, including small private liberal arts colleges, which grew rapidly during the "Golden Age." The libraries in many of these colleges were directly affected by this growth. New libraries were built on many campuses, others were remodeled and expanded. Book and periodical collections grew, and staffing patterns changed at both the professional and paraprofessional level. These libraries took advantage of new technologies, incorporated nonprint resources and services, added microforms to the collection, and encouraged the growth of special collections; the new clientele on campus required new methods of bibliographical support and the expansion of library instruction. But success and prosperity were not to continue indefinitely, and by the early 1970s colleges had begun shifting to a period of static or limited growth. This chapter will examine the effect this new era of limited growth has had on college library budgets by looking at small private liberal arts colleges in Ohio.

Ohio Library Budgets

Budgetary information is an integral part of academic librarianship, yet relatively few longitudinal studies have been made of library budgets. One notable exception is a book by Baumol and Marcus, Economics of Academic Libraries, [1] which used statistical methods to analyze data relating to library costs. Their data, though interesting, are of minimal value to small academic institutions today because, one, the book deals with the 1950s and 1960s, a period of academic growth for all institutions, and two, the data pertained primarily to university libraries.

The study presented in this chapter was formulated in order to illustrate budgetary trends that have had an influence on small academic libraries in the late 1960s and the 1970s. A sample of thirty-two private liberal arts colleges in Ohio with enrollments between 500 and 2,200 was selected. Since the enrollment size of a college is not necessarily indicative of its financial situation or its commitment to the library, two subsamples were identified. The first, or "elite" subsample, consists of nine colleges with 1977-78 enrollments of over 1,000, total library operating budgets of over $200,000, and book volumes in the library of over 100,000. These colleges can be assumed to have programs, facilities, faculty, and resources that would classify them as selective, relatively secure financially, and having high academic standards. The remaining twenty-three colleges constitute the second, or "developing," subsample. They are for the most part nonselective and less financially secure; they have adequate facilities and varied academic standards. These two subsamples will provide a clearer picture of budgetary trends for different types of libraries.

The longitudinal data for the thirty-two institutions were obtained from library statistics compiled by the National Center for Educational Statistics and by the State Library of Ohio. Budgetary information was collected for the years between 1966-67 and 1977-78. The results of this study, while suggestive, were obtained primarily from soft data and cannot therefore be considered conclusive; that is, the information used was obtained from secondary sources, rather than directly from the colleges themselves, and the opportunities for error multiply. [2] It is therefore important that the reader look at the information presented here only in terms of the overall trend of the institutions rather than looking specifically at one year compared with another.

In order to compare the budgetary information obtained for the Ohio colleges it is necessary first to look at the enrollment pattern for the total sample and the two subsamples. It is generally recognized that colleges and universities across the country experienced a period of rapid growth during the 1960s, followed by a decline in the 1970s. This same pattern is exhibited by the Ohio colleges in the sample, with the average number of students enrolled in the late 1960s and early 1970s slightly higher than in the latter half of the 1970s. When the two subsamples--elite and developing--are considered, the same trend holds true, with average enrollments being somewhat smaller in recent years.

Just as enrollment has become a common barometer to evaluate and measure the fluctuations of colleges and universities, the library budget has become a common measurement for academic libraries. Total operating expenditures can be defined as all costs associated with the library budget, including personnel, books, periodicals, equipment, memberships, supplies, binding, and miscellaneous. During the twelve-year period between 1966 and 1978 the average of total operating expenditures for all thirty-two institutions generally increased (see Graph 1), which would be expected during a decade of recurring inflation. Even more interesting, however, are the differences between the elite and developing institutions. From 1966 to 1978 the average total operating budget for the elite colleges increased by $143,409, or 85 percent. In contrast, the budget for the developing colleges increased by only 60 percent, or $47,137, for the same time period. Thus the average budget for the elite colleges was more than three times the size of the average budget for the developing colleges in 1966, but by 1978 the average "elite" budget was four times larger than the average "developing" budget. It is clear, therefore, that libraries in the elite colleges gained more financial resources than the developing colleges.

Yet what do these figures mean in terms of buying power? Graph 2 translated total operating expenditures into constant dollars, [3] which can be defined as expenditure costs minus inflation. As the graph shows, the library budgets generally kept pace with inflation through the 1972-73 academic year. After that period the libraries' ability to keep up with inflation began to decline. In fact, by 1977-78 the library budgets of the elite colleges could buy 5 percent less than they could in 1966-67, and the developing colleges were even worse off--the value of their budgets having declined by

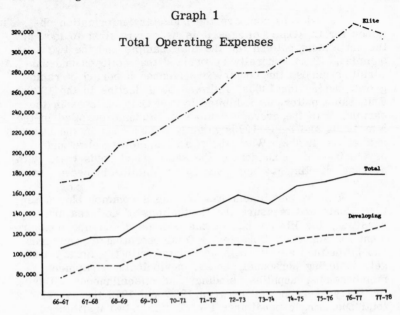

Graph 1

Total Operating Expenses

Graph 2

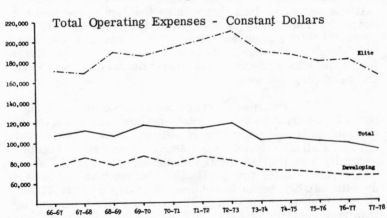

Total Operating Expenses - Constant Dollars

Graph 3

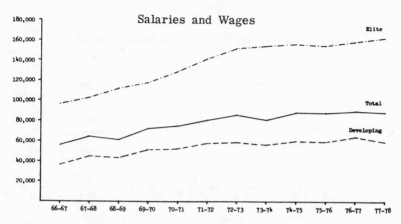

17 percent. It is apparent, therefore, that college libraries are losing ground in the struggle to keep pace with inflation, whether they are classified as developing or elite.

Two categories within a library's operating budget consume the majority of the funds--salaries and wages, and books and other printed materials. To get a better idea of budgetary trends in college libraries it will help to look at these areas in more detail. Taking salaries and wages first, Graph 3 shows that they too have increased from 1966-67 to 1977-78, with the elite colleges again outgaining the developing colleges. However, the two subsamples are much closer than in the case of total operating expenses; the elite colleges increased salaries and wages by 68 percent and the developing colleges by 62 percent. Since much of this increase occurred prior to 1972-73, it may have been that increases in the number of staff occurred before this time, while during the period from 1973-74 to 1977-78 increases in the salaries-and-wages category may have been due primarily to higher salaries of existing staff. In fact, it is possible that staff cutbacks occurred at some colleges after 1972-73 because the average for the total sample decreased for three of the five years.

With this smaller dollar increase in salaries and wages from 1966-67 to 1977-78, one would assume that the constant-dollar amounts for this budget category would show an even greater decline than that experienced by the total operating budget, and Graph 4 shows that this assumption

Graph 4

Salaries and Wages - Constant Dollars

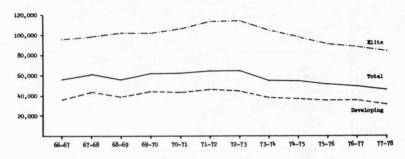

Graph 5

Budget for Books and Other Printed Materials

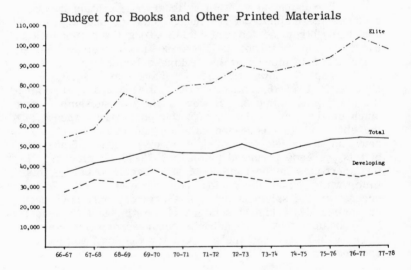

holds true.   The buying power of the dollars allocated for
salaries and wages declined 13 percent for elite colleges
from 1966-67 to 1977-78, and that of the developing colleges declined 16 percent.   Here again the demarcation
point for the start of the decline is the 1972-73 academic
year.

Turning to the book budget, the second major budgetary category, Graph 5 shows that the average expenditures
for books and other printed materials at the thirty-two colleges increased 44 percent from 1966-67 to 1977-78.   Comparing the two subsamples, we see that the trend for the
developing colleges roughly paralleled that of the total sample, although their rate of increase over the same time
period was only 33 percent.   On the other hand, the elite
colleges increased their budget allocations for printed materials by 78 percent over the twelve-year period.   It is
apparent, therefore, that the elite colleges have been placing a greater priority on increasing the book budget than
have the developing colleges.   Part of this emphasis is undoubtedly due to the elite colleges' commitment to maintain
the growth and quality of their collection.   But another reason may be that the greater financial resources of the elite
colleges allowed them to respond to the pressures of inflation to a greater extent than the developing colleges.

The next question is, of course, what has inflation
done to the book budget?   Graph 6 shows the book budget in
terms of constant dollars; clearly, the buying power of this
budget category has been greatly eroded for both the total
sample and the two subsamples.   Overall, book budgets at
the thirty-two Ohio colleges have declined 25 percent in
terms of constant dollars; the buying power for the sample
began to decline after 1969-70, reaching its lowest point in
1977-78.   The developing colleges followed this same pattern, with their constant-dollar book-budget average declining from a high point in 1969-70 to its lowest point in 1976-
77.   This average rose slightly in 1977-78; nevertheless, the
buying power of the developing colleges' book budgets dropped
31 percent from 1966-67 to 1977-78.   Even the elite colleges, which had budgetary increases in terms of actual dollars allocated to books and printed materials, experienced a
drop in buying power, decreasing 8 percent from 1966-67 to
1977-78.   The high point for the elite colleges in terms of
buying power was in 1968-69 and the low point was in 1977-
78.

While it is apparent from Graph 6 that academic

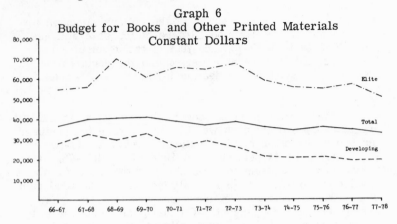

Graph 6
Budget for Books and Other Printed Materials
Constant Dollars

libraries are being handicapped by the eroding of the book
budget because of inflation, it must be pointed out that the
situation is probably even more critical than shown here.
The constant-dollar figure used was for the buying power of
the dollar, which declined from a base of 1.00 in 1967 to
.518 in 1978.[4] Yet if one looks specifically at hardcover
books, the price index declined even farther than the dollar,
decreasing from 1.00 in 1967-69 to .436 in 1978.[5] The situation has been even worse in terms of periodicals, with the
price index reacing a low of .314 in 1978.[6] Looking at these
figures from another perspective, they show that while there
has been an increase of 93 percent for all goods and services, hardcover books have increased 129 percent and periodicals 219 percent in the period from 1967 to 1978. And
these are only average prices for all books and periodicals;
in some fields, such as sociology, economics, and music,
the percentage of increase is even greater.

The data presented above give a general picture of
small college library budget allocations over time, yet to
see how the budgets themselves have changed, one should
also look at what has happened to the percentage of the total
budget allocated to the major budgetary categories. Graph 7
shows these percentages both for salaries and wages and for
books and other printed material. Only the data for the total sample of thirty-two colleges have been presented here
because the averages for the subsamples were very close to
the total sample for most years. Looking first at salaries
and wages as a percentage of total operating expenses, this
percentage rose from approximately 50 percent in 1966-67 to
56 percent in 1970-71 and 1972-73. After that time, how-

Graph 7
Salary and Book Budgets as Percentages
of Total Operating Expenses

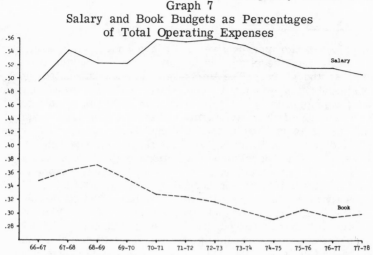

ever, the percentage began declining, reaching less than 51
percent in 1977-78. The book budget followed a similar pattern, although its highest percentage of total operating ex-
penses--37 percent--occurred in 1968-69 and then declined
steadily until 1974-75. For the latest year in which data
were collected, 1977-78, the portion of the total budget allocated to books was 30 percent.

Over the last twelve years both major categories of
the budget--salaries and wages, and books and other printed
materials--have declined as a percentage of total operating
expenses. The decline in the area of salaries and wages may
be attributed to any of several reasons. As salaries have
increased some libraries may have had to decrease their
staff and/or use lower-payed personnel, such as student
help, to reduce costs. Other areas may have had an even
greater priority because of rapidly increasing costs. Because of the inflationary trends in book prices it would seem
that the book budget would receive a greater percentage of
the money allocated to the library, yet this percentage also
declined. It is apparent, therefore, that other factors have
served to increase college library budgets. These factors
include such items as an increased emphasis on media and
media-related materials and equipment, and computerized
cataloging, such as that offered by the Ohio College Library
Center (OCLC).

Two Case Studies

To gain a better perspective on library budgets this section
will delve into the effect the budgets have had on the libraries over the years. The thirty-two colleges undoubtedly vary
considerably on this issue, depending on the money allocated
and the priorities of the libraries, and it is impossible to
discuss each of them at length.   Therefore two fairly typical
colleges, referred to here as College A and College B, were
selected from the sample.   Both of these colleges can be
characterized as developing institutions with enrollments generally in the 900-1,200 range, although both have experienced
enrollment declines in the second half of the 1970s.   Each
college has a library facility that was built during the 1960s,
and the two book collections are similar in size, although
College B's is currently about 15 percent larger.   Yet while
there are a number of similarities in the budgetary trends
of the two colleges, there are also some notable differences.

Graph 8 is a composite of total operating expenditures
for College A and three main budget categories--salaries and
wages, books, and periodicals. As the graph shows, total
operating expenditures of the library increased until 1972-73
and 1973-74, when declines were experienced. These declines occurred at a time when the college was experiencing
a rapid decrease in enrollment after a period of prosperity.
Although enrollments at College A continued at this reduced
level, total operating expenditures again began increasing
after 1973-74.

The three main categories within College A's library
budget tended to parallel the trend of the total budget.   Salaries and wages, for instance, dipped dramatically at the
same time total operating expenses declined, i.e., in 1973-
74.   This drop in salaries and wages can be explained by
the drop in the number of paraprofessionals employed at the
college (from six in 1972-73 to four in 1973-74); the number
of professionals remained the same at three.   While a reduced library budget may have forced a decrease in paraprofessionals, it is also possible that the loss of two paraprofessionals resulted in a decline in the total operating budget
for that year.

The book and periodical budgets for College A also
declined in 1973-74, but they have since increased each year.
Because of inflationary trends, however, the library purchases
in these areas have not risen in the same way.   Even when

Graph 8

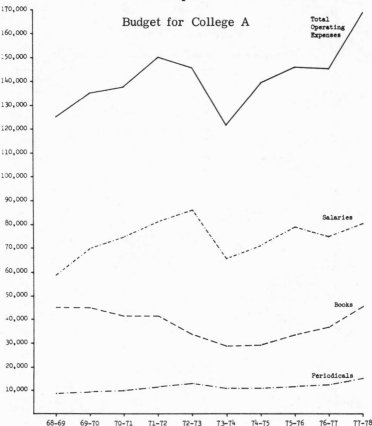

Budget for College A

the total book budget was increasing in the latter half of the
1970s the number of book volumes added to the collection
decreased for two of the four years. A similar pattern exists for the number of periodical subscriptions in College A's
library. After the prosperity of the early 1970s the number
of periodicals in the collection declined steadily, with a slight
upturn in the number of periodicals in 1977-78 (paralleling
the increase in the periodicals budget).

Turning to College B, an even more interesting picture emerges (see Graph 9). College B's library budget
shows two periods of rapid decline, 1970-71 and 1974-75.
The reasons for these declines are not as easily tied to enrollment decreases as was the case for College A, although

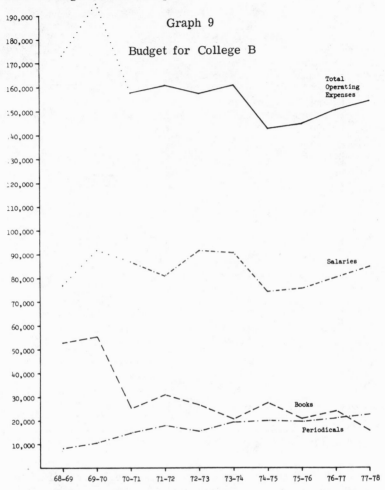

Graph 9

Budget for College B

that is much of the reason. In 1970-71 College B experienced a decline in enrollment for the first time in several years. In 1974-75, however, enrollment was almost exactly what it had been during the two previous years, but there was a sharp decline in salaries and wages. This was the year the professional staff was reduced from six to five. With enrollments holding stable, it can be assumed that the decrease in the budget was the result of the leaving of a staff member.

Another interesting aspect of the College B library budget is the trend in the books and periodicals categories.

Unlike College A, where these two categories remained roughly parallel over time, at College B the book budget has been declining overall for the past decade while at the same time the periodicals budget has been rising; in fact, by 1977-78 the periodicals budget was actually larger than the book budget. The number of periodicals in the College B library has been consistently at a higher level than at College A, and with the rapid rise in periodical prices it is not surprising that the periodicals budget was increasing even while the actual number of periodicals subscribed to was decreasing. Even more interesting, however, is the number of book volumes added each year. College B experienced sharp declines in the number of volumes added over the past decade, until the library added only one-fifth as many new books in 1977-78 as it did ten years before. It is obvious that the priority in this library is to maintain the quality of the periodical collection, but the question it faces is whether the current rate of 2, 600 new books each year will maintain the quality of the book collection in the decade to come.

Projections and Conclusions

The data in this study have shown several trends in the library budgets of small private Ohio colleges from 1966-67 to 1977-78. First, the total operating budgets, while increasing, have not kept pace with the consumer price index; even the elite colleges, which have had higher levels of funding, have not been immune from the effects of inflation. Second, the budgets for printed materials have experienced an even greater decline in buying power because of the rapid increase in book and periodical prices. And third, the increases in the salaries and wages budgets due to rising salary levels may have been minimized because of staff reductions in the late 1970s.

As the data for both elite and developing institutions have illustrated, there has been a downward trend in the buying power of library budgets over the last decade, and this trend will probably continue into the 1980s. Most of the college libraries in the Ohio sample have reached a point where within the next few years noticeable changes will have to be made in staffing patterns and in allocations for materials, supplies, and other library costs. Given this information, what will the 1980s bring to these Ohio private college libraries as well as similar private liberal arts institutions

throughout the country? The future holds four principal
areas of concern: personnel, services, collection development, and technology.

It seems clear that in the 1980s library personnel
patterns and costs will continue to be affected by societal,
economic, and demographic trends. Salaries and wages will
continue to increase, and for many colleges with shrinking
financial resources this could be an area of concern. Small
college libraries may therefore be faced with nonreplacement
of staff who leave the institution. Yet the demand for traditional public services, such as circulation, reference, bibliographical searching, and library instruction, will continue.
Thus it will be important for small libraries to examine
critically the work roles and functions of all employees.
Professional and paraprofessional staff may have to assume
new or different job duties, and student assistants and vol-
unteers may well play an expanded role in the operation of
the small college library. As a result, paraprofessionals
in small college libraries may be used more extensively in
the 1980s in technical and public services and may be involved more in bibliographic research and library instruction, which traditionally have been done only by a professional librarian. And professional librarians will find that
the demands on their time will increase, as the college librarian of the 1980s becomes more of a supervisor of paraprofessionals, student assistants, and volunteer assistants.

As personnel patterns and functions change in the
1980s, another critical concern will be in the area of collection development. Given continued inflation and the rising
cost of all library materials, it will become increasingly
difficult for small college libraries to maintain appropriate
and up-to-date collections. In addition, as colleges make
curricular changes in their quest to better their programs
and attract new students, the libraries will have to modify
their collections. Presently many college libraries use a
shared selection approach in collection development, in that
college faculty or departments are allocated a portion of the
materials budget. The amount of the allocation is usually
based loosely on enrollment in the department, number of
faculty, and number of lower- and upper-division courses,
although many institutions use only a standard amount or
increment for each faculty member or department. As the
library is faced with scarcer resources for collection development in the 1980s, there may be little money left over
after basic and required items are purchased, and as collec-

tions become outdated in certain disciplines more funds will
be needed for replacement.   As a result, book selection
could become more and more the province of the librarians,
who have more direct access to standard bibliographical and
collection development guides.

Technology will continue to be important in academic
libraries, but the direction and impact on the small college
library will be determined by the computer applications that
are feasible and applicable to the small college library.
During the 1970s the majority of the thirty-two Ohio college
libraries in this study have been using computerized technology developed by the Ohio College Library Center (OCLC).
Many of these institutions were charter members of OCLC
in 1971-72 and have been using the on-line cataloging system
to supplement or substitute for additional staff.   Recently
new services, such as an acquisitions and serials subsystem
plus an interlibrary loan system, have become available;
their adoption by small college libraries remains a clouded
issue, however, dependent on whether the benefits will outweigh the costs of these new automated services.   The costs
associated with OCLC have traditionally been moderate for
small college libraries in Ohio, but with the implementation
of new services and the formation of an Ohio network,
OHIONET, cost savings may well accrue only to large-scale
users.   Thus library technology will grow in the 1980s, but
the use of this service by small college libraries will be
heavily influenced by factors of cost and usefulness.

Given the demographic and economic changes in the
past and prospects for private higher education in the 1980s,
the library budgets of small colleges over the next decade
must reflect an entirely different set of standards, goals,
and costs.   Furthermore, to achieve their goals, private
liberal arts college libraries must begin to use more appropriate methods of budgetary preparation, justification,
and monitoring. [7]

There are several significant reasons to justify a
systems approach to the small college library budgeting
process.   In the past it was often thought that because these
libraries were small, planning and compiling studies were
time-consuming or really did not need to be done.   But the
potential seriousness of the financial condition in many private colleges has undermined this idea.   As economic factors become increasingly critical for the private college, all
units within the institution, including the library, will need

to justify their annual costs and expenditures. Synonymous
with this justification will be cost studies that will cover a
broad range of functions from circulation studies to workflow patterns in technical services. Libraries in small colleges will be competing with other units for basic funding.
Thus the planning stage of budget preparation will assume an
important role. Through the use of carefully documented
studies based on analytical evaluation of various services and
functions library budgets will be able to compete successfully
with other institutional budgets, such as those for departmental units, admissions, student services, and intercollegiate
athletics.

Another aspect of the budget planning of the future
will be the establishment of library goals and paralleling
these goals with those of the budget. In establishing goals
for the library each service and function of the library will
need to be measured and evaluated and associated with appropriate cost indicators. As the staffing level of the college library changes, for example, should the library staff
perform the same services? The amount of time it takes
to complete a task and the cost of that time coupled with
the cost of the product are measures that college libraries
will be required to answer.

The second factor in implementing a budgetary system
in a college library involves the issue of management. Most
libraries, even small college libraries, have operated from
a decentralized management system. But as accountability
in terms of the budget is emphasized, the role of the director of the library will assume new dimensions. It will become increasingly important for the director to establish library policy, delegate and administer library responsibilities,
and set library priorities. One would hope that the collegial
form of communication would be retained and that the director would continue to consult with the staff, particularly other professionals. But in order to provide the management
and planning required of the budgetary process in the future,
this form of administration or a system similar to it will
have to be implemented.

The third criterion of the new budgetary system involves budgetary control. Usually the control of the existing
library budget has been a function assumed as a responsibility of whoever maintained the library account--the business
office, the director of the library, or even the technical
services librarian. In the future the director will play a

much more direct role. Given the wide use of automated
budget systems by most small colleges, it will become increasingly important that the library and the business office
have a good working relationship and maintain close communication. Both units should keep accurate accounts of
expenditure levels and types of expenditures so that a continuous monitoring of all library accounts takes place. Over
time the information generated in this process will play a
determining role in the measurement and evaluation of existing library services and will influence the planning and management functions of the library budget process.

The implementation of an effective budgeting system
for a small college library lies in the thorough preparation
and justification of the budget. As Martin states:

> ... a budget is a statement which identifies in
> monetary terms the ways in which an institution
> will seek to achieve its goals during the period
> for which it is valid.... It implies control and
> feedback to measure both conformity to the ex-
> pressed or implicit goals and the degree of suc-
> cess in achieving those goals. [8]

By emphasizing budget preparation, management, and control,
small college libraries will have a greater chance of acquiring sufficient resources to maintain or even improve their
situation in the next decade.

Notes

[1]William J. Baumol and Matityahu Marcus, Economics
of Academic Libraries (Washington, D.C.: American Council on Education, 1973).
[2]The problem encountered by the author in collecting enrollment data for the sample institutions illustrates this
clearly. Since there was the possibility that the level of
budgetary funding for libraries would fluctuate according to
the enrollment level of the college, it was felt that the enrollment data associated with a particular budgetary year
should be the enrollment of the college for the fall of that
year. It turned out, however, that the library budgetary information collected from the colleges each fall is for the
previous budgetary year, while the enrollment information

requested is for the current year.   Thus the information
within one year's statistics was not comparable, at least
for the purposes of this study.   A further problem developed in terms of enrollment statistics.   In some years the
enrollment figures represented the actual head count of the
schools, in other years the full-time equivalent enrollments.
To make this information comparable across time it was
therefore necessary to adjust the head counts to full-time
equivalents.   Luckily, the statistical volumes used for the
early years of the study included the percentage of full-time
students as well as the head count, so for each non-FTE
year these percentages were used to adjust the figures and
make them more comparable.   There may be other instances,
of which the author is not aware, where data from different
schools are not comparable because of differing interpretations of what was requested by the persons compiling the
data or because the specific information requested changed
over the years.

[3]U. S. Bureau of the Census, Statistical Abstract of the
United States: 1978 (Washington, D. C.: Government Printing Office, 1978), p. 482.

[4]This index was used because index levels were readily
available for each year.

[5]The Bowker Annual of Library and Book Trade Information, 1979, ed. Filomena Simora with Nada Beth Glick (New
York: Bowker, 1979), p. 337.

[6]Ibid., p. 335.

[7]Murray S. Martin, Budgetary Control in Academic Libraries (Greenwich, Conn.: JAI, 1978).

[8]Ibid., p. 25.

A MODEST MANAGEMENT APPROACH

Susan Lee

In past years when library resources were plentiful and scrutiny was all but absent, it was of little consequence that management decisions did not always result in the most service being provided for each dollar expended. In years past libraries provided a minimum of services; they were caretakers and maintainers, not developers or innovators. But because college libraries are now responsible for the delivery of a growing range of services directly related to the quality of education and scholarship, the importance of improving management has increased.

Recognizing this, librarians have become management-conscious. Modern management tools, such as statistical modeling, systems analysis, and computer applications, are being promoted with enthusiasm. But while most of these management techniques are of value to university and research libraries, they are impractical for the college library administrator who is without a planning department or even a single systems analyst. For the college library director the need for balancing costs with utility often rules out the adoption of sophisticated methodologies that would be more appropriate for larger, more complex organizations. The problems and particularities of the college library call for a more modest management approach.

In regard to the management process, perhaps the most significant aspect of the college library is the lack of accepted and quantifiable criteria for measuring its performance. Without such standards it is most difficult, if not

impossible, to judge if the business of the library is being
performed well or poorly. Librarianship has no equivalent
of games won or lost, earnings per share, or return on in-
vested capital. Unlike a for-profit business, a college library has few accepted measures that permit us to evaluate
its performance objectively. In addition, this lack of performance measures makes it most difficult to evaluate the
probable benefits that might result from a considered course
of action.

Recognizing this difficulty, we must move beyond it.
We cannot allow this absence of performance standards to
keep us from improving the management process. While we
must as a profession strive toward the articulation of standardized performance measures, we must in the meantime
recognize the contribution to improved performance that better management planning can make.

Peter Drucker, an insightful and prolific writer on the
subject of business performance and management, has most
emphatically supported the proposition that the performance
of not-for-profit service organizations can be improved by
strengthening the process by which they are managed.[1] In
all probability our efforts to strengthen the management
process will enable us to accomplish more with the available resources. For the purposes of this article I will
leave the question of performance standards unanswered.
Acknowledging the difficulty of measuring the "ends," I will
approach the "means" of management--specifically, the
planning process.

Although long-range planning in business has been
growing rapidly, many college librarians either have no
long-range planning program or are dissatisfied with the one
they have. Many college librarians are thinking about creating a formal long-range planning program, yet there continue
to be widespread expressions of doubt about the process. In
the planning area, as in so many areas of management, serious semantic problems exist. Many organizations do not
use the term "long-range planning" but substitute such
phrases as "integrated planning," "comprehensive planning,"
"programming," or just plain "planning." Justice Holmes
once observed that:

> A word is not crystal, transparent and unchanged.
> It is the skin of a living thought and may vary
> greatly in color and content according to the
> circumstances and the time in which it is used.[2]

This observation is true of the words "long-range planning." But although the words may mean different things to different people at different times, basic principles and patterns exist. Whatever term is used, planning means thinking ahead, and extending our time horizon.

Much of what is uniquely attractive about small organizations proves to be a barrier to planning. The informality of the small organization discourages written plans while encouraging spontaneous personal judgments. In the college library time is also a significant barrier to the development of a formal planning process. The director must wear many hats. Management levels are thin and daily demands are many. The temptations to drift along until serious problems arise are great. Day-to-day crises draw our attention and our energies, thus perpetuating a vicious cycle in which crises proliferate because of the lack of planning.

Also, the college library director usually has had little direct management training. Library schools continue to produce skilled librarians but in most cases neglect the management side of the professional role. Nor does librarianship usually attract those who aspire to manage. We usually identify ourselves with more traditional visible library functions and feel most comfortable with the operational side of librarianship. Nevertheless, it is often our duty to manage, even when the task is unfamiliar and perhaps somewhat frightening. So in writing this I address myself to the college library director who has neither the luxury of a staff consultant nor released time for advanced management training. Much of the existing literature deals in abstracts; I shall try to present observations and suggestions that are both realistic and more immediately useful to my colleagues.

Stepping Back to Look at the Forest

Planning can minimize a fledgling manager's discomfort. It can enable both manager and staff to see the organization from a new perspective, leave off counting the trees, and instead concentrate on visualizing the shape of the forest. Planning that is long-range raises fundamental questions and gives all staff members a share in the "agonizing reappraisal of the crucial problems and opportunities facing the organization."[4] Occasional preoccupation with such questions as "where are we going?" is replaced by frequent consideration of such questions as "are we making satisfactory progress with respect to the plan?" and "are our plans still valid?"

By planning in a continuous cyclical process we can constantly survey our destination and continuously reevaluate our position.

The planning process also provides the means for reinvigorating the staff, certainly a significant concern for all library managers. Sooner or later most organizations run out of steam, reach a plateau, or lose their way. As John Argenti points out in his book on corporate planning, [5] two reasons for an organization "going off the boil" are either that the organization does not have a clear objective or that it does not know how to achieve it. I would suggest that these two problems are addressed by the planning process. So, at least, planning should prevent stagnation; at best it will provide stimulation.

The specific planning technique presented below must be adapted by each director to his or her unique situation. The actual operational details will vary among libraries, reflecting a variety of factors unique to the individual library. Yet there clearly are underlying analytical steps that are important for the development of an efficient planning sequence.

Starting

If you find that starting is the highest hurdle in this planning process, do not feel alone. According to a survey of over 100 small businesses, the most difficult point in planning is the start. [6] A simple, easily used tool is the standard list of bookkeeping accounts, adapted for long-range planning purposes. This can work well for a small organization that has a fairly limited number of accounts. The trick is to have few enough so that they can all be kept in view. The "List of Accounts ..." (p. 69) presents a partially completed form indicating a shift in personnel. The chart indicates both quantitative and qualitative personnel changes with associated changes in related areas. A full-time professional librarian will be added to the reference staff, and a position in the cataloging department will be cut from that of a full-time professional to a thirty-hour subprofessional. These moves have already been decided upon, but the changes in organizational objectives have yet to be articulated. These two related decisions indicate a shift in priorities that will be placed in context as the planning process develops.

The completion of this form will give you something

<u>List of Accounts, Adapted for Planning Purposes</u>

Item	Change Next Year	Comment
ACQUISITION DEPARTMENT administration gift and exchange order division serial division binding	M, m	more catalog card sets arriving with books from the jobber. additional acquisitions due to new professional
CATALOG DEPARTMENT administration monograph cataloging serial cataloging searching section filing section catalog maintenance	m	more dependence on externally produced cataloging, less original cataloging
CIRCULATION administration college circulation community circulation reserves	S	increased circulation due to bibliographic instruction
REFERENCE DEPARTMENT administration reference division interlibrary loan newspapers and microtexts film rental service	l S	the addition of a reference position and the downgrading of a cataloging position
PERSONNEL Professional Clerical Students	L, l M, m	
CAPITAL EQUIPMENT	S	new typewriter
OFFICE SUPPLIES	S	additional office supplies. less catalog cards needed
SPECIAL ACCOUNTS photocopy service publications travel professional expenses equipment maintenance and repair	S	allocation for new position

INSTRUCTIONS:
All changes are estimated in relation to the preceding year. If a qualitative change is anticipated, use the following symbols: l, large; m, medium; s, small. If a quantitative change is anticipated, use the following symbols: L, large; M, medium; S, small. Note that the notions of small, medium, and large changes are obviously subjective and will vary with the person using the form. The notion of qualitative change would cover such items as the changes resulting in ILL from entering a cooperative group or the using of a new source of supplies or equipment repair.

concrete that you can discuss with your staff. This form
when filled out is not entirely self-explanatory, but it will
point out topics that need discussion. In our example the
completion of this form made us look at the related changes
that need to be planned for, equipment and supplies that will
be needed, peripheral effects on related departments, and
anticipated shifts in demands for services affecting the whole
organization. The use of this planning form will make public what up to this point has been kept in the privacy of the
director's mind. In addition, it will facilitate the beginning
of the formulation of goals and objectives.

Involving your professional staff in the discussions
will give them a feel for where the library is going and the
various problems to be confronted. Involving your staff in
this process will encourage them to think of the organization
as a whole rather than only about their particular speciality.
Participating in the planning process encourages them to
clarify their contributions in terms of the whole. To do
this they must develop a sense of the library's mission, its
character, and its importance. Looking at the overall picture will give them a certain detachment, a certain perspective on their day-to-day activities. It will be beneficial to
all concerned if the staff, through their participation in the
planning process, begin to develop an executive point of view.

Staff participation in all institutional planning is superior to long-range planning done solely or mainly at the departmental level. Staff participation is particularly advanta-
geous when two different planners are competing for limited
resources, and a choice has to be made between them. The
ability to present an overall plan that the professional staff
has participated in is one way to impress an administration
with the cogency of one's arguments.

High professional performance must be encouraged in
the organization, but it must always be related to the needs
of the whole. Surely individual workmanship is essential.
Without it no library can flourish. In fact, an organization
becomes demoralized if it does not demand of its members
the most scrupulous workmanship of which they are capable.
But as Peter Drucker points out so clearly, we always run
the risk that true professionals will believe that they are ac-
complishing something when in effect they are just "polishing
stones or collecting footnotes."[8]

Information

The next step in planning comes with the realization of the
need for information. You will realize that certain gaps exist, and you may have to gather particular data on present
operating conditions. Imaginative thinking cannot be done in
a vacuum; measurements make things visible and concrete.
The measurements we use will determine what we pay attention to. The things we decide to measure become important,
and the things we omit are passed over. Direct usefulness
in the planning process is an excellent filter through which
to sift our various statistics. Do you really need attendance
figures by the hour or will a sample provide you with the
necessary information in a less cumbersome way? If you do
not need them for planning, chances are you do not need
them. Any set of figures not an integral part of the planning process should be carefully scrutinized.

In our example specific figures on expected operating
changes of both departments are needed. In terms of the
reference department, the addition of the reference position
indicates that we had to gather information on the additional
numbers of hours reference-desk services would be available
and the number of classes to be instructed each semester.
In terms of the cataloging department, we will want to look
at the number of monographs to be cataloged in the respective years, the percentage of original cataloging this will include, and the percentage of revision expected to be necessary. Qualitative differences indicated need to be specified.
In this case the downgrading of the cataloging position means
more reliance on commercially produced cataloging with minimal in-house revision. The more frequent use of commercially produced catalog card sets supplied by the book jobber
and arriving with the books has created both qualitative and
quantitative changes in the cataloging department.

Objectives

Like a Molière character who discovered that for forty years
he had been speaking "prose" without knowing it, your staff
has been operating on as-yet-unarticulated objectives. The
formulation of organizational objectives is one of the major
steps in the planning process. Having looked at the current
situation and the factors that led up to it, one is now in a
position to select appropriate goals and to formulate a set
of objectives.

In the situation referred to in the "List of Accounts
..." less emphasis is being placed on the development of
complete and exact bibliographic records; greater emphasis
will now be placed on the use of externally produced cataloging. Also, more emphasis will now be placed on direct
user services. How is this to be reflected in the written
objectives of the library? When carefully examined, these
staff changes indicate fundamental changes in the mission of
the library. The library is no longer seen by the director
as a mere storehouse of knowledge but rather as the deliv-
erer of information. A dynamic objective needs to be formulated, one that catches the aggressiveness of these changes.
The library staff might define this goal as, "To help our
students, very actively, to acquire a variety of basic intellectual skills and habits of thought." The library, by stat-
ing such a goal and designing strategy to meet that objective,
may be able to take a more aggressive role within the college, no longer merely passively serving as a warehouse.

The statements of objectives are the crux of the planning process. Everything you have done up to this point has
been done to produce them, and everything you and your staff
do from this point on is based on them. Keep in mind that
objectives are fundamental to the nature of your organization.
They are therefore meant to last. They are the reasons for
its very existence, that for which it came into being and for
which it now exists.

Do not dictate to your staff your list of objectives:
ask them what they think. Your task here is to introduce a
decision-making system, not to make all the decisions. Certainly you should challenge their answers if you are not satisfied, but your overall strategy should be the result of
much discussion.

This process cannot be approached casually. It takes
time and a great deal of patient work. Your staff must
come to respect you and the process enough to tell all they
know, to share their ideas, and to discuss the future of the
organization, and hence their own future, with you. Your
special role is that of leader, contributing quality to purpose
through the projection of quality of person. The director's
function above all is to be the exemplar of a permanent human aspiration, the determination to devote one's powers to
jobs worth doing. 9

Strategy Formulation

In formulating strategies to reach our stated objectives we need to ask ourselves three questions: "What might I do?" "What can I do?" and "What do I want to do?" This is probably the most difficult and complex section of the planning process. Prepare a list of actions that you and your staff might take in order to achieve your goals. In the previous step you have given yourself an objective. Following our example, we have the goal of "actively helping our students acquire a variety of basic intellectual skills and habits of thought." The means by which part of this task is to be performed already exists in the present operation. Even if the existing services are carried out in just the same way as in the past some contribution will continue to be made. Now the challenge is to find better ways and means of adding to these services. The result will be the establishment of coordinated plans that blueprint the manner in which the organization should be able to reach its objectives. You will need to specify each action, who will do what, when, where, and why. The detail of the "how" will be up to the appropriate department.

Distinctive Competence and Value Added

In formulating strategy management should emphasize that which its organization can do best. Philip Selznick refers to that which a company is particularly good at as its "distinctive competence." Size is certainly a factor limiting the resources of the college library, but it is also a factor that facilitates a distinctive competence. The staff of the college library must find and adopt a strategy that makes the greatest use of its size as a strength. To plan a multimedia presentation for library orientation would be a near-suicidal project for a college library with limited equipment and production talent. But to take the individualized personal approach of informal talks to small groups of students would not only be feasible but also would exploit the personal atmosphere of the college library.

This personal approach provided by the college library is its distinctive competence and part of the value added. "Value added" is the difference between the physical object of production (a printed book) and the total product received by the customer (the printed book plus the service involved in getting that book to the particular user). Genuine concern for an individually known patron, personal contact of management with the customer, and a high level of personalized service can make for one happy customer.

There is a common attitude within our profession that our task is to provide the greatest possible amount of physical product per dollar spent. While the importance of cost cannot be denied, it is a serious mistake to visualize our job as one of merely reducing or controlling costs. Our consumers respond to atmosphere, staff attitudes, and many other intangible aspects of service. In planning our strategy we must realize that the product that our customers get when they come to the library encompasses a great deal more than merely the physical object. Of course, there is nothing startlingly new here. Now, however, college librarians can begin to capitalize deliberately on the strength of their relative smallness, and to see this as a distinctive competence that greatly increases the value added. We can stop feeling inferior because we do not have all the fancy toys the universities have and start to take a new pride in our uniqueness.

Daniel Gore points out that what makes the practice of librarianship possible is the narrow range of interest that any library clientele will have in the totality of published writings, and the narrow range of really necessary tasks. [10] If we think in terms of the user we will be able to find simpler ways of doing that which must be done. We can no longer afford the insular professional thinking that has us cataloging for catalogers. The myopic artist who paints for a narrower and narrower audience eventually becomes meaningless to the people.

It is a matter of priorities. Because of its size the college library can be more flexible in responding to individual student desires, can offer far more intimate student-staff relationships, and can afford much more experimentation. The college library can capitalize on its distinctive competence by providing a product to the students that is different and in some ways better than that provided by much larger institutions. There can be a togetherness that is simply not possible in larger institutions, an opportunity for students to see the library staff up close.

This close personal contact cannot be brushed aside as unimportant. My guess is that for certain kinds of young people it may be more constructive and helpful than exposure to the largest of book collections. If smallness is seen as an asset in strategy formulation it can generate actions and programs that will use the unique characteristics of the college library. Smallness can be an advantage if it is recognized and planned for in the college library.

External Resources

Of course, each of us cannot think of everything. Our closeness often keeps us from being effective critics. It is like trying to proofread your own paper; the words on paper so closely match what is in your mind that effective distance is impossible. Because the college library administrator is without a management team, he needs to look outside the library for professional counsel in the planning process. Here is where we can really help each other, and at no additional cost. Sophisticated planning experience is not necessary. Rather, what is needed is a check on our thinking in the formulation of a workable planning approach. Because we are nonprofit we can afford to be open with our peers in other institutions. Periodic meetings for long-range planning discussions would be a fruitful activity for our many blossoming cooperative groups. Perhaps only our egos detain us.

There also could be much more fruitful contact between the college librarian and our faculties of business administration/management. My experience has been that most professors are eager to help and can indeed be a most valuable asset. In addition, faculty who are brought in on discussing the planning process for the library seem to gain a new appreciation for the management problems faced by the library and a new admiration for the professional skills of the library staff. And we can always use more appreciation and admiration from our faculties.

Opportunity Costs

In planning our long-range strategies we should evaluate the various alternative activities under consideration in terms of their opportunity costs. According to the economist's definition, the cost of producing a certain product is the value of the other products that the resources used in its production could have produced instead. [11] It represents a forsaken alternative, so the "cost" differs from the usual kind in the sense that it is not the outlay cost that managers typically encounter and evaluate. For example, the cost of producing library services is the value of the goods and services that could be obtained from the labor, equipment, and materials used currently in producing these services. The costs of the inputs to an organization are their worth in their most valuable alternative uses.

The costs incurred by a library are often thought to include the money expended to obtain necessary resources. However, the library's money outlays are only part of the costs. Since our resources are limited, when they are used to produce a certain good or service less can be produced of some other product that could be provided from these same resources. A given amount of staff time can be used to provide cataloging, bibliographic instruction, book selection, or reference desk coverage. When staff time is used in one activity some value of alternative activities is given up.

A fixed resource is fixed only in relationship to a given period of time. The longer the time period, the more alternatives open to us. Thus the alternative uses of a resource will expand as our time period lengthens. For example, the college library staff has as alternative activities only those services that use present skills or less skilled activities, but given time the members of the staff can acquire other skills. In the long run alternatives tend to be greater and more varied than in the short run. Long-range planning that encompasses staff-development programs can greatly expand the alternative uses of staff time, allowing greater flexibility and diversity.

Change takes place in most libraries with or without planning. But when left to itself change will usually follow an expansion of present activities and similar services, without taking into account alternative uses of resources. Planning looks at the long run, providing an accurate estimate of alternatives, and thus providing greater alternatives. In the long run inputs are variable, so the optimal combination of resources can best be determined through careful long-range planning. William Hazlitt has observed that "man is the only animal that laughs and weeps; for he is the only animal that is struck by the difference between what things are and what they ought to be." Systematic long-range planning can help us to narrow this gap between the way things are and the way we would like them to be.

By this point in the process we should have a plan that says something about our goals and how they will be attained. It is what statisticians would call a "decision rule" and what systems engineers would call a "standing plan." When Hannibal inflicted the humiliating defeat on the Roman army at Cannae in 216 B. C. he led a ragged band against soldiers who were in possession of superior arms and better training. His plan, however, was so superior that those advantages proved relatively insignificant. Once we have an explicit plan we have something that can be evaluated and improved. While the planning process does not guarantee success, it is a vital ingredient in determining our future. Crawford H. Greenewalt, who chairs the Board of Du Pont, recently observed:

> The difference between a notably successful institution and one whose record is simply run-of-the-mill is seldom very great. It does not consist of brilliant and inspired flashes of genius--certainly not over a considerable period of time. The difference rather is in the small increment of extra performance, diffused over a very large number of individuals at all levels of the organization. [12]

Long-range planning of the type described in this chapter can furnish a stable foundation for this added difference.

Conclusion

Two conditions must exist for successful planning: the dedicated support of the library director and the full involvement of the professional staff. Long-range planning is the responsibility of the library director, who guides the destiny of the organization. And if the final plan is to be energetically supported by the operational staff it must recognize their problems and encompass their ideas. If these two conditions exist the planning process will successfully help the library manager to step out of the restricting confines of day-to-day problems and to take a challenging look at present operating methods, procedures, and philosophies. By providing a rational approach to decision making, planning will assist managers in evaluating proposals. In the fullest sense it is an aid to determining the best thing to do and the best means of doing it. At the same time, long-range planning can never provide a complete or final solution. The library profession itself is in transition; the future is beset with uncertainties. As library administrators we can only be certain that there will be no lack of problems and that nothing will turn out as we anticipate. This of course, is the real challenge in what we do.

Notes

[1]Peter Drucker, Management: Tasks, Responsibilities, Practices (New York: Harper and Row, 1974).

[2]George A. Steiner, ed. , Managerial Long-Range Planning (New York: McGraw-Hill, 1963), p. 131.

[3]Ibid. , p. 9.

[4]John Argenti, Corporate Planning: A Practical Guide (London: Allen and Unwin, 1968).

[5]Raymond M. Haas et al. , Long Range Planning for Small Businesses, Small Business Management Research Reports (Bloomington: Indiana University, Bureau of Business Research, 1964).

[6]Roger A. Golde, "Practical Planning for Small Business, " Harvard Business Review 42 (September-October 1964): 147-61.

[7]Peter Drucker, The Practice of Management (New York: Harper and Row, 1954), p. 122.

[8]John V. Petrof, Small Business Management: Concepts and Techniques for Improving Decisions (New York: McGraw-Hill, 1972).

[9]Daniel Gore, To Know a Library: Essays and Annual Reports, 1970-1976 (Westport, Conn. : Greenwood, 1977).

[10]Edwin Mansfield, Microeconomics: Theory and Applications (New York: Norton, 1970), p. 156.

[11]George A. Steiner, ed. , Managerial Long-Range Planning (New York: McGraw-Hill, 1963), p. 4.

PERSONNEL ADMINISTRATION IN THE COLLEGE LIBRARY

H. Palmer Hall, Jr.

Management courses in most library schools adequately cover most problems met by the new director of a college library. This is true even though the school experience may be five to fifteen years in the past by the time the librarian gets his or her first directorial position. With little management background beyond that obtained in the library management class and other library school classes the new director, assuming the existence of some modicum of common sense, can prepare an adequate cost estimate of new, proposed programs; can work with the physical plant staff on building and maintenance needs for the library; can even argue convincingly, though often unsuccessfully, for increases in the acquisitions budget. All that is needed is a reasonably facile mind, a firm grasp of the English language, and a basic knowledge of research methods. Aside from this the director needs to have kept up with the profession since leaving library school, must be able to assimilate the needs of the college community, and must be able to develop an idea of where the library needs to go in order to meet those needs.

For the administrator of the college library the one problem area not covered well in that management course is personnel administration. The new library director is probably as well prepared, though more nervous, as most older library directors to deal with the information explosion, with new concepts in librarianship, with the desire for increased automation combined with the realities of the budget. With

experience and knowledge of research on such matters, the
director feels reasonably confident of handling them well.
Combined with that is the additional benefit that the people
to whom he or she reports are generally not well informed
about the library and its operations. The administration of
the college will react well to almost any proposal for change
that is well written, shows a combination of good research
and good thought, and doesn't require a large increase in
the library's budget. A director opposed to change in the
library will normally be successful in this opposition. The
chances of impressing the college administration are weighted
heavily in the director's favor--with one possible exception.

That exception exists, unfortunately, on the library
staff. Personnel problems can become a time-consuming
"cancer on the directorship." While personnel problems exist in libraries of all sizes, the director of the college library faces problems unknown to the director of a large research library. I like to think of the director of the large
library as insulated in a large office, protected by a circle
of superprofessionals, assistant director for this, assistant
director for that, personnel officer, unapproachable secretary.
That insulation keeps the director from some of the problems encountered by the counterpart in the smaller library.
I doubt that the director of the large library has significant
contact with the library's nonprofessional staff. Although
possibly familiar to the lower-echelon professional staff, the
director does not really have that much of an association
with them. Involved in meetings with branch library heads,
with budget preparation teams, with meetings with provosts
and vice-presidents, the director is unlikely to develop true
personal relations even with the other professional librarians
below, at least, the department-head level.

In the small library the director knows everyone and
knows them well. This is both an advantage and a disadvantage: an advantage because this familiarity with the whole
staff prepares the director for personnel changes and provides information about the staff's capability to adapt to
change; a disadvantage because the director is continually
consulted over many staff problems that in a larger library
would be handled at lower levels of responsibility. A director of a small library, seeing that work isn't being done
properly by a member of the clerical staff, will normally
inform the professional supervising in the clerk's area and
hope that the professional can handle the problem. In some
cases it becomes embarrassing for both the director and the

professional to have to have such conferences. There are
also many cases in which a member of the clerical staff
feels free to go to the director to make a complaint.

While the case-study method of teaching personnel administration is no longer considered the sine qua non, I
would like to point out a few examples of the clerk/director
relationship that may be likely to happen in the small academic library.

Salary problems. This is particularly important in
light of recent and scheduled increases in the minimum-
wage law. In many small colleges and universities, forced
to comply and, generally, wanting to comply, the new
minimum-pay scale created new problems for employees
holding higher-ranking clerical responsibility and several
years of seniority. A finite amount of money is available
for salary increases within a single year on any college
campus, and when a whole group of employees has to be
brought up to a higher minimum employees already earning
more than that minimum will probably be disappointed in
their comparatively smaller pay raises. The situation currently in effect in many college libraries is that the range
in salaries from the lowest-level nonprofessional salary to
the highest is frequently less than $.50/hour. This is not
just, and the director will hear about it from some of the
more valuable and now most unhappy members of the clerical staff. The only solution is absolute honesty about the
situation and sincerity in explaining that once the most recent series of minimum-pay increases has been effected,
the situation will revert to a more normal pay sequence.

Does this approach really handle the problem? Probably not. The injustice is there and will remain there until
the next year's pay raises go into effect. The clerical staff
remains disappointed and should be expected to remain disappointed until the situation is righted. The library director
is in a "no win" situation. The director who is genuinely
concerned about the problems with lower-paid clerical workers and who responds honestly in such situations has a better chance of maintaining good relations with the staff than
the director who merely makes an announcement and does
not face the staff in person. At the risk of sounding con-
tentious, the head of the large library does not normally
face this kind of problem. This director may have a personnel director in the library to handle such matters or a
library clerical staff committee, representing the workers,

to whom he or she can issue an answer to such enquiries.
But, generally speaking, the director will not have to face
the disgruntled employee in a one-to-one situation.

Interdepartmental quarrels. This may be prosaic and
obvious, but it is not always possible to determine which department in a library has control over a particular item when
it is ordered or arrives. A library may purchase, using
funds from the book budget, an item that comes into the
building on a weekly basis, is cumulated monthly and then
annually. Sometimes this is necessary when using line-item
budgets if the library staff wants to purchase a new index
while preserving the periodicals budget. The acquisitions
clerk feels that since the index was purchased with funds
from his department, he must retain control of the materials. The periodicals clerk feels, just as properly, that
anything arriving that frequently should be under her control.
The professionals in charge of the two departments agree
with their clerks, meaning they disagree with each other.
The problem comes to the library director's office.

The problem would not reach the director's office in
a large library. A professional dubbed "assistant director
for technical services" would probably reach the ultimate
decision about the matter. But in the smaller library there
is frequently no one else to turn to. With a staff of from
three to nine librarians, the director does not normally have
the luxury of appointing a brace of assistant directors and
department heads. "Too many chiefs, not enough Indians"
is as bad for a small library as for a tribe of Indians. The
solution in the library that did have the problem was to insist
on further departmental cooperation. It would be absurd to
set up a separate "periodicals" check-in unit within the acquisitions department, but the periodicals department could
inform the acquisitions department if any shipments were
missing--thus assuring control of funds.

Staff jealousy. The A/V clerk doesn't do as much
work as the rest of the clerks, complains a member of the
cataloging staff. Whom does she go to? To the chief cataloger? She has no authority over the A/V department. The
A/V professional? She's too likely to defend her own clerical staff. The library director? Why not? After all, he
has responsibility for the whole staff.

Would such a situation spring up in a large academic
library? Possibly, but it isn't very likely. In the large

library, departments are more likely to be segregated from each other. The clerical employee in cataloging may not even know the clerks in the other departments, but in the small library everyone works closely together and can see what everyone else is doing. I sometimes think the staff believes I have the easiest job in the library. They can see me reading journals, writing, having pleasant chats with the Academic Vice-President, with departmental chairs, and with other faculty members. The director doesn't really do very much when there isn't formal budgetary preparation or planning sessions. Or so, at least, they must think occasionally.

Such problems do spring up in the small library, and the director must be able to resolve them at least to the point where everyone can continue to work together smoothly. In this case the library director implemented a staff-development program for all of the clerks in the library. For two hours every other week the entire clerical staff was sent to one particular department (varying each time) to see what really does go on. The professional librarian in charge of the department and the clerks who actually do most of the work demonstrated and explained what they were doing. I do not say that this kind of approach would make the cataloging clerk happy about the work done by the A/V clerk, but at least after such a program she would have a basis for complaints.

If these three cases make any particular point it may be that the case-study approach is not really appropriate for personnel management. It is, however, the most common method for teaching the subject. In the final analysis there are only a few rules for personnel administration of the clerical staff:

1. Select good librarians for those supervisory roles. If the librarian/supervisor is sympathetic and efficient, problems will be nipped in the bud before they have a chance to bloom and canker.

2. Be honest about all situations affecting the clerical staff. This may not make the individual clerks happy, but it should make you happier and should show them that you are trying to cope with their problems.

3. Be flexible and understanding. It is quite possible that your clerical staff has good ideas that could help the library run more effectively. Don't block off this source of information.

    4. Finally, be aware that the nonprofessional staff is composed of thinking, human individuals. Treat them so.

    The professional staff can also cause problems for the new director. Whether the library has three librarians or ten, there will probably be someone who is certain that the college could have made a much better choice of a director than it did. If a new director is brought in from the outside there will be at least one person who feels that promotion should have come from within the ranks. If the promotion was made from within the ranks at least one person will feel that the wrong librarian was promoted or that a new librarian with new ideas should have been brought in from outside the area.

    But even after acceptance by the library faculty there will be problems. Major components for the library budget are always good fodder for a small-scale war. The periodicals librarian may feel that the library is devoting too large a share of the budget to books; the acquisitions librarian argues for more funds for the book collection; and the forces of the avant-garde, the media staff, yowl for more money for nonprint media. The library director, in his or her not-so-divine wisdom, who does not involve faculty in determining the proper distribution of a too-small budget is heading for serious trouble. Consultation is an absolute necessity for the small library and participation in determination is probably even better. If nothing else, the library director can dissolve faculty resentment (and here I speak of the library faculty) of "his" or "her" policies if those policies become "our" policies.

    In their classic essay on "The Changing Role of Directors of Academic Libraries" (CRL, March 1973, pp. 103-25) Robert Downs and Arthur McAnally appear to be most shocked, in discussing elements of the university that prompt the demise of the director, that the staff is among those elements. While the authors pointedly refer only to large research libraries, saying that, "Oddly the chief librarians of colleges and junior colleges do not appear to be affected," the fact is that the library faculty can make even the director of a small library very uncomfortable. There are several methods: in the small college the library faculty is normally on good terms with the teaching faculty. All the librarian has to do to make an enemy for the director is to respond to a question about cancelation of an expensive periodical by saying, "Oh, that decision was made by the director. He feels that the library can't afford to purchase such titles, " or, "I would love to purchase films, but the Director ...," or even "She just doesn't understand the college. " In a well-working consultative process such statements could not be made.

A problem is beginning to crop up that may make librarians in small libraries very resentful, if not openly angry. I refer to the relatively new appearance in standard advertising media for librarians with "experience in large academic or research libraries. " If this trend continues it may mean that librarians who begin their careers working in smaller libraries will have little opportunity to effect a career change if they later decide that they would prefer working in a large library. This could result in dissatisfaction among the staffs of smaller libraries. At the very least it reflects a kind of elitism about the large libraries of the country, a feeling that they are somehow doing work of a significantly different nature from that of their colleagues at the college level.

It is becoming more and more apparent that the library director or staff search committee for new librarians must take overall goals of the librarian applying for positions into careful consideration. A new librarian, fresh from library school, desiring to work in a large academic library, should probably not be employed in a small academic library. The graduate's career goals will not be met, and the small academic library may be stuck with an unhappy librarian. If the staff were large such unhappiness could be easily overlooked, but on small staffs it could make a significant demoralizing impression.

In general, dealing with the staff at the professional level requires the same candor as discussed earlier in relationship to the clerical and paraprofessional staff. If the A/V librarian must attend that important conference in Boston, 2, 000 miles away, and your travel budget cannot possibly justify such an expenditure, it is necessary to be open and honest about the situation. A better method is to involve all librarians in the budgeting of the library. If you do so each will be more likely to understand fiscal restraints.

It is also true that the small library is less likely to have the wonderful new innovations that place large libraries in the forefront of the profession. With computer systems

as expensive as they are, regardless of industry disclaimers
that the price of computers is the only thing going down in
the economy, most small libraries cannot purchase new automated circulation systems, on-line catalogs, COM catalogs,
dedicated terminals for on-line searching, and so on.   Librarians working in small libraries may begin to feel that
they really are in the hinterlands and are being passed by
by technology.   Because of a sense of inevitability, that this
is the future of libraries, it is important that the staffs of
those libraries that cannot currently afford such technology
remain aware of the field.   The only way to do this is to
afford through the budget the means of acquiring the professional literature, of attending workshops, and of visiting
other, larger libraries.   Continuing education for librarians
is at least as important in the small library as in the large,
probably more important.

        The most important thing to remember about person-
nel relations in the small academic library is that personnel
relations are actually human relations.   In the small library,
with closer interrelationship among all parts of the staff, the
human-relations component of personnel relations is of primary importance.   Without good human relations the library
director had best call it quits (or, perhaps, try to move to
a larger library).   Thus the most important quality for the
director of a college library is not to be able to budget, to
be able to plan for the future, to keep abreast of the literature, to be a good bookperson, to know bibliographies, to be
able to do adequate self-studies or research proposals.   The
most important qualification for the library director is to be
human, to have feelings and recognize those feelings in staff
members.   The other things can be learned or have already
been learned before the librarian gets a first supervisory
position.   Good, practicing "human relations" must be acquired before the librarian can obtain a second administrative office.

EQUAL EMPLOYMENT OPPORTUNITY
AND THE COLLEGE LIBRARY ADMINISTRATOR

Jeniece Guy

College librarians tend to consider equal employment questions a worry for only large public institutions, but recruiting, selecting, hiring, and all other aspects of employment
are much more closely regulated by laws and government-
agency regulations now than in the past, and college libraries are subject to these laws and regulations no less than
are other employers.

Perhaps those that cause the most confusion and mis-
understanding are the Equal Employment Opportunity laws.
Five major laws form the core of Equal Employment Opportunity legislation. The Civil Rights Act prevents discrimination on the basis of race, national origin, sex, or religion.
The Age Discrimination Act of 1967 prohibits discrimination
against people aged forty to seventy. The 1974 Equal Pay
Amendment to the Fair Labor Standards Act prohibits differences in pay based on sex. The Vocational Rehabilitation
Act of 1973 prohibits employers with federal contracts of
$2,500 or more from discriminating against the handicapped.
Finally, the Vietnam Era Veterans Readjustment Act of 1974
extended EEO protection to Vietnam War veterans and employees with federal contracts of $10,000 or more.

Although the terms "equal employment opportunity" and
"affirmative action" are often used interchangeably, they are
really two different concepts. Equal employment opportunity
means that the same opportunities are available to all regardless of status. Affirmative action goes beyond equal employ-

ment opportunity and requires employers to make special
efforts to recruit, hire, and promote certain groups protected
by equal employment opportunity laws. Not every group protected by EEO laws is covered by affirmative action. Employers are required to take affirmative action to hire wom-
en, Vietnam War veterans, the mentally and physically handicapped, and certain racial and ethnic minorities (designated
as protected groups): blacks, Hispanics, Asians, and American Indians. Affirmative action is not required for those
over age forty or for religious minorities, even though both
groups are protected by Equal Employment Opportunity laws.

While the equal employment opportunity laws apply to
all but the smallest employers, affirmative action applies to
only those employers who are federal contractors or recipients of federal aid or grants. Most large universities and
many smaller colleges are required to take affirmative action and to have written affirmative action plans. Public
colleges are likely to be part of a municipal or state government that is required to have an affirmative action plan.
Voluntary affirmative action is also permissible under civil
rights legislation, so colleges and universities that do not
receive enough federal aid to make affirmative action mandatory may still choose to have voluntary affirmative action
plans. Normally the affirmative action plan will be developed and administered by the college affirmative action officer or the college personnel office. Nevertheless, the college librarian should be familiar with the components of the
affirmative action plan since that plan affects the employment
decisions the college librarian will make.

The affirmative action plan has several components.
The first is a statement of the institution's commitment to
affirmative action, which also assigns the responsibility for
affirmative action to a specific campus office or offices.
The next major component is the Workforce Utilization Analysis, which is an evaluation of the current utilization of
women, minorities, and other protected groups in the college. This section of the affirmative action plan usually
contains charts showing all of the major job classifications
in the employing institution and the number of women, minorities, handicapped, etc. in each job classification. Such
an analysis makes it possible to determine which jobs have
or do not have a satisfactory representation of women and
minorities. The next component in the affirmative action
plan is to set goals for the hiring or promotion of women
and minorities in those areas of the institution where they

are underrepresented. Finally, the plan contains a timetable for achieving the goals, and a plan of action.

The numerical goals for employment of nonprofessionals will be based on the percentage of the work force that is minority or female in the geographical area from which the college recruits employees. There is reason for caution here, because courts may sometimes take the position that employers must recruit from a wider geographical area when there are insufficient numbers of minorities in the immediate geographical area.

While the nonprofessional goals will be based on the composition of the local work force, professional employees are normally recruited nationally; thus the employment goals for librarians will reflect the composition of the profession as a whole. The college librarian may be asked to assist the college affirmative action office by supplying data or sources of data on the racial, ethnic, and sexual composition of the library profession. Although the U.S. Census does contain this data, the 1970 census is now out-of-date and the data from the 1980 census may not be available before 1982. Since 1972 the American Library Association Office for Library Personnel Resources has conducted an annual survey of the racial, ethnic, and sexual composition of library school graduates. This survey can be used as a supplement to update the 1970 census figures until the 1980 figures are available.

Affirmative action for the handicapped usually does not consist of numerical hiring goals but of job analysis and physical modifications of the work area to remove barriers to the employment of the handicapped.

Although it is advisable for the college librarian to be aware of both legislation governing the employment process and the affirmative action regulations, the college librarian will probably be most interested in which day-to-day work practices are affected by existing federal, state, and local regulations and how these work practices are so affected.

Recruiting

Recruiting is the first step in the employment process, and the recruitment of employees is an important element in the college's affirmative action plan. The college librarian needs to be concerned with both where and how employees are recruited. Excessive reliance on word-of-mouth recruitment is inadvisable especially in situations where minorities and women are underutilized. Jobs should be advertised as widely as possible to ensure an applicant pool that is large enough to be representative of the work force. Furthermore, the college must make special efforts to encourage minorities and women to apply. Ads should indicate that the employer is an equal opportunity employer and, if appropriate, an affirmative action employer. Nonprofessional recruiting includes placing ads in minority or women's publications, running ads on local minority radio stations, and using the state employment service.

The college librarian, likely to be more directly involved in the recruiting of professional applicants, may be at a loss when informed by the college's affirmative action officer that it is necessary to make a special effort to recruit minority librarians or to recruit women applicants for administrative positions. Library administrators frequently ask where minority librarians can be recruited. Areas suggested for affirmative action recruiting are:

1. Library schools with a large number of minority students. Two accredited library schools, Atlanta University and North Carolina Central, have a large black student population and can be used as a source of black librarians. The University of Arizona has an institute for Spanish-speaking librarians and is thus a source for recruitment of Spanish librarians. Many library employers who list positions with library schools list only with those schools in their geographical area; however, if employers would also list positions not only with the abovementioned library schools but with library schools on a nationwide basis, there would be a greater response from minorities.

2. Minority caucuses within the profession. The American Library Association Office for Library Personnel Resources publishes a list of minority and women's organizations in librarianship. Some of the newsletters of these organizations have job listings, and when they do not the chairperson may be able to suggest sources for minority recruitment.

3. Advertising in local minority newspapers and radio stations. Library employers should not overlook the

local minority press and media as a source for advertising both professional and nonprofessional jobs. Directors of minority media including minority newspapers and minority radio stations can be found in Affirmative Action: A Comprehensive Recruiting Guide. [1]

Employee Selection

Once the recruitment activities have provided a sufficient applicant pool the next step in the employment process is the selection of the employee. Contrary to what is sometimes heard, affirmative action regulations do not require an employer to hire an unqualified woman or minority-group member. The employer must make certain, however, that the selection process is free from bias and must be able to demonstrate that the person who is hired is the most qualified applicant for the position. All pre-employment inquiries, whether in an interview or on an application blank, must be carefully designed to ensure that there is no bias. Bias goes beyond overt discrimination. It has also been interpreted as that which has a discriminatory effect. For example, an employer can no longer ask a woman applicant whether she is married, what her husband's occupation is, or the ages of her children. While there is no federal law that expressly prohibits such questions, use of those questions may be evidence of discrimination against women. Some states also have more specific restrictions, so it is necessary to be familiar with local regulations as well as federal ones.

Another example of a pre-employment inquiry that may be considered discriminatory is a question about arrest records. Questions about criminal convictions may be acceptable, however, if the applicant has been convicted of a crime related to the job. It is all right to refuse to hire someone convicted of embezzlement for a job as a bank teller; it is less defensible to refuse to hire that same person for a job that does not involve handling money. Other questions that should be excluded from the pre-employment inquiry are those concerning sex, height and weight, and national origin.

In a secular college religious background is probably not likely to enter the pre-employment inquiry unless the issue is raised by the applicant. Religion often becomes an issue, however, when the applicant's religious practices require some sort of special consideration. The need to avoid work on Saturdays and Sundays, to be home before sundown on the eve of the Sabbath, or to wear certain clothing, or religious prohibitions against union membership are often of concern to job applicants. Courts have held that employers must make reasonable accommodations to an applicant's religious beliefs. An employer should consider letting an applicant begin work an hour early or shorten the lunch hour in the case of the person who must be home before sundown on the Sabbath. On the other hand, the employer does not have to disrupt the entire organization to accommodate one employee's religious beliefs. If a no-Saturday or a no-Sunday work schedule can be easily accommodated, then the employer has a duty to allow the employee to work that schedule. If, however, allowing the employee to have the Sabbath off requires that many other employees change their schedule, this is an undue hardship on those employees, and it is not necessary to accommodate the individual employee.

Employers often ask, "If there is so much that can't be brought up in a job interview, what can be asked?" There are many things that may be discussed in a job interview; the critical factor for the library administrator to remember is that the questions must be job-related and must not have a discriminatory effect on any of the protected groups, i.e. minorities, women, the handicapped, and persons aged forty to seventy. Questions must also steer clear of national origin or religious practices. Among topics that can be discussed are the applicant's work experience and work record at the previous job, attendance record, and reason for leaving the previous job. The key point to remember is that the questions must be job-related.

EEO considerations also apply to other aspects of the selection process as well. Whenever there are questions of adverse impact on any of the protected groups, the employer must be able to show that the job requirements or qualifications are necessary to perform the job. An employer cannot ask for a B.A. degree from a library assistant, or a second Master's and two years of college library experience for a reference librarian, unless it can be demonstrated that those requirements are absolutely essential for the performance of the job. One way to help prevent discrimination complaints arising out of job advertisements is to have alternative qualifications, such as a B.A. or four years of relevant experience. The problem with this approach is that the employer still must be able to prove that both sets of requirements provide the applicant with the necessary skills to do the job. Detailed job analysis is usually the only way this can be done. Job analysis can be an expensive and time-consuming process requiring the use of industrial psychologists; however, the librarian should consult the college personnel department, which may be able to assist the librarian with a job-analysis project. Some employers are expressing job requirements in terms of demonstrated competencies rather than in terms of formal education or years of experience. Such competencies for the library assistant might read "typing skill 45 w. p. m. , and ability to handle public contacts tactfully and courteously." Even such competencies as these should come from job analysis; however, the skills, knowledge, and abilities required by the job are probably easier to establish than the relationship of the skills, knowledge, and ability to formal education and years of experience.

Another procedure that was once popular in the process of employee selection was pre-employment tests. Many such tests had an adverse impact on minorities and were also shown to be of no value in predicting on-the-job success. For this reason federal requirements now state that pre-employment tests must be job-related, that is, a valid predictor of job success. The validation process is, once again, an expensive and time-consuming process requiring the services of a psychologist or specialist in testing. Because of the complex requirements for pre-employment testing, many employers have now limited pre-employment tests. The college library employer, with limited funds for test validation, would do well to confine pre-employment tests to actual work samples, e. g. , typing tests for typists, putting numbers in order for shelvers.

Once the employment decision is made the employer must be aware of the provisions of the Equal Pay Act, which prohibits paying men and women differently for jobs that are equal or substantially equal.

Other Employment Practices

Other aspects of the employer/employee relationship that are affected by EEO considerations include promotion, performance evaluation, disciplinary action, and termination.

Promotion decisions are subject to the same requirements as initial hiring decisions. Questions that should not be asked in an initial applicant interview also should not be asked of an in-house applicant, nor should such information be taken into consideration. Refusal to promote a female staff member because she has preschool age children is illegal sex discrimination just as much as is refusal to hire a woman with preschool children. Of course, if the woman staff member with preschool children has job-related problems, such as poor job performance or poor attendance, the promotion can be denied on those grounds. Once again, job-relatedness is the key.

Since affirmative action guidelines suggest that job openings be advertised widely, with special emphasis on advertising sources that will be utilized by women and minorities, employers sometimes wonder if these requirements prevent promotion of an internal candidate. While it is usually necessary to advertise vacancies, particularly professional ones, where there may not be a large enough internal pool of minorities or women, this does not prevent promotion of an internal candidate as long as he or she is the best qualified applicant and as long as minorities or women have been given a chance to apply and have been considered on equal terms with other candidates. Indeed, a policy of promoting internal candidates can be an important component of an affirmative action plan in that it can provide opportunities for minorities and women in entry-level positions to advance.

An employer is required to ensure equal treatment not only for job applicants and internal candidates, but also for all employees. Thus performance evaluation is another area of employment practice that has come under the scrutiny of the courts. Court decisions have held that performance evaluators may be discriminatory if:

1. the performance-rating method has not been shown to be job related or valid;

2. the content of the performance-rating method has not been developed from thorough job analyses;

3. raters have not been able consistently to observe the ratees performing their work;

4. ratings have been based on raters' evaluations of subjective or vague factors;

5. racial, sexual, etc. biases of raters may have influenced the ratings given to ratees;

6. ratings have not been collected and stored under
standardized conditions.

These guidelines suggest that college libraries would do well
to consider more objective forms of performance evaluation
than the graphic rating scales or trait-based forms that are
so commonly found in libraries. Employers must also be
sure that disciplinary measures and terminations are handled
in a nondiscriminatory manner. The best way to ensure this
is to have well-defined personnel policies that are clearly
explained to employees in a manual or orientation booklet.
In many colleges the personnel office may furnish a booklet
for new employees that explains policies adequately; however,
when the college personnel office does not furnish such a
booklet or when library policies differ substantially from college policies the library would do well to consider issuing a
personnel manual. A useful guide is The Personnel Manual:
An Outline for Libraries[2] published by PAS/LAMA. A well-
thought-out grievance or appeal procedure for both professional and nonprofessional staff is also useful in ensuring
equal treatment of all employees.

Librarians of smaller libraries often tend to have one
of two reactions when first confronted with the many state
and federal regulations. Some librarians believe that because
their library is so small it cannot encounter problems--"it
can't happen here." Other librarians go to the opposite extreme and believe that their hands are completely tied by a
confusing array of laws that generally makes every personnel practice illegal. In reality neither of these extremes is
correct. The college librarian, even in a small college,
must be aware of legal regulations governing employee decisions. Complaints have been filed against small colleges
as well as large ones. Although college librarians should
not cultivate a false sense of security, neither should they
feel totally stymied.

A general awareness of laws and regulations governing the employment process will guide the college librarian
through most of the day-to-day employment problems, and a
knowledge of where to turn for help will alleviate the more
difficult problems. Your college's affirmative action officer
is the first person to ask for help. The college personnel

department is the first place to turn if there is no such officer. The college's legal counsel can help with the more
technical aspects.

The college librarian who wishes to use outside resources or who does not have access to on-campus resources can contact the American Library Association Office
for Library Personnel Resources. The OLPR can provide
limited advisory service, publications that explain how to
develop an affirmative action plan, and data on the racial,
ethnic, and sexual composition of the library profession.

Finally, a useful principle to remember is that fair
and equal treatment of employees requires personnel practices based on job-related criteria. This is a principle of
good personnel practice, which people should follow even
without legislation and government regulations.

Notes

[1]Robert Calvert, Jr., Affirmative Action: A Comprehensive Recruitment Manual (Garrett Park, Md.: Garrett
Park Press, 1979).
[2]American Library Association. Personnel Administration Section. Library Administration Division, The Personnel Manual (Chicago: American Library Association, 1977).

CLOSE ENCOUNTERS OF DIVERSE KINDS:
A MANAGEMENT PANORAMA FOR THE DIRECTOR
OF THE SMALLER COLLEGE LIBRARY

Charles B. Maurer

Following what is evidently a national trend toward rethinking
the place and function of management in modern society,
contributors to the library literature have recently been urg-
ing the profession to equip itself with the mechanisms of
leadership and control developed by industry and enterprise.
These are the methods, it is claimed, by which librarians,
in their capacity as managers, can meet the challenge of
fiscal responsibility in the hard times ahead.   During the
past few years management-consultation firms have obliging-
ly been offering us high-powered--and high-priced--seminars
on management style and directorial efficiency.   The Council
on Library Resources is fostering a program to assist college libraries in reviewing and improving their administrative
procedures, a program based on a successful predecessor
formulated by and for the Association of Research Libraries.
As the director of a smaller academic library (240,000 volumes counting bound periodicals), and as someone who takes
his responsibilities with proper seriousness, I appreciate
whatever help I can find in meeting the demands placed upon
me, but I wonder sometimes if management seminars and
sympathetic peer review would have as much value for me
as might a tour of duty with our director of physical plant.

         Consider the leadership structure of your own institu-
tion and the different kinds of responsibilities the director of
the college library is expected, in the normal course of things,

to assume. Who other than the library director must deal
with the sum of: a professional staff; a nonprofessional
staff; student assistants; the entire faculty; the entire student
body; a large and complicated budget; a complex procurement
and storage operation, including the need to keep abreast of
new items of various kinds; long-range planning, but also the
day-to-day functioning of a many-faceted system comprehending innumerable small details; upkeep problems for one or
more buildings; and concern for public relations with people
beyond the campus? The president has responsibilities in
some of these areas, the provost and the dean must cope
with their share, and departmental chairpeople face some
of them, too. But it is only the director of the physical
plant who can be put on the level of the library director in
terms of diversity of responsibility. A president's or dean's
job may be more difficult, more demanding in some ways,
but no one's attention is pulled in so many directions simultaneously as those officers in charge of maintenance: physical maintenance on the one hand, information maintenance on
the other.

Once this fascinating insight has been achieved, there
follows the regrettable conclusion that it is of precious little
practical use for running a library. It does not help the
director of the physical plant much either. Yet there may
be some value for directors of smaller academic libraries,
for those who aspire to such positions, and for those who
hire them, to be fully aware that the basic requirement for
success in the job is the ability to do everything and to do
it all at the same time.

The key word in this situation is "smaller." Administration at any level falls potentially into four categories:
personnel, planning, public relations, and budgetary matters.
In large organizations, including large libraries, the director
has assistants for some or all of these areas and in addition
is insulated by the size of the operation from day-to-day
concerns; department heads or section chiefs or area super-
visors handle that. On a small staff, however, a director
who delegates to others comes face to face with their decisions from the subordinate's point of view whenever he or
she stands a reference watch or fills in at the circulation
desk. A director who does not delegate faces his or her
own decisions at those times. In any case, the director
will sometimes be on reference or circulation duty, and will
not have personnel specialists or budget managers to take
care of the details of those concerns. In our era of growing
specialization this library head is one of the last generalists.

Size influences personnel policies as well. The scientific approach to personnel management has proven its efficacy in situations where many employees interact and a number of people are on hand to fill an unexpected vacancy. In such cases the manager can maintain a certain aloofness, use personnel evaluation forms to good advantage, and consider the appropriateness of management by objective over other approaches. In a shop where each person does two or more jobs, however, and where the only individual available to fill in is the director, a formal personnel structure and chain of command are hard to live by. One of the director's largest tasks in this situation is to foster cooperation and mutual understanding in the staff; inept employees can usually be more readily helped to improve by being made to understand the effect of poor performance on coworkers rather than by poor annual evaluations. And if, as is often the case, the entire staff of the smaller library lives close to each other in a small community, sociology of the family may be a more pertinent study for the director than management theory.

If the staff is considered a family, however, the director is head of it ex officio, and this fact adds another dimension to his or her personnel responsibilities. When there are problems within the library the director is expected to solve them to everyone's satisfaction, and if administrative decisions outside the library annoy the staff, it is usually the director, being the one authority figure within reach, whom they get mad at. The director is an authority figure, even though the size of the operation precludes the luxury of authoritarian behavior; paradox can be a way of life.

Serious planning is best done at times when the staff is not angry at the director, because that is the area where staff cooperation is most important, both in formulation and implementation. The job description may say that it is the director's responsibility to "set and initiate policy, consistent with overall college policy, for library operations ...," and there may even be a usable statement of overall college policy, but it is the size and capacities of the staff that determine what is possible, and it is the expertise of each individual staff member that keeps the director, safely within the bounds of the possible, from stumbling occasionally into the impractical. Whether or not participatory management is the official style, the manager of a small organization who does not regularly test plans against staff opinion is taking a considerable and unnecessary risk of failure.

Yet even the most cooperative staff cannot relieve its director of the most significant planning responsibility, namely, predicting with steely certainty what is going to happen the next year, five years, ten years, and twenty years. Surely this was never an easy task, but how can it be properly performed in the era of burgeoning automation? The profession has had enough experience with the new electronic marvels so that by now directors of smaller libraries can have some idea of what they would like to achieve with them. But how to go about achieving it is quite another matter. Theoretical developments come so fast and new products spring up in such profusion that the very act of trying to keep up all but eliminates sufficient time for making decisions. Perhaps rather than management theory or sociology, the dedicated director should study electronics?

Not practical. Yet one does have to keep abreast of these things--at least of what the machines can and cannot do and how much they cost. Here again major institutions usually have built-in assistance--in the form of comfortably staffed computer centers and engineering departments of various kinds. Directors of smaller libraries are largely on their own. Networks and network staffs have helped, and the hard-pressed director of the campus computer center does what he or she can, but journal reading and conferences are the price one has to pay for living and trying to work effectively in technological times.

Journals and conferences cover many topics aside from automation, of course, and every professional can benefit from them. But from which ones most? A glance at American Libraries' monthly calendar as it unrolls throughout the year reveals that a conscientious library director could spend nearly 360 out of each 365 days at potentially useful conferences or workshops on one or another pertinent subject. And the journals: three major ones on libraries and librarianship in general, at least two dedicated to academic librarianship, and newsletters of ALA divisions! The Chronicle of Higher Education might be thrown in. Two automation journals are worthy of attention; the director of a smaller library, doubling in reference, or acquisitions, or cataloging--or anyplace needed--should really keep up with the titles dedicated to those special areas (RQ, for instance). Moreover, the list never stops growing; while writing this I received an eight-page brochure proudly announcing "New Library Periodicals"! A director who reads nothing else, and loves to read, might

be able to cover them all, and having done so, claim the
best possible preparation for planning duties.

This approach, however, is likely to detract from
the public-relations function. Any academic library director
faces a particular public-relations problem not experienced
in other kinds of libraries, namely, the faculty. The difficulty arises from the fact that faculty members know something about libraries--but not enough. All academicians have
made their professional way at least to some extent via the
library, an experience that often trains them to some extent
as to how libraries work. What they usually have not learned,
and do not know that they do not know, is why libraries work
as they do. I doubt that anyone who has not actually toiled
on a library staff could ever appreciate the mass of interre-
lated detail that makes a library a functional unit, and not
very many people really care much, as long as the library
is a functional unit. When functions break down--as they
occasionally will--it is always the director's fault on a
smaller campus, because everyone on the faculty knows him
or her (in large libraries breakdowns are the fault of the
system), and the director can usually be assured of constructive criticism from genuinely interested faculty colleagues
who know what needs to be done but have no idea how complex the doing of it might be. Explaining all the troublesome
details does not soften the fact that things may not at the
moment be going as they should, and the director can expect
little admiration for a profound understanding of the problem.
To gain faculty's respect the director must meet them on
their terms, and know a little--or better, a lot--about their
fields; reading must therefore go far beyond the library literature.

The question of the director's status on campus is an
important one, and not--or not only--for reasons of ego, but
because of the library's unique position within the academic
community. It is an institution run by members of one profession for the benefit of members of a different profession
who serve a larger institution that encompasses the library.
Granted, this description is an oversimplification, implying
that students are passive recipients of faculty service (not
so), but it is nonetheless useful, because the college library
does its job best when it is satisfactorily supporting what
the faculty is trying to do in the classroom. To reach this
goal the library must have faculty cooperation in a number
of areas, but faculty members frequently do not know how
to cooperate effectively, because they are dealing in the

library with members of a different profession, and the requirements for performing in that profession are in many
ways different from the ones the faculty is familiar with.
One of the library director's most important functions is to
integrate the requirements--and the potentials--of the two
professions, and to achieve this the director must be accepted in both camps.

Developments in librarianship over the past twenty or
so years have vastly increased the importance of this medi-
ating role, but it may be the one place where directors on
smaller campuses have been least successful. Librarians
are well aware of the potential automation puts into our hands
and are eagerly awaiting the benefits a national bibliographic
network will provide us. But these benefits will be real for
the academic community only if the teaching faculty is persuaded to make use of them and to have their students make
use of them. Till now, however, librarians have not been
able to involve their teaching colleagues to any great extent
in these developments. Nor has general faculty cooperation
been obtained for librarianship's new efforts at bibliographic
instruction (exceptions to this, e.g., at Earlham College,
are much admired as examples of what can be achieved when
requisite cooperation is forthcoming). It is usually the case
that intensive faculty interest in the library indicates dissatisfaction with the service it is providing. When all is
going well no one but the library staff thinks much about it.
Directors must assume the added obligation of working hard-
er to gain faculty understanding for the larger part academic
libraries can play in the educational process.

If relations with faculty are the principal public-
relations task of the library director, duties in this area
certainly do not end there. Students represent the largest
part of the patronage, and their needs must be looked after--
in ways they are able to recognize. Directors are at a disadvantage here, because their contact with students often
concerns problems ("I did bring that book back! I brought
it in with a whole pile of others, and I remember that one."),
but such devices as the library handbook, letters to the campus newspaper, and specialized services (e.g., pathfinders or
subject bibliographies) can foster the impression that the library is trying to be helpful, and directors must support
staff efforts toward developing effective contacts with all patrons. Service on faculty-student committees, as tiresome
as that can be, often affords the director, and other staff
members, opportunities to create positive attitudes toward

the library. So does attendance, formal or informal, in courses on campus.

Beyond the campus there is the local community to react to, other libraries to stay in contact with, library organizations to keep track of and take part in, government agencies to please. There is a public-relations aspect to all these activities, just as there is to the upkeep of buildings and equipment. The director must see to it that patrons are comfortable, and properly served, and in a smaller library that means, often enough, taking a hand personally. It may well be the director who gives first aid to an ailing Xerox machine or unsticks a pamphlet file drawer; and who is there but the director, after the janitors have left, who can cope with a social indiscretion casually committed by a transient puppy? I wonder if things like that are covered in management seminars.

Budgetary matters, of course, relate to everything the director does in any size institution; one cannot do what one cannot afford. The biggest problem in budget management, however, is not getting the money but spending it all before the end of the fiscal year. In times of financial stringency this appears to be a paradox, but it follows naturally from the normal budgetary cycle. The cycle starts usually somewhere between November and May, before a fiscal year beginning in July. The director (with suggestions from the staff) decides how much will be needed over a period commencing approximately half a year hence and lasting a year beyond that. To be decided is not just what the total should be, but how much is necessary for each budget item listed (e. g. , salaries, books, periodicals, travel; my own budget has twenty-nine lines). The reader will remember the steely accuracy of the director's predictions; long-range planning provides a sound basis upon which to make guesses at the sums the director will need to keep functioning when that nebulous future has become a troublesome present. Carefully justifying each request, the director submits the budget to whatever authority he or she is responsible to, and waits for reality to start.

That moment comes when the actual budget is made known, and the director learns what there is to work with. Some real plans can be made at that point, and a provisional spending schedule established for the entire fiscal year. There may not be enough money to do what needs to be done, but at least a firm estimate can be made of what can

104 • College Librarianship

be done for the money available. As the fiscal year pro-
gresses circumstances invariably require adjustments in the
plans, and constant surveillance of expenditures is a regular
part of the director's routine. With care, all money will
not have been used up during the first six months; with luck--
a lot of luck--there will be precisely nothing left on the last
day of the fiscal year. Running over the budget is, of course,
frowned upon by the institution's fiscal authorities, and with
watchfulness it can be avoided. Where luck is necessary is
in figuring out what portion of outstanding materials will actually arrive before the end of the fiscal year and how much
discount there will be on those orders. There is, alas, no
way for the director to control this, and the end of each fiscal year becomes a kind of bibliographic roulette in which a
balancing of surpluses in some budget lines against actual or
anticipated deficits in others gives a theoretical sum of zero.
I was relatively new at this game in 1973, but if ever again
ALA meets at Las Vegas I shall feel far better prepared
than I was then.

    A new area of uncertainty is developing for library
budget managers, one that must be given considerable attention in the years ahead. Cooperation and technology both
cost money, money that may have to be squeezed from materials budgets, and that at a time when materials themselves are making unprecedented financial demands. Amidst
all the other duties the director of the smaller academic library must learn to make the right fiscal decisions so that
the attained balance of materials, equipment, and interinsti-
tutional cooperation provides the best possible service for
patrons. A lot of luck may be needed for solving this problem, too.

    In light of the preceding litany of perplexity, the ob-
vious question presents itself: why would anyone want to do
it? Consider the alternatives. Be a college president and
spend your time cultivating reluctant donors? Try the provost's job dealing with a morass of government agencies?
Accept the dean's responsibility of keeping educational ideas
alive in a period marked by anti-intellectuality? Or assume
the directorship of a large academic library, where the very
massiveness of collection and staff tends to strangle the service the library is there to provide? Rather not. The welt-
er of responsibility surrounding the director of a smaller library is sometimes pierced with a glow of satisfaction derived from a difficult task well performed, a long-range plan
carried through--and even a reference question adroitly

answered. Amidst the complaints it is my lot to hear I occasionally receive a comment about how helpful someone on my staff has been. The chance for moments like that is not easily relinquished.

Still, it is desirable to face reality, and the reality is that there is more to do than any one person can do well, that anyone who accepts the director's position in a smaller library will be less successful in some areas of responsibility than others, that the experience is something like looking at life through an unfocused kaleidoscope. Like Hesse's magic theater, it is not for everyone; the ideal candidate for the job would be a combination of Mozart's Sarastro and Rossini's Figaro. People like that are hard to find, so lesser ones will have to accept the task. Let them know in advance: if variety is the spice of life, the director's job in the smaller academic library deserves at very least an R rating.

THE ESTABLISHMENT OF AN ARCHIVES
IN A SMALL COLLEGE LIBRARY

Martha Counihan

A college librarian confronted with the task of establishing a
college archives or taking over the administration of a pre-
existing archives is at a disadvantage in comparison with a
colleague who is shifted from one area of the college library
to another. The small body of literature concerning the establishment and development of college and university archives
pays scant attention to the needs of the small institution.
Concomitant with this gap in the literature is the frequent
"lumping together" of college archives with rare books and
manuscript librarianship. New college archivists are apt to
have had far less course work and experience--especially if
they are primarily educated as librarians--than curators and
catalogers of rare books collections. There is a paucity of
helpful, practical advice to new archivists; too few individuals
who combine responsibilities of both archives and library service have shared their expertise. As a result, information
about the management of academic institutions' archives is
written by full-time university archivists whose programs and
problems are larger and different from those of the small
college.

Planning an Archives

The decision to establish a college archives should be made
by more than one person. Ideally, a committee including
the college president, library director, and representatives

from the board of trustees, history department faculty, alumni association, and student body should share in the decision and establish general goals. Part of this planning would include a job description of the person to be hired to serve as archivist.

In the small college library the job description would probably include the requirement that the applicant be a professional librarian who will serve the college library in another capacity in addition to being the archivist. This is not an unreal expectation in a small institution. Whether an archives is being founded, or if one already exists in an informal office and the decision has been made to establish a more formal archives, the selection committee must decide upon the desirable qualifications to expect in candidates who will have two roles to fill. A minimum of a graduate course in archival management that included actual experience in an archives can be expected. The college might consider subsidizing the cost of additional archives workshops, once a candidate is selected. [1] Unfortunately, aside from library school and limited graduate history department courses in archival management, little training is available; therefore it would be unrealistic to expect much more in a beginner. And since archival work is so specifically centered upon its own collection, experience is the best form of education--the person chosen to serve as the college archivist will eventually have the necessary experience that cannot be taught in a graduate course.

Archives work requires an individual who can organize, someone who has training in history, or, at least, has an interest in it. Familiarity with the history of the college or its sponsoring organization would also be an asset. Discretion and the maturity to conduct oneself both professionally and personably, are important qualities; the archives is no place for "difficult" personalities. Ability in public relations is valuable anywhere, but especially in a small college, where personal contacts often pave the way for an archivist who is personally approaching officers or faculty about turning their noncurrent records over to the college archives.

Archivists often work with records that, potentially or actually, contain highly sensitive information. The need for discretion cannot be overemphasized; any information that might prove embarrassing to an individual or to the college is to be treated as confidential. Unlike the librarian, whose tasks do not include inquiry into the purposes for which a patron seeks information from the library collection, the archivist does have the responsibility to determine how requested information is to be used. The access policies that govern the administration of a college library are very different from those of the college archives.

If an archives is being established and the person to be hired will also be employed in the college library, it would be wise to determine what the archivist's status will be within the college's organization. If the professional librarians have faculty status, so should the archivist. Maynard J. Brichford, in his article "University Archives: Relationships with the Faculty,"[2] argues that faculty status for the college or university archivist is more important than to whom the archivist reports, but the question of the reporting structure is certainly a central concern. The archivist of a college may well be directly responsible to the library director, but should also be expected to make regular reports to the college president.

Reporting to the Librarian should not, ipso facto, indicate that the archivist is solely under his or her jurisdiction, especially in regard to the annual budget. A number of archivists advocate placement of the archives budget within a separate budget category. Kenneth Duckett strongly argued this opinion in his 1967 paper at the University of Illinois' Graduate School of Library Science conference on archival administration of small institutions.[3] The basic expenses of setting up or maintaining an archives, when added to the perennially-too-small budget of a college library, may easily appear too much to a budget-conscious library director. Bills for dry cleaning, extra shelving, and paper restoration can seem frivolous in a budget that must include such basic library needs as salaries, books, periodicals, and equipment.

A final step in the planning stages of an archives is a "mission statement," issued by the college president or board of trustees. Such a statement informs the college community about the foundation of the archives and authorizes the archivist to survey, designate, collect, process, and preserve the records of the college that the archivist and the officers of the college deem vital. Although a college president may be reluctant to take so formal a step, failure to entrust the archivist with specific authority and responsibility will be a source of frustration to both. The college president should not have to be consulted by other offices about turning over records to the archives. Even a less-than-formal memorandum to the various offices and faculty can delegate authority to and define the role of the archivist. Where lack of planning precedes the establishment of an archives, the unfortunate results echoed in a 1951 survey of college archives can be repeated in the 1980s:

> The whole problem of college archives appears to have its origin in lack of funds, and, more basically, lack of administration policies which require preservation, centralization, and organization of the official and non-official materials. [4]

The archivist and the appropriate officers should devise a collections policy and a description of how materials will be received, processed, and made available for use.

Location of the Archives

The physical location of the college archives will be a concern to the archivist as well as to the college's space-allocation committee. Few colleges have the necessary funds to erect a secure, climate-controlled, fireproof, well-designed facility. Archives are often located within the college library building or within the administration building. Although not the ideal solution, location of the archives within the library does physically unite the college's own records with the college's center of learning and research. An archives, however, has a few requirements that differ from those of a library; security is probably the most important of these. A remote location in which records can be processed and housed is preferable to more public areas. The archivist should insist that areas designated for smoking and eating not be nearby. Sufficient space for storing unprocessed materials, a processing space with large tables, and a secure archives vault or other enclosed area are minimal spatial requirements.

If temperature and humidity control (twenty-four-hour, not just when the library is open) systems are impossible, regular use of a dehumidifier and careful avoidance of temperature extremes will suffice. Light is another enemy of paper, and efforts should be made to store records out of sunlit areas or to cover window glass with special filters. Filter sleeves can also be fitted over fluorescent lights to lessen the deleterious effects of ultraviolet rays. A dark, relatively dry, evenly cooled location is ideal, but few archives begin under such conditions. Papers that have been stored for years in damp cellars or in attics that are alternately hot and cold will benefit from even slight preservation measures and from relocation.

What Constitutes Archival Records

Planning an archives, selecting a suitable archivist, and allocating space for processing and storage are preliminary steps. What the new college archives will collect is the next question to be addressed. Decisions must be made about what records to collect, how to collect and describe them, where to shelve them, and how to make them available for use. Knowledge of what to collect is necessary, and reflection on what constitutes vital, archival, records will be enlightening.

> Those records of any public or private institution which are judged worthy of permanent preservation for reference and research purposes and which have been deposited or have been selected for deposit in an archival institution. [5]

This is how the noted American archival theorist, T. R. Schellenberg, defined the word "archives," and he so defined it in very general terms. In the case of a college the decision about what constitutes archival records rests chiefly with the archivist. This presumes that the archivist is already familiar with the history of the college, the background of its organizational and administrative changes, and its goals. For a person who is new to the position or the institution, this is a difficult decision. However, the official administrative history of the college is generally found in the minutes, memoranda, and reports of the board of trustees and the presidents. It is also found in the records of all academic and administrative committees including the faculty senate; archivists should normally collect the records, reports, and correspondence of the chief academic officers, directors of student services, deans, and other executive officers. Annual budget and audit reports, legal papers, and records of the college's academic departments all constitute vital records, as do the records of the registrar, director of admissions, offices of institutional research and college development, alumni, student organizations, and

personnel records of retired, resigned, and deceased faculty
and staff. The less legally or administratively important
the records are to the creating office, the less importance
they will have in the overall accessioning; e. g. , the contracts of Professor X from the president's office will be of
more value than the report of the 1964 Oktoberfest Food
Committee.

Nonofficial records will also have an important place
in a college archives. Examples of nonofficial (in the sense
that they were or are not integral in the shaping of the college's administrative, academic or fiscal policies) records
would include college publications, the official bulletin, and
audiovisual materials that document the history of the college
and persons associated with it--films, photographs, and nega-
tives, oral-history interviews, and audio- and videotapes.
Faculty publications, scrapbooks, student letters and papers,
and memorabilia like programs, posters, and small articles
are also nonofficial records that can have a real and useful
place in the college archives. Storage and the special care
such articles might require must be considered before one
solicits these. Any librarian knows the burden that some
"gifts" can cause; the archivist must also be aware of this
before advertising for donations to the college archives. [6]

Steps in Setting Up the Archives

An archivist in a newly established program, or one taking
over a previously established but possibly informal, operation can best determine the extent of the work to be done by
making a survey of the college's records. This survey can
be general or detailed, but one should begin by informing
the college offices of this intention. The Society of American Archivists' Forms Manual[7] has several examples of
forms that have been used in such surveys; these can help
a new archivist devise one of his or her own. In visiting
the various offices of the college one should discover before-
hand who is the person most knowledgeable about the records
of that particular office; new deans and secretaries can be of
less help than persons who have been employed longer in a
department. The archivist should remember to ask if old
records are stored elsewhere than in the office; this question will often lead to forgotten or semi-secret storage areas
(which are often, climatically, terrible places).

A survey is time-consuming, but it may well turn up

records that have been lost, forgotten, or neglected for
decades. A survey can enlighten the new archivist, more
than any article on the topic, about which records have been
considered vital and, therefore, have been kept. It also
gives the archivist a clearer idea about the volume of the
college's records; with this knowledge, a schedule for examining and processing these records can more realistically
be drawn up. While long-term storage is not the only criterion for transferring the archives, such records do enlarge
the archivist's knowledge of the history of the college's administration. The data collected in this survey could later
be used in planning a records-management program.

Processing and Preservation of Records

The actual reception and preparation of records for archival
storage are carefully described in several publications, among
which are the SAA Manuals, Appraisal and Accessioning, by
Maynard J. Brichford, [8] and Arrangement and Description,
by David B. Gracy;[9] Kenneth Duckett also details these processes in his Modern Manuscripts. [10] The individual archivist must decide on the necessary detail with which to describe accessioned materials.

Rarely do records arrive in the archives ready for
immediate storage. Discarding duplicates and files that do
not originate in the office that sent the files are all-too-
common tasks performed by the archivist. Furthermore, a
carton of files will display a confusing provenance unless the
archivist is well informed about the organizational structures
of the college's offices.

All records need at least a cursory survey, during
which time simple preservation steps can be taken--
unfolding, removal of metal staples, paper clips, and rub-
ber bands, dusting, and sandwiching acid-laden news clip-
pings between leaves of acid-free bond paper. Time taken
to care for records before they are stored and described
will add years to their life and potential use. Even if the
archives budget cannot allow for the immediate purchase of
special acid-free file folders and storage boxes and deacidi-
fication processes, the above measures will, to a certain
extent, slow down the process of disintegration.

Preservation for its own sake can become an exag-
gerated concern; it is important, but an archives can function

without the best available preservation materials and techniques. As custodians of the past, archivists must make
every effort to preserve the information contained in the
records under their care; an original document, especially
if printed on poor-quality paper, cannot become so important that its preservation results in the neglect of other
records. Modern photocopying equipment can cheaply and
easily reproduce information printed on disintegrating news-
print and other highly acid papers so that the information
contained thereupon is not lost--if time and finances cannot
preserve the original.

The archival profession does not have the classification schemes available to librarians; the attempts by the
National Archives to develop such a system have proved
highly unsatisfactory. Archives are such unique institutions
that they do not lend themselves easily to classification systems. The principle of provenance--organization by source
of records rather than by subject--best governs their relocation in an archives. Again, knowledge of the organizational
history and its changes is helpful in determining provenance.

The actual shelving plan of storage containers need
not be complex; the system that is logistically most workable
and practical is probably the best one. Additional growth
space must be provided in the shelving plan. More specifically, this might mean the arrangement of records from the
board of trustees--minutes, agenda, reports--in one range of
stacks, and nearby, the collections of the chief administrative
officers--presidents, deans, and provosts. Nonofficial records
of various forms--bound copies of college publications, photograph collections, scrapbooks, etc.--can be shelved elsewhere
with their form and interrelatedness determining the proximate
locations.

Accession sheets and shelf and box lists that briefly
describe holdings can be made available as reference aids to
users; relying on the memory of the archivist is a poor substitute for precise location and contents information. While
the archivist's knowledge of the collection will assist users
in discovering related collections and series, other reference
materials and finding aids are necessary.

Services of the College Archives

Communicating with the various sectors of the college about

the transfer in noncurrent records and sorting, processing,
and storing these records are the primary tasks of the archivist.   These, however, are services that take place behind the scenes.   The public service functions of the college
archives are not to be overlooked; these must be regularly
evaluated, since, broadly speaking, the archives' goal is to
serve the entire college community, past, present, and future.

     One instructional service that the archives can per-
form is to encourage the novice historians among the student
body by assisting them, under the supervision of the archivist or a professor of historiography, to use some of the
facilities of the archives in their course work.   Collaboration
with faculty in various departments can result in student
projects that make use of the primary research materials in
the students' own institution.   These papers can, in turn, become valuable additions to the college's own history.

     The college's publications are another area in which
the archives can serve to inform the public of its resources
(and, simultaneously and judiciously, appeal for donations);
histories of persons, departments, and events are of interest
to persons who are or have been associated with the college.
If the archives has a good photography collection, copies can
be made available for use in college publications.

     The occasion of an anniversary celebration is another
opportunity not to be missed by the archivist.   An anniver-
sary calendar, address book, or brochure that is illustrated
with materials from the archives and includes significant
(and not-so-significant) events pertinent to the institution's
history is relatively inexpensive to produce for sale.   Such
a project can be initiated by the archivist, but produced by
the publications or public-relations office.   The archivist
should be prepared for such special events and anniversaries
with appropriate historical information relevant to them.
Displays are another way in which the archives can inform
students about the college's history, touch the memories of
alumni, and provide generally unknown information.

     Copies (not originals) of archives photographs can be
made available to the office of publications for inclusion in
the college bulletin, admissions literature, development
brochures, and alumni magazines; the local newspaper might
appreciate similar copies for their own photograph files on
the college.   Another service that the archivist might consider

is lecturing to local and college groups; relating the past to the present facilitates college relations with groups that otherwise might have little contact with the college students. Authoritative information goes a long way in demythologizing local misconceptions or letting alumni know that the college and its students reflect both the traditions and the progress of society and the college.

Within the college a public service that the archivist can offer is a ready-reference file of significant information about dates, persons, events, and buildings. A card catalog or file of facts can answer desperate questions in a hurry. Who designed the gym? When did Professor X retire? When were parietals first established? These facts cannot be found together elsewhere. If the archivist can provide a ready answer, the credibility and value of the archives program increases.

In order to serve the college community the archives has to be able to justify its existence in competition with other departments, and, possibly, with the library itself. Everyone is concerned with acquiring a share of a very limited amount of funds and space. In a time of tight budgets it is possible that only if the more evident effects of the archival program are demonstrable will the college have reason to continue its support. Herein lies the value of an archivist who relates well with the public, performs efficiently and reasonably, and knows how to provide creatively for and advertise the services of the college archives.[11]

Notes

[1]Case Western Reserve University, Cleveland, Ohio, offers an annual workshop devoted solely to college and university archives. The five-day workshop includes both introductory and advanced groups featuring experts in the fields covered, at both levels.

[2]Maynard J. Brichford, "University Archives: Relationships with Faculty," American Archivist 34 (April 1971): 174.

[3]Kenneth Duckett, Archival Program: Location, University of Illinois Graduate School of Library Science Occasional Papers, no. 88 (Champaign: University of Illinois, 1967), p. 12.

[4]Mary Elizabeth Hinckley, "The Role of the College Library in the Preservation and Organization of the Archives of Its Own Institution" (M. A. thesis, Columbia University, 1951), p. 52.

[5]T. R. Schellenberg, Modern Archives: Principles and Techniques (Chicago: University of Chicago, 1956), p. 16.

[6]The Subcommittee of the Society of American Archivists' College and University Committee has prepared a useful draft of proposed guidelines for college and university archives, which appeared in the January 1979 SAA Newsletter. The proposed document covers the following topics: Core Mission Administration, Service, Personnel, Facilities and Equipment, Supporting Services, and Records Management. The work outlines a complete archival facility; it does not attempt to serve as a step-by-step guide nor is it a model of an ideal facility.

[7]Society of American Archivists, College and University Archives Committee, Forms Manual (n. p. : SAA, 1973).

[8]Maynard J. Brichford, Archives and Manuscripts: Appraisal and Accessioning, Basic Manual Series (Chicago: SAA, 1977).

[9]David E. Gracy, Archives and Manuscripts: Arrangement and Description, Basic Manual Series (Chicago: SAA, 1977).

[10]Kenneth W. Duckett, Modern Manuscripts: A Practical Manual for Their Management, Care, and Use (Nashville, Tenn.: American Association for State and Local History, 1975).

[11]This article describes the planning and organization of a college archives that does not expand its collections to include literary and historical manuscripts or special collections of books and printed material that do not directly touch upon the college itself. However, the college archivist who lets it be known that he or she is seeking papers about the college and its history will eventually be confronted with an offer of manuscripts or local-history materials. A perennial confusion of manuscripts and special collections with archives persists to this day. The history of the development, in American colleges, of special collections, manuscript collections, and archival materials is illuminating in regard to this confusion. Until the post-World War II era's interest in more uniform archival techniques introduced separate description and handling of these materials they were often stored together in the college library, possibly separated into a "Rare Books," "Special Collections," and "Archives" (or combination of these) Room. Before the recent development of modern techniques, therefore, these materials

were cataloged and stored together, and the logistics and cost of changing this practice were too great to consider a reversal. For this reason in a number of institutions, particularly older ones, archives, special collections, and manuscript collections continue to be cataloged, serviced, and shelved in the same division of the college library.

FACULTY STATUS IN THE COLLEGE LIBRARY

William Miller

The issue of faculty status for college librarians has not
been faced honestly on most campuses. American colleges,
on the whole, have sidestepped the issue, striking a variety
of local compromises and ad hoc arrangements not grounded
in any consistent theory. Unlike the university situation, in
which such classifications as "Librarian I-IV," or "Catalog
Librarian with the rank of Assistant Professor" have evolved
nationwide with a large degree of consistent definition, and
are understood not to be the equivalent of true faculty status,
"faculty status" in the college library has no predictable
significance. It can mean anything from true faculty status,
i. e. complete parity with those normally defined as faculty,
to little more than a willingness to allow librarians to sit in
on faculty meetings--often without a vote. In the university
library the size of the professional staff has facilitated the
concept of "library faculty" with its own Dean (the library
director), its own governance structure, a multiplicity of
committee assignments within the Division, and the possibility of peer review for staff evaluation and tenure. In the
colleges, where there are not enough bodies to make a separate governance structure viable, librarians have so far
looked almost exclusively to the already-existing faculty
structure of the institution for their own definition and
protection--often with disastrous results.

Dimensions of the Problem

As college librarians come up for tenure consideration it

118

often becomes painfully clear that their colleagues on the faculty have never accepted them as true equals, and occasionally some public fiasco dramatically reveals the danger inherent in the vague definitions of "faculty status" under which most college librarians now operate. A case in point was the dismissal of Rose Smith as Head Librarian at Milton College in Wisconsin in 1976. When Smith and seven other (nonlibrarian) faculty members were dismissed for reasons of financial exigency, most turned to the Faculty Grievance Committee for redress. In Smith's case, however, the Grievance Committee declined to act, determining that she was not a faculty member, contrary to her own assumption of long standing. Upon investigation, the American Library Association's Staff Committee for Action, Mediation, Arbitration, and Inquiry (SCMAI) could not definitively unravel whether or not Rose Smith was in fact a member of the faculty, the administration, or the support staff:

> The members of the college faculty and the administration ... were in agreement that Rose Smith was not a member of the faculty. There was little agreement, however, as to what the status of Rose Smith actually was while she was head librarian. Some saw her as a member of the college administration; others saw her and the other librarian in some kind of support-staff role.
>
> Despite the testimony and evidence indicating that the head librarian was not a member of the faculty, the Subcommittee reviewed documents and heard testimony which confirmed that Rose Smith attended and voted at faculty meetings, that the head librarian had served as secretary to the faculty, that the professional librarians held ten-month contracts, that the form of contract given Rose Smith for the 1975/76 academic year was the same as for members of the teaching faculty. [1]

Both the librarians and the other faculty at Milton College had in fact evaded the question of faculty status, preferring instead to operate in an ill-defined limbo, which in the short run pleased everyone, but in the long run only brought the issue home with more force. The Milton College faculty had approved the 1972 Joint Statement on Faculty Status of College and University Librarians, [2] "contingent upon subsequent faculty approval of all standards and processes of implementation," [3] but it never approved any such standards or processes, nor, apparently, did Rose Smith press for implementation. Smith, one imagines, would have

worn her "emperor's new clothes" indefinitely, rather than
press the faculty for an answer to the question of her real
status.

The SCMAI committee found "ambiguity surrounding
the role of the librarian in the college ... central to the
matter of Rose Smith's termination, "[4] and it is almost certainly ambiguity and lack of definition that have accounted
for the remarkably high rate of faculty status for college librarians, as reported by college librarians themselves during the past thirty years. In 1948 Gelfand, surveying status
in colleges and small universities in the East, found that 72
percent of the head librarians and 24 percent of the professional library staffs "had faculty status," at least according
to the head librarians. [5] Dennis Reynolds, in a 1978 survey
of college librarians reported upon elsewhere in this volume,
found that almost 90 percent of college library directors nationwide report themselves as having faculty status; approximately 75 percent of head catalog librarians and reference
librarians report themselves similarly. If such figures were
in fact true, of course, they would mean that college librarians have now achieved parity with their traditional faculty
colleagues in overwhelming numbers. Clearly, however,
such parity is for the most part an illusion, based upon so
amorphous and various a set of definitions that the results
cannot be taken literally.

Why Faculty Status?

"Faculty status" is indeed a figurative concept for most of
us. The job advertisement section of College & Research
Libraries News warns, in every issue, that the terms "faculty 'rank' and 'status' are ... ambiguous" and should be
investigated to determine their meaning in any given situation. How did it come about that college librarians place
so much stock in a concept they have failed to define? It
is, after all, as Virgil Massman has noted in his book Faculty Status for Librarians, "rather unusual for a professional group to argue for something without first defining precisely what it wants."[6]

The simplest explanation for why academic librarians
have sought faculty status so eagerly and so uncritically lies
in the emergence and development of librarianship itself as
a profession and in the failure of librarianship to develop
well-defined professional standards, goals, and rewards.

Academic librarians, who as a group lacked respect for themselves and their work situations, found themselves in close contact with the faculty, a well-respected, well-organized, self-confident group. It was natural, then, for academic librarians to attempt to model themselves on the teaching faculty as they searched for a satisfactory way to define themselves. This desire for emulation goes far to explain Arthur McAnally's seminal 1957 definition of faculty and academic status. McAnally based his optimistic definition on the belief that librarians would in time acquire the education and training that would compel the faculty to recognize them as equals:

> Faculty status for librarians is defined as the possession of all or most of the privileges of the classroom teaching faculty, including faculty rank. Academic status is held to be the possession of some but not all usual faculty privileges, with definite classification as academic but always without faculty rank. Academic status thus may be considered a kind of reduced faculty status. Because faculty status and academic status are quite similar, and for convenience, the term academic status is used loosely ... to apply to both forms.[7]

Here we have all of the essentials of today's confusion. Academic librarians were to think of themselves, for whatever reason, as fledgling faculty members, lacking only the education, which in time they would acquire. In the meanwhile McAnally sanctioned a broad, muddled, imprecise, and presumably temporary area, that of "academic status," in which almost any ad hoc situation was provisionally valid.

To do him justice, McAnally did not use the term "faculty status" to sanction any number of diverse situations, but it was an easy and perhaps inevitable step for academic librarians to do so. The kind of compromise for which McAnally called was obviously well suited to the needs of academic librarians and acceptable to college and university faculties, because his muddled definition remains the norm. On college campuses today, through mutually agreeable lack of definition, almost everyone can agree that librarians have faculty status, when, in fact, any strict definition of the term would shatter this fragile belief. Librarians have not, as a group, acquired the education and training that would compel the faculty to accept them as equals; indeed, one wonders if education and training alone could ever compel such acceptance, there being so many who insist that the practice of librarianship is not substantially equivalent to the practice of teaching. Nevertheless, college librarians continue to seek faculty status, and they have yet to articulate any alternatives to it on a nationwide scale.

Definitions of Faculty Status

Before looking more closely at possible alternatives to faculty status one should first have a clear idea of what "real" faculty status for college librarians would entail, and how such status would differ from "academic status." Virgil Massman defines academic status as "an official recognition by the institutions that librarians are part of the instructional and research staff."[8] Academic status, then, is simply a recognition that librarians have some more involved relationship to the instructional process than do, say, admissions counselors, or college relations and development officers. Academic status such as this is an honor, but not much more, and it is certainly not to be confused with faculty status. Academic status, as Massman defines it, is in fact what most college and other academic librarians actually mean when they assert that they have faculty status. Real faculty status, for Massman, would consist of these eight factors:

1) title and rank
2) commensurate salary
3) eligibility for sabbatical and other leaves
4) access to research grants
5) eligibility for tenure
6) voting privileges in the institution's governing body
7) eligibility for election to faculty committees
8) vacations identical with those of other faculty members. [9]

Judged by such standards, one suspects that Gelfand's and Reynolds's high percentages of college librarians with faculty status would melt away rather quickly to single-digit proportions.

Similarly devastating would be the American Library Association's own criteria, "Standards for Faculty Status for College and University Librarians."[10] This document, which uses the terms "faculty status" and "academic status" interchangeably, urges all institutions to adopt nine standards for all academic librarians:

1) assignment of professional responsibilities only, and review by a committee of peers
2) governance by a "library faculty"
3) membership in college governing bodies
4) equal compensation for equal education and experience; academic year appointment; salary adjusted upward for extra contract days
5) eligibility for tenure
6) eligibility for promotion, with titles and ranks identical to those of other faculty
7) eligibility for leaves on equal basis with other faculty
8) equal access to research grants
9) academic freedom

This document, as the ACRL Academic Status Committee itself acknowledged at a recent meeting, has been honored principally in the breach, rather than in the observance, and while it is at least theoretically applicable to a university situation it is clearly inapplicable, in many of its particulars, to a college one. Even those colleges willing to grant equal pay and length of contract to academic librarians would balk at the creation of a "library faculty" consisting of three or four people who would govern the library on equal terms with the rest of the school's faculty, evaluating its own members for promotion and tenure, and parceling out research funds and sabbaticals to its members. If there is ever to be true faculty status for college librarians, it will have to come about through full integration with the rest of the college faculty, using a model such as Massman suggests.

The Survey

How well does faculty status for college librarians today measure up to the criteria proposed by Massman? To answer this question I conducted my own survey recently, the methodology of which was impressionistic rather than quantitative. Forty-one college library directors around the country were asked to define faculty status for librarians at their institutions; thirty-one responded. The results, though difficult to quantify and dangerous to extrapolate from, suggest that faculty status for college librarians is almost a myth, and that it is defined and treated so variously that one would need an in-depth interview at every institution, and a lengthy written profile for each, simply to account adequately for the vagaries of each situation. Any simple tabular questionnaire would only gather and summarize misleading information. What follows here, therefore, is a prose summary and analysis of the written responses. [11]

Of the thirty-one respondents only six said that there was no faculty status for librarians at their institutions. In six other libraries only the director had faculty status (self-reported). In three other libraries the respondents were for one reason or another unsure whether or not they had faculty status--and in at least one case the ambiguity was considered preferable to a certain knowledge.

The majority of college head librarians, therefore, define themselves and the other librarians at their colleges as holding faculty status. Beyond that there is little uniformity. In approximately half of the cases librarians are part of the college's governing body, usually (though not always) with a vote. While most colleges allow librarians to serve on committees--especially ones not closely connected with faculty affairs--there is some sense among these librarians of being looked down upon, and discriminated against, when it comes to placement on committees. Library directors, more likely to be given committee assignments than are the members of their staffs, are also secretaries of faculty governing bodies out of all proportion to their numbers.

Librarians' fringe benefits are usually comparable with those of faculty members, but salaries are not, though in many cases they do not lag very far behind. The question of salary, of course, depends closely upon that of contract year. In no case are librarian and faculty work periods identical, and, where salaries for college librarians approximate those of other faculty, the reason is usually that college librarians work extra days for the same amount of money. A basic nine- or ten-month contract, with a required supplemental summer contract, is the norm, though ten- or eleven-month contracts are also common. Holidays and vacation time are not equal to those granted to the other college faculty, but are greater than those given to university librarians, principally because colleges tend to close down more fully during major national holidays and between terms.

Approximately one-third of college librarians are eligible for tenure; two institutions report that they rejected their college's offer to be considered for tenure, because the continuous appointment policy now in force effectively gives them tenure, while at the same time presumably obviating the need to meet faculty tenure requirements.

In approximately one-third of responding institutions librarians are theoretically eligible for sabbaticals, though in many institutions this privilege has never been exercised, and librarians wonder how real it is. Any leave granted to librarians at colleges is more likely to be termed "administrative leave" than "sabbatical." In one institution a reference librarian's faculty sabbatical recently resulted in an absence of reference service at the college for the entire year, a situation that perhaps points out the college's low regard for the library, and also points up the kinds of problems that make implementation of the ACRL standards unlikely in a college situation.

Perhaps the clearest test of how well librarians are perceived as colleagues in colleges is the degree to which they have access to college grant money and other funds for research and faculty development. Thus it is probably significant that in only five of the thirty-one institutions are librarians eligible for such money.

In three of the thirty-one institutions librarians hold administrative rather than faculty appointments. Nevertheless, interestingly enough, they appear to have all of the privileges accorded elsewhere to librarians with "faculty rank," except for the possibility of tenure and, of course, faculty status itself. As is the case with those who assume that they have faculty privileges, however, it is not clear how many of the privileges theoretically held by these administrative librarians are actually illusory.

Approximately half of the responding head librarians indicated that librarians at their institutions were being accorded a rank and title substantially equivalent to that accorded other faculty. One institution offers an "Associated Faculty Rank," which is, apparently, what we would call academic status, conferred in recognition of professional work that is closely allied to that of the academic departments. This rank, like the administrative ranking mentioned above, appears to entail most faculty privileges except for sabbaticals and tenure. Several other institutions offer faculty rank only to those librarians who also teach a course in an academic department; this rank, apparently, is little more than a courtesy, and never entails the possibility of tenure by virtue of any association with the particular department.

A number of practices are peculiar to particular institutions. In one library the director and cataloger are on eleven-month contracts, while the other three professionals (two in reference, one in special collections) have ten-month appointments. At least one other school recently began to offer staggered ten- and eleven-month contracts, as a way of staffing the library continuously through the summer vacation period. In one college librarians receive twelve-month Trustee appointments, which provide them with virtually all faculty fringe benefits, although they are not allowed to teach courses or serve on most committees. Finally, in one library, librarians are appointed as ex officio members of the "General Faculty, " a group that includes librarians and administrators, and is distinct from the Teaching Faculty. These librarians have neither faculty rank nor the possiblity of tenure; however, they are eligible for sabbaticals.

What can we conclude about this multifarious state of faculty status for college librarians at present, as revealed in this survey? When we compare the present state of affairs with the ideal as presented in Massman's criteria, or in the ACRL standards, we can certainly conclude that college librarians, taken as a group, do not presently have faculty status, despite their varying degrees of belief that they do. They have, in large measure, gained academic status, mostly because such status is perceived to be both feasible and warranted by their backgrounds and job responsibilities, and their relationship to the educational mission of the college. However, they have not come to be the equals of their teaching colleagues, despite all of the arguments about the teaching function of the college library. Moreover, given the size of American colleges, and given the financial, social, and political structure of these colleges, it is not likely that more than a few of the wealthier and more liberal institutions will ever grant true faculty status to their librarians.

Arguments For and Against Status

So far, I have avoided the question of whether or not librarians in colleges should have faculty status. This question has been hotly debated over the years, without resolution. On the one hand, there are those who point idealistically to librarians' role in the educational process, and to librarians' own educations, as strong arguments for status. The ACRL "Standards for Faculty Status for College and University Librarians" gives clear expression to these arguments, and is worth quoting at length:

> The academic librarian makes a unique and important contribution to American higher education. He bears central responsibility for developing college and university library collections, for extending bibliographical control over these collections, for instructing students (both formally in the classroom and informally in the library), and for advising faculty and scholars in the use of these collections....
> Without the librarian, the quality of teaching, research, and public service in our colleges and universities would deteriorate seriously and programs in many disciplines could no longer be performed. His contribution is intellectual in nature and is the product of considerable formal education, including professional training at the graduate level. Therefore, college and university librarians must be recognized as equal partners in the academic enterprise, and they must be extended the rights and privileges which are not only commensurate with their contributions, but are necessary if they are to carry out their responsibilities.

It is good to read such a strong defense of academic librarians. However, as we have seen, the "Standards" have not really had much impact on the granting of faculty status for college librarians. The idea that librarians need "full academic recognition in order to play a more effective role in the academic program"[12] has not gained much credence in the college community, nor has the M. L. S. program impressed itself upon the teaching faculty as a credential that merits granting of equal recognition--although at the junior college level, where most faculty do not have Ph. D. 's, the M. L. S. is a much more influential equalizer. The only other rationale for faculty status that is commonly advanced is a bread-and-butter one: faculty status, or something resembling it, provides the most attractive form of job security most college librarians can think of, and they will not relinquish the possibility of such security easily.

There are, however, many librarians who have argued against the concept of faculty status for librarians, and they have raised serious questions about the rationales for it. Patricia Knapp, for instance, questions the centrality of the library to the student-teacher relationship, which she considers the essential part of the educational process. She compares the library to the pharmacy department of a hospital, in which doctor-patient relationships are paramount: "Such enterprises are essential to the achievement of the purpose of the parent institution, but they are subordinate, and the position of those responsible for them is often anomalous."[13] To Knapp "the key relationship in the college is between teacher and student,"[14] and, as a classic article has asserted, "College Librarians Are Not Teachers,"[15] but rather administrators.

Robert Balay has also undercut the argument for academic librarians as teachers by pointing out the disparity between librarians' and faculty members' educations, and Balay further points out that a large percentage of academic librarians never really see, let alone teach, patrons. While this argument has less force in a college setting, where all professionals tend to take a turn at the reference desk even if technical service is their primary task, it still has considerable relevance in the college library.

Perhaps the most devastating argument against faculty status for academic librarians is a sociological one: both librarians and sociologists have looked upon the quest for faculty status as a misdirected plea for recognition. Faculty status is, as Knapp said in 1955, "an important and convenient symbol of status,"[16] and college librarians have naturally reached for such a symbol; however, they have never been able to convince the college community as a whole that they merit it, nor have academic librarians themselves ever been totally convinced by their own arguments, though few have seen fit to say so publicly. One who has done so recently, Pauline Wilson, describes the desire for faculty status as an "organization fiction," a sociological construct that a group employs to "overcome an unfavorable stereotype," "buttress a status claim," or "relate the profession and its members to the public or to other professions."[17] According to Wilson, the claim for faculty status has no objective validity, serving merely to comfort academic librarians, while at the same time diverting them from more fruitful attempts to upgrade their positions in society.

Ultimately, whether or not the claim for faculty status

is justified is probably a psychological, sociological, and political, rather than a rational or theoretical, question. Those who want to believe that academic librarians should have faculty status will continue to claim broad powers for academic librarians and attach great importance to their functions; those who believe that librarians are not teachers and scholars will label the whole notion of faculty status for librarians as ridiculous. We can say, however, that whether or not the notion of faculty status is a justifiable one, it is in either case unlikely to make much more significant headway in colleges, where the Ph. D. is the normal prerequisite for acceptance as a faculty member, and where the centrality of the library to the educational process has rarely been a reality. The claim that college librarians as a group are teachers, though advanced with more justification in colleges than in the highly stratified university situation, remains a weak one.

Alternatives to Faculty Status

What, then, are the options for college librarians in regard to faculty status? The most likely course of events is a continuation of the status quo, a somewhat demoralizing but nevertheless livable compromise (except for the occasional Rose Smiths), in which the majority of college librarians have some form of academic status that they can, if they so choose, consider to be faculty status. Acceptance of this ersatz faculty status entails reduced rewards and prestige, along with considerable uneasiness for many; on the other hand, it also reduces the demands on librarians and minimizes their risks. Academic status, human nature being what it is, represents the path most college librarians will choose to follow.

Some college librarians may press their claim for true faculty status, with varying degrees of justification and acceptance, depending upon their educations and functions within the library. Those with Ph. D. 's as well as M. L. S. 's, whose jobs fall into the area of public service, will find it easiest to gain faculty acceptance; those with only the M.L.S. who work in technical services will experience much more opposition. Any librarian seeking true faculty status will have to be prepared to meet the same criteria for promotion and tenure that other college faculty must meet, and this most college librarians will probably not be prepared to do, either by training or temperament. Those college

librarians who do want true faculty status will also have to
overcome the considerable prejudices against them as a
group, both justified and unjustified. Evidence indicates
that college faculty members are prepared to admit individual librarians into their ranks, even while maintaining a
poor opinion of the group as a whole. [18]

Other alternatives to faculty status currently within
practical range for college librarians include affiliation with
nonprofessional union groups; acceptance of some other status as administrators or trustees, with no organizational affiliation; or affiliation with Administrative Professional groups
(a more common pattern at universities), either as administrators, as "Associated Faculty," or as "General Faculty."
Although such affiliations would provide an alternative status
for college librarians, and a measure of security for them,
each of these alternatives also entails giving up, to some
degree, the "organization fiction" that librarians, as academicians, are central to the educational process, an idea
that, even if a fiction, is nevertheless useful and more
worth maintaining, perhaps, in the college situation than in
any other.

As Pauline Wilson suggests, however, there are alternatives to faculty status as a universally desirable goal--
although these alternatives may not make us comfortable or
secure in the near term and will probably raise a new set
of questions about our professional identity if implemented.
One new approach, suggested by Willis Bridegam of Amherst
College, involves multiple tracks for librarians within the
same institution. In this system the reference people could
opt for faculty status, the catalogers for technical status,
and the director for administrative status. Such a solution
tends to indicate that librarians have no common ground professionally, and would tend to fragment any group of working
individuals within a single library; nevertheless, it might
make sense in some situations. For instance, a reference
librarian with advanced degrees and an active library instruction program, who in fact has more contact hours than many
faculty and who feels comfortable competing for tenure, may
consider faculty status vital for the credibility of the instructional program. Under this system the librarian could compete for faculty status without fear of damaging others in the
library who wish to opt for academic status, administrative
status, trustee status, technician status, or General Faculty
status (depending, again, on local arrangements).

A more radical alternative to faculty status for college

librarians, and an alternative that I personally find more
attractive, is to organize more strongly as a profession,
and to seek recognition and status as librarians. It is
ironic that this should be a radical alternative; it seems
rather like the natural and inevitable one, if librarianship
is ever to come into its own and if we are ever to see ourselves as an integral profession. Robert Balay notes that
"for librarians in public or special libraries, the issue of
academic status simply does not exist," and he suggests
that academic librarians of all kinds "must decide where
their primary loyalty lies, with their own profession or
some other."19 The desire for faculty status may or may
not be a "false claim to status," which must necessarily be
"rejected by legitimate holders of the sought-after status,"20
as the sociologists tell us; but in either case it is clearly a
devisive and somewhat unnatural desire, and it also places
many academic librarians in the position of being unable to
fulfill the requirements expected of them as faculty, when
they should in fact be judged by different criteria.

What can we do, then, to organize as librarians, and
end the voluminous, acrimonious, and ultimately fruitless
debates about faculty status that have raged in the pages of
College & Research Libraries for many years? Robert Balay
suggests that we might, first of all, seek recognition as librarians within individual institutions.

> A recent management study at Columbia ... recom-
> mended three general classes for university staff,
> officers of instruction, officers of administration,
> and officers of the library. Something like this,
> providing recognition for librarians as a separate
> academic group, is to be preferred to straight fac-
> ulty status, since it would go a great way toward
> resolving the profitless debate about faculty status
> in which we now find ourselves. 21

In addition to ending the debate about status such a solution
would also relieve much of the tension and anxiety felt by the
many academic librarians now struggling to match their academic colleagues. Balay's suggestion that librarians organize within institutions as a separate group is less viable in
colleges, with their small numbers of librarians, than it is
in universities, but the idea is still cogent; there is no reason why college librarians could not be classified as a separate academic group, "officers of the library."

By what standards would Balay's separate groups of

library officers be judged? Ultimately, if librarianship is
to come of age as a profession, it will have to be judged as
such, and here our teaching colleagues do offer us useful
models in AAUP and in their individual disciplinary associations (such as the Modern Language Association or the American Historical Association). It is to the American Library
Association and to professional associations of librarians that
we will have to look, not only in academic librarianship but
in all of librarianship, if we are to come of age. As we upgrade our profession we will also have to insist on increasingly stricter standards of performance, and on higher levels
of education and professional competence, from our members;
only then will we compel respect, on our own terms.

The National Librarians Association, still a fledgling
group, has gone farther than any other association toward
delineating a course that would lead to the recognition of librarians, as a unified group, on the basis of national standards. The NLA has proposed state boards of certification,
which would base their judgments upon nationally-agreed-upon
standards of education, continuing education, and professional
practice. Under this plan librarians would have to be re-
certified periodically, and provide other evidence of continuing intellectual and professional growth and development.
Such a system of self-evaluation and self-recognition, were
it carried out conscientiously, would facilitate the process of
self-identification, and discourage the kind of fragmentation
of the profession that the desire for faculty status creates.
Following the NLA model, librarians, like lawyers or phar-
macists, would certify themselves, and choose to affiliate
primarily with their peer group, rather than with an outside
group. This alternative, while it would not provide immediate job security, might help satisfy the status demands of
librarians, and help them to explain, both to the outside
world and to themselves, what the librarian's place is in the
intellectual scheme of things. One can see academic librarianship becoming a specialty within librarianship, which would
demand advanced degrees, in much the same way that specialties within other professions require advanced study. The
recognition granted to academic librarians, as people who
have chosen such a specialty within their own profession,
might ultimately provide them with the status and gratification they currently seek through the present system of faculty status.

For the present, however, the reality is that the
mass of college and other academic librarians will continue

the tantalizing quest for faculty status, which they will assume to be their only proper aspiration. Faculty status will be much wished for by librarians, but rarely attained and imperfectly realized. Academic status, in its various forms, will continue to be the norm. College librarians will remain becalmed on this motionless sea until some strong wind sweeps through academia, giving them new direction in their quest for status and a sense of professional identity.

Notes

1Marjorie Sibley et al., "SCMAI Case Report," Ameri-can Libraries 9 (January 1978): 55.

2Ibid. The "Joint Statement on Faculty Status of College and University Librarians," originally published in College & Research Libraries News 33 (September 1972): 209-10, was reprinted in C&RL News 35 (February 1974): 26, and also in Faculty Status for Academic Librarians: A History and Policy Statements, compiled by the Committee on Academic Status of the Association of College and Research Libraries (Chicago: American Library Association, 1975), pp. 35-37.

3Sibley, p. 55.

4Ibid.

5Morris A. Gelfand, "The College Librarian in the Academic Community," in The Status of American College and University Librarians, ed. Robert B. Downs, ACRL Monograph no. 22 (Chicago: American Library Association, 1958), pp. 151-52.

6Virgil Massman, Faculty Status for Librarians (Metuchen, N.J.: Scarecrow, 1972), p. 11.

7Arthur M. McAnally, "The Dynamics of Securing Academic Status," in The Status of American College and University Librarians, p. 29.

8Massman, p. 5.

9Ibid.

10This document, first printed in C&RL News 33 (September 1972): 210-12, was reprinted in C&RL News 35 (May 1974): 112-13, and again in Faculty Status for Academic Librarians: A History and Policy Statements, pp. 31-34.

11It is interesting to compare the results of my survey, detailed below, with a survey conducted by the Association of Research Libraries' Systems and Procedures Exchange

Center (SPEC) in December 1979 and reported on in SPEC Flyer No. 61 (February 1980). In this survey of 111 ARL libraries, "twenty-seven libraries report full faculty status for librarians, while 25 indicate academic status with some faculty rank and benefits. Thirteen report academic status with no faculty rank and benefits, 10 report non-academic status, and fifteen of the libraries were unable to categorize librarian status within the survey's headings.... It appears that criteria for appointment, promotion, and tenure and areas of equivalency with teaching faculty vary considerably from library to library." The ARL survey indicates that on the university level there is likely to be equivalency between librarians and faculty in the areas of leaves of absence, access to travel funds, and protection of academic freedom; there is not likely to be equivalency in the areas of salary, vacation, tenure, and length of contract year.

[12]Raleigh De Priest, "That Inordinate Passion for Status," C&RL 34 (January 1973): 153.

[13]Patricia B. Knapp, "The College Librarian: Sociology of a Professional Specialization," C&RL 16 (January 1955): 66.

[14]Ibid.

[15]H. Glenn Brown, "College Librarians Are Not Teachers," Library Journal 65 (November 1, 1940): 910-11.

[16]Knapp, p. 67.

[17]Pauline Wilson, "Librarians as Teachers: The Study of an Organization Fiction," Library Quarterly 49 (April 1979): 147.

[18]See Knapp, pp. 67-69.

[19]Robert Balay, letter to the editor, C&RL 34 (July 1973): 305.

[20]Wilson, p. 158.

[21]Balay, p. 306.

COLLECTION DEVELOPMENT FROM A
COLLEGE PERSPECTIVE

William Miller and D. Stephen Rockwood

Collection development today is certainly a most inexact
science. As Michael Moran demonstrates in his recent article "The Concept of Adequacy in University Libraries,"[1]
there is really no way, at present, for any of us to determine whether a collection is or is not adequate.   Formulas
exist, but these are arbitrary constructions rather than validated criteria.   This inexactness need not concern university
collection-development officers very much, for they have the
comfort of aiming for total coverage in many, or perhaps
even in every field; they might even have the funds to acquire near total coverage.   For small college collection-
development officers, however, the situation is quite different.   They have neither the funds, nor the space, nor the
staff to attempt total coverage.   Unfortunately, they also
have little in the way of theory to guide them in their quest
for enlightened selectivity.

Review of the Literature

Where can college library collection-development officers
look for guidance?   The locus classicus would presumably
be Guy R. Lyle's Administration of the College Library.[2]
Lyle provides common-sense advice about considering the
nature of the curriculum, the composition of the faculty,
the amount of funds available, the initial size of the collection, and geographical location, among other factors.   For

instance, a college surrounded by institutions with significant collections can engage in cooperative acquisitions and might not need to acquire certain items (expensive sets of legal materials or science abstracts, for example). Isolated college libraries, on the other hand, might wish to acquire such items not only for students and faculty, but also as a service to the surrounding community.

Lyle's recommendations are good advice and have yet to be superseded. There is, however, no special guidance here for the college collection-development officer. These factors are precisely those that university development officers would also have to consider, were they trying to spend their resources according to a formula. Indeed, one might even say that the factors that Lyle suggests for consideration are misleading for college collection-development officers, because they are generally applicable principles and are not especially relevant to their special needs. This problem was illustrated well by the pioneering citation analysis that Gross and Gross, two small college chemists, did in 1927 for their department. [3] Interested in reducing its periodicals budget, they hit upon analyzing footnotes in journal articles to eliminate subscriptions to journals that were little used. What Gross and Gross ignored, however, was that they were analyzing the use patterns of researchers and publishing scholars, not of the college undergraduates. They had unwittingly conducted a study that was perhaps relevant for the college faculty members, or for university use patterns, but irrelevant for their primary college audience. [4]

Their study was archetypally off-base. It is only recently that librarians have conceived of the college library as an institution at all distinct from the university library. Newton McKeon's 1954 article "The Nature of the College-Library Book Collection"[5] illustrates this lack of awareness well. McKeon, more interested in faculty than in student needs, stated that the college library had the responsibility to supply the faculty with "working materials for scholarship in their fields."[6] These "working materials" included journals, proceedings, official documents, reprints of manuscripts, and original source materials of all kinds, most of which would in practice undoubtedly have proved irrelevant to student needs. McKeon contended, however, that such a collection would serve students as well as faculty, because a "rewarding educational experience"[7] required the very best available resources. Clearly, McKeon's intention was to create a university library in miniature at every college.

How colleges could afford to do this was left unsaid, and whether such attempts at universality are desirable was left unquestioned. As for the execution of his development plans, it was all art and intuition, a "spirit of team play" between librarians and faculty members, chance conversations, informed suggestions, and inquiries about unfulfilled needs. Nevertheless, this is probably still the state of the art at many institutions.

By 1963 Stuart Stiffler, in "A Philosophy of Book Selection for Smaller Academic Libraries,"[8] had realized some of the inherent differences between college and university libraries and was stressing the need for college libraries to select materials not only for their intrinsic merit but also for their ability to complement the existing collection and the college's educational philosophy and program. Stiffler correctly noted that a book collection "consists of ideas, or themes, events, and interpretations"[9] that combine to form a distinctive entity. Stiffler did not eschew subjective criteria for collection completely, but he subordinated them to criteria based upon a conception of the existing collection, perceived as an ideationally and structurally coherent whole. Stiffler's article was quite abstract, and he never grappled specifically with how we might define a collection in order to build upon it. Yet his inherent recognition of college collection building as different from university collection building remains valuable.

Recent Theory

Recent college library collection-development theory is best represented by Evan Farber's work. Many people now realize intuitively that college libraries cannot be small versions of university libraries, because they cannot afford to be, financially. But to rest there is to define college libraries in the negative; Farber takes a more positive approach. He has worked actively to create an alternative to the "University-Library Syndrome" that affects so many college librarians. According to Farber, college libraries differ from university libraries "not only in quantitative terms but in their educational roles."[10] The college librarian must build a collection that directly fulfills student needs, which means, most importantly, "a collection of cultural and recreational materials that can expand students' horizons."[11] Farber's ideal college collection must be a cultural center and do more than serve basic curricular needs. It must also have a "good reference collection that will serve as a key to the immediate library and to resources elsewhere."12 The reference collection is the link that puts users in touch with the universe of resources their library does not, because it cannot, and perhaps should not, have. The reference collection, along with a strong program of bibliographic instruction, is also the key to making full use of the collection the library <u>does</u> have and justifying the library's material and processing expenditures. As an advocate of the no-growth library, Farber believes that the present financial difficulties of colleges are not necessarily bad, because as librarians have to curtail expenditures, they will have to pay more attention "to what a college library should be doing."13

Implications of the Literature

As we analyze the trend in collection philosophy from McKeon to Farber, one point stands out: the trend is toward emphasizing the differences between college and university libraries. One can no longer pretend that collection development for the college library is simply a lilliputian version of university collection development; more attention is now being paid to the goals of the small college and to the library's role in the fulfillment of those goals. Instead of bridling at the restrictions forced upon the college librarian by financial exigency, Farber and his followers now glory in the singular nature of the small academic library. They want us to emphasize our differences and to turn our limitations into creative assets. Thus the attitudinal change in twenty-five years has been great.

Corresponding to the change in thinking concerning the purpose of the small college library, there has also been a change in the view of the selector's position. McKeon advocated selection by intuition. Stiffler called for "hard analysis of the individual title in its relation to some conceptualization of the book collection."14 This was an advance, abstract concept though it is. Farber would endorse Stiffler's analysis of the individual title but would do it even more critically. By committing himself to a "no-growth" library he has increased the need for discipline in selection. The selector of a fixed-sized library must continually evaluate the collection and for every book added must weed a book out. This places greater responsibility on the selector, both as acquirer and as weeder, because it magnifies the impact of mistaken decisions.

In this post-"University-Library Syndrome" era we
wish we could offer college collection-development officers
validated, scientific guidelines with which they could confi-
dently make the hard decisions they face daily. We cannot
offer such guidelines, however; as Michael Moran's article
suggests, we doubt that they can ever be formulated. Therefore all college collection-development officers will continue
to use Choice, use standard lists, involve faculty in collection decisions, give special attention to the existing strengths
of their library, consider the holdings of other area institutions and the willingness of such institutions to extend their
resources to others, make interlibrary loan arrangements,
and try to anticipate the changing nature of the college curriculum. We hold these practices to be self-evident. Yet
we think that something more emerges out of a consideration
of college collection-development theory in recent decades.

Student-Centered Libraries

First, we must now recognize very frankly that our primary
client is the student and not the faculty member and collect
with that fact in mind. This is radical doctrine, one that
many faculty members would undoubtedly find unpalatable,
but it is the inevitable conclusion we draw from Farber's
work. As undergraduate teaching institutions, colleges cannot afford to devote much of their resources to highly specialized research materials, even when these would facilitate
faculty dissertations and publication. The reference collection can and should be the link, for faculty, between their
needs and the universe of resources available at research
institutions, resources that their own college library very
properly does not have. Their research, important as it
may be, is secondary to the primary mission of the college,
and the faculty member's needs are secondary, for the library, to those of the students. The reality of our college
curricula today is that at most institutions, a basic work
(such as, for instance, the Twayne series on standard authors) is more valuable to an undergraduate than a more
sophisticated work that focuses on minute aspects of an author's work.

We do not mean here to demean scholarship, and we
would not like to be accused of pandering to student taste or
taking students' perceptions as the ultimate measure of what
is valuable. As working librarians, however, we cannot ignore the obvious disparities between what faculty too often

request and what students actually find useful. The college
library needs to have a written collection-development policy
that specifically names its primary clients and attempts to
delineate as far as is practical the kinds of books that are
and that are not appropriate for its primary collection goal.
With this policy in hand the librarians can contend with the
professor of English who wants to spend his department's
remaining thousand dollars on first editions of Arnold Bennett, or the biologist who has a list of specialized journals
that she considers essential for her research.

College faculty members at first view this attempt to
rationalize acquisitions as a usurpation of prerogative or an
abridgment of academic freedom, but they can usually be
made to understand and admit the difference between college
education as a process and university training as a specialized inculcation of particular facts and information. Once
they accept this distinction they are likely to become part-
ners in the endeavor to collect a useful working collection,
on a fixed budget, for undergraduates.

Periodicals Collections

A second principle becomes evident as a corollary to the
proposition that the college library exists primarily for the
benefit of the student. It is that the periodicals collection
should not be apportioned by department. The result of departmental apportionment is a haphazard collection of journals designed for no particular purpose. If periodical collections in colleges are to be as useful as the book collection, they should, for the most part, reflect the titles covered in the major indexing tools that the library receives and
that students are most likely to use. There should probably
be a core collection of indexing tools that are most appropriate for undergraduate work and that are essentially surro-
gates for the periodicals collection. Such a core-collection
concept, presently being employed at Alma College, has been
defined by Peter Dollard to include Readers' Guide, Humanities Index, Social Sciences Index, and the new General Science Index. Copies of these indexes are prominently shelved
as a group and are given special treatment in bibliographic
instruction.

Of course, the library will also have indexes and abstracts that refer users to resources to which they would
not have immediate access. Thus the core indexes are

essentially analogous to the card catalog and signal clearly
to the user that "this is what you can have, immediately,
in our library." The other indexes and abstracts would be
analogous to specialized bibliographies; library instructors
could say of these, in effect, that they "are for the more
scholarly, sustained, or adventuresome projects. Be forewarned: we do not have all, and perhaps not even many, of
the items included here, so you may have to use interlibrary
loan, or go elsewhere, to obtain your materials."

University librarians need not worry very much about
the rationale for their periodicals collection and can confid-
dently expect a collection of 30,000 to 50,000 periodical titles to satisfy any average student user, from any department. College librarians, however, may be expending half
of the materials budget on only 700, 1,000, or at most
2,000 periodical titles. To accept the proposition that all
periodicals, and the indexes and abstracts, are created
equal, is to accept a formula for perpetual student frustration and dissatisfaction. It is folly for college libraries to
attempt to satisfy research needs on a hit-or-miss basis; it
would be much more sensible to conceive of periodical acquisition primarily in terms of a core of indexes, which students could easily be instructed to use and which would lead
the students, with confidence, to the articles themselves.

Of course, the library should also have indexes and
abstracts that refer the users to resources to which they do
not have immediate access, but the personality and the ten-
acity of undergraduates is such that they need quite a bit of
positive reinforcement in their periodicals searching. We
have never seen this consideration built into calculations of
what percentage of user needs a library should be expected
to satisfy, but clearly college undergraduates demand more
immediate gratification than do university graduate students
and faculty. The typical first contacts of college students
with the library occur when they are under immediate time
pressure to produce a paper. If they learn that the indexes
and abstracts exist only to point out to them material that
is, for their practical purposes, unobtainable, they will not
soon return. We suggest, therefore, that the college librarian's first periodicals priority is to subscribe to journals whose articles the students will surely be directed to
when they use the standard periodical indexes. Even if
another library exists in close proximity and holds these
same journals, their purchase is still justifiable. The time
to wean students from excessive dependence on the Readers'

Guide is after they have mastered its use and after they
know that they can always fall back upon it for quick references if PAIS or the other indexes point them to too many
unobtainable items.

Characteristics of Undergraduates

In a discussion of student frustration and the disparity between their needs and those of the faculty, a third principle
becomes evident for college librarians, a principle that
McKeon would have rejected but that Farber would probably
endorse: just as we should not consider college libraries
to be miniature university libraries, so we should not assume that college students are all scholar-adventurers. We
should not ignore the personalities of our primary user
group any more than we should ignore their need for materials.

Perhaps the major difference between the library use
of the average college student and the average graduate student or faculty member is that college students rarely need
to use the library as anything more than a study hall or a
reserve room. Human nature being what it is, they will
not generally use the library one whit more, or more intel-
ligently, than they have to. This is a consideration university collection policies need not concern themselves with, at
least where their graduate students and faculty are concerned.
These people will have to learn how to use the library, and
they will need to discover where the important materials are.
Collection development can thus proceed in an abstract intellectual vacuum. Subject specialists can procure abstruse
materials, secure in the knowledge that the appropriate people will appreciate the acquisition and make proper use of it.

College librarians can assume nothing of the sort.
Therefore they cannot conduct their collection development in
a vacuum. It must, first and most importantly, be tied in
to library instruction at introductory and advanced levels.
One might even end up purchasing more expensive materials
for departments that will encourage students to use them or
for courses whose faculty members will be cooperating in
the library's instructional program. To a great extent the
college library can generate whatever level of bibliographic
expertness its students acquire, and it can control (and justify the cost of) expensive items by instructing students in
their use. This is not the place for a lengthy discussion of

the merits of bibliographic instruction, but it is clearly here that the library discharges a good bit of its instructional responsibility, and collection development must focus on areas of heavy instruction. Here again, a written policy, coupled with a check on how often expensive materials are used, may defuse resentment and even result in more sober assessments of the library's place in the instructional life of the campus. Departments that have resisted bibliographic instruction should very properly have their book budgets cut, and if they complain, it should be easy to explain and defend the move.

If there is a place in the college library for specialized materials, or computerized versions of them, it is in the reference collection. Here, the faculty and more sophisticated students can become aware of those resources their library does not stock. Here, also, the interlibrary loan and cooperative-lending processes are facilitated. As more indexes and abstracts become available on-line, departmental and reference-materials budgets should probably be channeled away from traditional, expensive, and little-used hard-copy bibliographies and indexes and toward the computerized versions of them.

We doubt that on-line reference work, which has become a part of university library activity, will become an integral part of the college library very soon, expecially because college budgets will not permit extensive on-line searching. Undergraduates will not usually be willing to, and should not be made to, bear the cost of searches that would be just as valuable, at their level of inquiry, if done manually. Yet some of the more specialized indexes could conceivably be eliminated in favor of on-line work, if it were readily available. There is a danger here of limiting access and of frightening away timid potential student users. We judge this hazard to be more theoretical than real, however, especially if such services are advertised as a regular part of reference service and are underwritten as a normal part of departmental and reference-budget expenditure. Undergraduates are unlikely to care to go beyond Readers' Guide and the other core searching tools, but if they do, a readily available computer search may stimulate as much sophisticated research as it stifles.

Microforms

Should the curriculum warrant a small college's attempt to

acquire research-strength holdings in a particular field, the preselected microform collection might be an acceptable alternative. As such subjects as black studies, women's studies, and popular culture enter the curriculum, librarians often discover that their collection lacks the resources to support work in these areas. Retrospective collecting is time-consuming and expensive under the best of circumstances, and, lacking subject bibliographers, most college libraries are not set up for it. Thus a microform collection on a discrete subject can save staff time, ensure reasonable coverage of a subject, save expensive space, and make material quickly available, with minimal processing, for student use.

One must expect undergraduate resistance to microform use, especially among the minimally motivated, and for that reason we would not recommend acquiring the more popular, or heavily used, periodical titles in this format. Microform presents a number of barriers that will too easily frustrate the students who will not persevere. However, the ability to use microform is a skill that college libraries should probably be teaching, and one should not shy away from acquiring microform when it represents desirable material, including replacements of missing periodical volumes, that could not otherwise be conveniently acquired.

Curriculum-Centered Collecting

In order to discharge their collection-development responsibilities adequately college librarians must, to a much greater extent than university librarians, know the curriculum, the existing collection, and the students and faculty at their particular institutions. Though it may sound harsh and elitist, the truth is that the level of academic sophistication varies considerably from college to college. A collection that would support the curriculum and serve the students well at one college might prove entirely inadequate, for any number of reasons, at another. Librarians have to collect for their individual schools, not for some ideal abstract institution. They should be cautious in approaching standard lists or in using such selection aids as Choice. They should also try to anticipate academic developments and curricular change, so that the library can evolve along with the college. Finally, they should secure control of their acquisitions budget, if they do not already have it. In too many colleges, academic departments control and expend their budgets

according to no discernable criteria. While the faculty may
know their subjects, they probably know little about how students use the library, and their judgment as book selectors
is questionable. As Massman and Olson point out, faculty
members are too often either "overburdened with other duties," lacking in their knowledge of books, uninterested in
books, unconvinced that library materials are really of value
in instruction, prone to selecting only narrow research works
on the one hand or textbooks on the other, or simply too
lazy to care what happens to their book budget, even though
believing that "only they are capable of selecting."[16] It is
probably only the librarian who can see the collection as a
whole, as Stiffler suggested, and select material that is relevant to the students, the curriculum, and the existing collection.

Summary

Given the proposition that college libraries are not simply
small versions of university libraries, four guidelines that
college collection-development officers should follow become
evident. First, college librarians should recognize their
primary obligation to collect for undergraduate students.
Second, in the same way that book acquisitions should reflect student needs, periodical acquisitions should be based
primarily upon major periodical indexes, which students
would see as analogous to the card catalog. Third, college
librarians need to take into account the undergraduate personality, for instance avoiding microform material where it
would tend to be most discouraging to the weakly motivated
student. Finally, college librarians, to a much greater extent than their university counterparts, should know their
institution's curriculum and exercise maximum control over
their materials budget; extensive faculty selection, too common at colleges, is liable to result in haphazard collections.

Notes

[1]Michael Moran, "The Concept of Adequacy in University
Libraries," College & Research Libraries 39 (March 1978):
85-93.
[2]Guy R. Lyle, The Administration of the College Library
(4th ed.; New York: H. W. Wilson, 1974).

3P. L. K. Gross and E. M. Gross, "College Libraries and Chemical Education," Science 66 (October 1927): 385-98.

4Evan Farber notes the inappropriateness, for undergraduates, of existing citation studies, in "Limiting College Library Growth: Bane or Boon?" in Farewell to Alexandria, ed. Daniel Gore (Westport, Conn.: Greenwood, 1976), p. 39.

5Newton F. McKeon, "The Nature of the College-Library Book Collection," in The Function of the Library in the Modern College, ed. Herman H. Fussler (Chicago: University of Chicago, 1954), pp. 48-61.

6McKeon, p. 52.

7McKeon, p. 53.

8Stuart A. Stiffler, "A Philosophy of Book Selection for Smaller Academic Libraries," College & Research Libraries 24 (May 1963): 204-08.

9Stiffler, p. 205.

10Evan I. Farber, "College Librarians and the University-Library Syndrome," in The Academic Library: Essays in Honor of Guy R. Lyle, ed. Evan I. Farber and Ruth Walling (Metuchen, N.J.: Scarecrow, 1974), p. 22.

11Farber, "Limiting College Library Growth," p. 39.

12Ibid.

13Ibid., p. 40.

14Stuart A. Stiffler, "A Footnote on Confusion: Book Selection in the Smaller College Library," Ohio Library Association Bulletin 40 (July 1970): 18.

15For an alternative viewpoint on the place of microform collections in the small college library see Stiffler, "A Footnote on Confusion," p. 18.

16Virgil F. Massman and David R. Olson, "Book Selection: A National Plan for Small Academic Libraries," College & Research Libraries 32 (July 1971): 271-79.

COLLECTION DEVELOPMENT FROM A COLLEGE
PERSPECTIVE: A COMMENT

Evan I. Farber

To begin with, I agree fully with the main thrust of the
previous article--that the approach to building a college library's collection must be very different from that for a
university library and that it is really the college librarian's
responsibility, not the faculty's, to ensure the collection's
usefulness. I do, however, have several reservations about
specific points.

　　　1.　Periodical collections "should, for the most part,
reflect the titles covered in the major indexing tools the library receives. "

　　　To be sure, whether or not a periodical is indexed
should be an important consideration, but it is also important to have as many of those titles as possible that are
important for supporting course work. Restricted to indexed periodicals, most college libraries would not consider
subscribing to Paris-Match or Der Spiegel, for example, because they're not in the generally available indexes, even
though students taking French or German should be able to
see them.

　　　A periodical not covered by the indexes needs to be
examined very carefully for possible subscription but should
not be eliminated from consideration on that basis alone.
Its being indexed is important, of course, because that
makes its use more likely. If other factors, such as class

147

assignments or even student browsing, ensure its use, whether or not it's indexed is not as important.

There's another reason for not using indexing as a primary goal. It takes a while for any new periodical to get into an index--and that is particularly true, of course, of the Wilson indexes, for which inclusion of particular titles is determined by subscribers' votes. I think, however, that a college librarian has a responsibility for adding new periodicals--not constantly or hastily, but judiciously, with as much or more care than is given to book selection.

Among the titles our library has added within the past year are some not covered yet by any index, but I can defend the selection of each of them on some other basis of selection: Omni, Grants Magazine, Asia, Bennington Review, Public Opinion, and the Cornell Review. In a few years they probably will be indexed, but it's up to librarians to make sure that students do find out about them before then. Encouraging students to read, to browse, to become familiar with new books and periodicals is part of a college librarian's responsibility, and what the indexing services have chosen to cover cannot obviate that.

2. Another objection stems from the authors' overemphasis on bibliographic instruction, their claim that it should be the most important criterion in determining additions to the collection. Now this may seem a strange comment from one who is so closely identified with bibliographic instruction, and I'm sure our agreements about it are more numerous and important than our differences. But the suggestion that "departments that have resisted bibliographic instruction should very properly have their book budgets cut" simply runs counter to what I think is the desirable, even necessary, approach to bibliographic instruction.

Such a punitive device will hardly engender that spirit of cooperation, that sense of common endeavor between teaching faculty and librarians that is the sine qua non for an ongoing program of bibliographic instruction. It's too easy to forget that bibliographic instruction is not an end in itself--its justification and primary purpose are the enhancement of the teaching/learning process. Together with teaching faculty we college librarians are in the business of education; regarding and approaching bibliographic instruction as an end in itself, without considering its educational context, can only be counterproductive and result in an unsupported and eventually dismantled program.

I think that one source of the authors' error here is their implicit assumption that all teaching has the same thrust, that bibliographic instruction can be equally useful for all disciplines, or even for all types of teaching. For example, after all these years I still find it difficult to relate bibliographic instruction to mathematics courses or to foreign-language courses that emphasize language skills. One might respond that, okay, then these departments don't need much library support, but that's very different from saying that they should "have their book budgets cut."

Librarians must understand and appreciate that there are many approaches to teaching, and not every one, not even some of the most successful ones, entail use of the library. To be sure, we believe that good teaching can be made even better if students are required to use the library and are given instruction in that use, but that does not extend to every course.

We need to respect the different approaches to pedagogy and work with those that are appropriate for bibliographic instruction. Our creativity and energy should be focused on the teaching faculty with whom we can work--there's enough to be done just with them. Penalizing others will only put faculty on the defensive and ruin a working relationship that was probably fragile enough to begin with.

3. Librarians "should secure control of their acquisitions budget, if they do not already have it.... While the faculty may know their subjects, they probably know little about how students use the library, and their judgment as book selectors is questionable."

I'm not quite sure what Miller and Rockwood mean by "secure control," and if they mean the librarian is responsible for allocating the budget and supervising its expenditure over the fiscal year, I cannot argue with that. But if, on the other hand, they mean (and this is what I think they do mean) that the librarian should initiate all ordering or at least have to approve every request, I can't agree.

First of all, it's not wise politically and will surely test the fragility of that relationship I spoke of earlier. More important, though, it assumes that librarians know more about the content of disciplines than most do, or even more than they should be expected to know. It is unfair to categorize faculty members (even with a qualified "too often") as "lacking in their knowledge of books, uninterested in books ... prone to selecting only narrow research works on the one hand or textbooks on the other." My experience is that the few faculty members who fit that description will not even bother to order, and then the librarian can fill that gap.

It is more likely that most faculty members can't be depended upon to maintain some sort of balance in the library's collection, but that is where the librarian comes in: to suggest titles for filling in gaps and, more important, to work with faculty and help them develop a wider perspective. The library collection is not an end in itself: it exists primarily to support the teaching program, and teachers should be interested in making sure the collection does that. If they do not, then it's up to the librarian, but he or she should always be conscious of faculty expertise and responsibility.

COLLECTION DEVELOPMENT FROM A COLLEGE PERSPECTIVE: A RESPONSE

William Miller

We appreciate Evan Farber's thoughtful critique, which gives us an opportunity to clarify several matters. Farber senses, quite rightly, that our article is somewhat rigid and doctrinaire. It is so because we were attempting to define some theoretical, objective criteria and then explore what the logical consequences of these criteria might be, ignoring for the moment the political and social context in which the library exists. In real life, of course, we do not ignore the political and social context, and as a result we end up behaving very much as Farber suggests that we should.

Nevertheless, we thought it valuable to theorize, with this question in mind: "If I were not running the risk of offending department X, and if I did not need to do a favor for professor Y, what objective criteria could I apply to my acquisitions process to provide maximum educational benefit to the greatest number of students, given a budget that does not allow me to purchase everything I want?"

This question is complex and frustrating, so much so that many college librarians refuse to accept its legitimacy, preferring instead to follow whims, hunches, and prejudices and to bemoan the inevitably insufficient budget.

A second group of college librarians acknowledges the question but says, in effect, "Although we cannot order everything that every faculty member might theoretically want, we

can and will order anything any faculty member actually does request." We see little difference between the first and second responses; in both cases librarians are refusing to make professional judgments.

We suggest a third response: "Although I have the money to order any particular item and could order it if I wanted to, I do not want to unless it fits into a collection-development policy built around an objective set of criteria, which I have already defined." With that third response in mind, we should like to respond to Farber's three specific reservations.

1. In emphasizing that periodical collections should reflect titles covered in indexing tools, we acknowledge we are out on a limb and would like to address important questions he raises.

There are many thousands of fine periodicals, all of them potentially useful for course work. But which ones will students actually use? Clearly, they will almost always use the most highly indexed periodicals, because indexing provides their most important subject access. There are, of course, bibliographies that students might use, and they may be introduced to periodicals in several other ways. But how can one rationally build a small periodicals collection based on these other ways? On the other hand, we know for certain that students will be using the periodicals suggested to them in Readers' Guide and the other more common indexes.

We have no wish to make demigods out of the people at H. W. Wilson, and we recognize that there are other bases on which to collect periodicals, but they are weaker, more subjective, and too dependent on individual needs that may be transitory. Therefore for small academic libraries we have no hesitation about calling the acquisition of highly indexed periodicals the primary task in the development of the collection, assuming that the primary goal of collecting is use, and not the creation of that mythical budget-eating monster, the "balanced collection."

Der Spiegel illustrates our point well. Any large academic library should have it, and any small academic library should have it, if it is actually playing a part in the instructional program. But we would hate to see a library of 700 or 1,000 periodical titles subscribing to Der Spiegel simply because someone believes that it is the most important

German newsmagazine, something that one "must" have. We
would ask librarians at such an institution: "As far as you
can tell, do any students actually use it?" "Is there any
faculty member who seriously (and not just wishfully) supports the subscription as an aid to the instructional program,
or who expects students to use it?" If the answers are "no"
on both counts, then the subscription should be canceled--
unless there is a political consideration that outranks one's
normal criteria. Certainly, after cancelation, there may be
an occasional person who asks for Der Spiegel. But how
many students ask, every day, for more common titles that
the library cannot supply?

2.   Perhaps we were too insistent about library instruction. We do counsel an aggressive instruction program, but
Farber is right to make a distinction between departments
that are noncooperative and those that simply cannot accommodate library work into the structure of their courses. A
hostile attitude toward either kind of department is certainly
inappropriate and self-defeating.

We like Farber's distinction between consulting with
departments about their reduced need for support rather than
telling them that their budgets are being cut. The difference
can certainly be substantive as well as semantic and political.
At the same time it is also appropriate to make special efforts to enrich the collections in those areas where bibliographic instruction has created increased demand.

3.   By "securing control of their acquisitions budget,"
we meant that librarians should apportion a large part of the
acquisitions budget among departments, expecting departments
to initiate the bulk of their own book ordering but standing
ready, not only to expend departmental funds, but also to
exercise judgment on all departmental orders.

We do think that librarians should reserve the right
to approve every request, but this does not mean imperious,
arbitrary action; it means questioning and negotiating requests that seem too specialized, too expensive, too redun-
dant, or otherwise inappropriate. We think also that librarians should retain approximately 25 percent of the budget for
discretionary buying. Here, and in their control of the departmental funds, librarians would be exercising their professional judgments.

ACQUSITIONS IN COLLEGE AND UNIVERSITY LIBRARIES

Walter P. Hogan

In his well-known article "College Librarians and the University-Library Syndrome"[1] Evan Farber was primarily concerned with collection development from a public service perspective. The "University-Library Syndrome, " however, has equal applicability to the technical services. Acquisitions policies and procedures have a profound effect upon collection development, and the acquisitions practices of college libraries ought to be very different from those of the universities.

In the college library, for instance, a high percentage of the actual volumes acquired ought to receive individual attention from the professional librarian throughout the acquisitions process. A university library with $500,000 for books might be processing (very roughly) an average of 150 books per working day, and the sheer volume of ordering reduces the amount of time that university acquisitions librarians can spend with individual titles; thus a high percentage of orders is handled entirely by nonprofessionals. A college library, on the other hand, acquiring perhaps one-tenth as much material, can treat each acquisition with greater care.

The small academic library has a much greater opportunity to develop a uniquely appropriate collection, and to pursue acquisitions methods that best contribute to such development. This opportunity, however, can be eroded not only through inflation and reduced book budgets, and by allowing faculty to take over all selection, but also through mismanagement of routine acquisitions procedures. For example, the choice between paper and hardbound editions, decisions on whether to retain books ordered or sent in error, replacement of missing books--these are all crucial factors in collection building, but they are all too often regarded even in college libraries as technical services matters and considered on the basis of cost and convenience, without sufficient regard for their effect upon the shape of the collection. How can college acquisitions librarians deal with some of these issues, and how are their options different from those of university librarians?

Paperbacks

Because of the volume of ordering the university library is likely to develop a standard policy on paperback or hardcover editions when the book selector has not indicated a preference. Depending upon the nature of the collection and other factors, such as binding costs if the paperbacks are to be bound, a university general library will tend to arrive at a blanket policy concerning the desirability of acquiring paperbacks.

College acquisitions librarians, however, ought not to be hampered by a set policy either for or against paperbacks. Not only because of the smaller volume of orders, but also through their knowledge of the collection and how it is used and their familiarity with the faculty members who have ordered the books, college acquisitions librarians ought to be allowed to decide on a case-by-case basis whether any given title would be better ordered in paper or hardcover format. Searchers can be told to list both prices when two versions are available, and librarians can then decide in each instance which edition should be ordered. Criteria for making this decision would include the cost differential between the two editions and the type and amount of use that the book is likely to receive. It might be decided that some paperbacks should be bound cheaply, others should receive high-quality binding, while some ought not to be bound at all. In any case, these decisions can be made by the acquisitions librarian, perhaps in consultation with others on the staff, and this provides him or her with an excellent opportunity to exercise and develop professional judgment. The cumulative effect of thousands of these small decisions over a period of years will make a great deal of difference in the size, appearance, and use of a college collection.

Returns

The return of damaged books and books ordered or shipped in error is another decision-making area for college librarians. As with paperbacks, because of the large volume of business the university library will probably have a routine policy for the return of such items. For example, it could be decided as a matter of policy that any book costing less than $20 shipped from certain foreign countries would not be worth returning under any circumstances. By contrast, college acquisitions librarians can personally examine each damaged book and every book ordered or sent in error. Knowing the collection, they can determine whether a damaged item, duplicate copy, or wrong title might better be kept than returned. It seems likely that a college library would return a higher percentage of such books because (1) with a small book budget funds cannot be wasted on unwanted duplicates, and (2) in a collection that is more narrowly circumscribed a smaller percentage of new titles sent or ordered in error would be appropriate.

In sum, this is another area in which college librarians have the opportunity to develop a personal style of decision making and simultaneously exert a considerable influence upon the shape of their libraries' collections. In their dual role as acquirer and collection builder they span the technical/public services dichotomy that generates so much red tape in larger libraries.

Replacements

Dealing with missing and withdrawn books and their replacements is a difficult problem for any library but one that can be handled much more easily in the smaller institution. A routine procedure is ordinarily established in both large and small libraries for the compilation of missing reports, a series of thorough searches, withdrawal of records from the catalog, and reorder decisions. This can easily get out of control in a university library, where there are thousands of books circulating at any moment, hundreds if not thousands of missing reports, and very complex expensive procedures for withdrawal of records from the various library files. In addition, shelf inventory to identify missing items is obviously more difficult in direct proportion to the size of the collection. There is no excuse for the small academic library not to stay right on top of the situation, not to maintain good

records and statistics, and not to acquire, speedily, needed
materials that are known to have been lost.

An example of a technique available in the small library that would not be feasible in a university collection is
that of checking on "haves." In a small library each time
it is discovered that a book order duplicates a title already
cataloged a student can be assigned to search the stacks
and then the circulation records to make sure that the book
is actually owned and not missing. If it turns out that such
a book is missing, the order card can be used to generate
an order for a replacement copy, rather than being sent back
to the book selector as a "have." In a large library such a
procedure would probably not be cost-efficient, or even
possible--but as a result, many of the "haves" returned to
university library book selectors actually represent items
that have been lost from the collection. A missing title
might be ordered several times over a period of years,
with the order card being returned each time as a "have"
and the book finally going out of print without ever being
replaced.

Being up-to-date on what is missing from the library
is but one of the many ways in which college acquisitions librarians can develop a feeling for their libraries' collections--
for the collections' strengths and weaknesses, growth and
losses. Because the collections are smaller, the librarians
can get to know them more easily; and because they are not
pigeonholed into technical services functions, they have the
opportunity to influence the development of the collections,
for better or for worse. This sense of being in touch with
a living collection can be one of the most rewarding aspects
of librarianship, and it is an experience that is more readily attainable in the smaller library.

Selection

In major university collections nearly every item listed in
current bibliographies, such as Weekly Record and British
National Bibliography, is ordered immediately or received
automatically on blanket order. Selection is mainly a matter of not missing anything: reviews are generally irrelevant, since new books are ordered long before any critical
assessment appears, and remainder sales are of little significance because the university library already owns all but
the rarest materials. Envious of such extravagance, college

librarians will quite naturally bemoan their comparatively small materials budgets. This very limitation, however, has the effect of amplifying the significance of each selection decision they make. The small library cannot order thousands of new monographs as soon as they are announced, nor can it casually commit itself to continuing orders and to approval or blanket plans. Instead, much of the book ordering must be retrospective, so that the college library can base its selections upon reviews and bibliographies and take advantage of publisher and clearinghouse sales whenever possible. Of the thousands of academic books published each year only a small percentage are of lasting value. With its acquisitions vacuum cleaner, the university library will acquire all of the most important books but also a great number of less useful items. Additional copies of those books that turn out to be valuable can be ordered later, while the great silent majority, destined never to circulate, quietly gather dust in the stacks by the hundreds of thousands. [2]

Needless to say, college librarians cannot afford this extravagance: every one of their choices is crucial to the students at their colleges, because each purchase effectively cancels other possible purchases. [3] Thus in selection decisions as well as in technical acquisitions strategies college acquisitions librarians have the greater potentiality to shape their libraries' collections.

The Joy of Specialization

Thus far we have emphasized the advantages that college acquisitions librarians have over their university counterparts. The latter, however, have the advantage of being surrounded and supported by the superior bibliographic, economic, and human resources available at a large institution. While college librarians usually participate in a wide range of tasks, university librarians--particularly if they are employed in a central technical services unit rather than a divisional library--tend more to be specialists. Their range of duties may be relatively limited, but they have the opportunity to become expert at those functions to which they are assigned. The development and use of such expertise is as satisfying to university librarians as involvement in a broader range of services is to their college counterparts. In terms of acquisitions functions, this tendency is most clearly illustrated by the contrast between the searching procedures of large and small academic libraries.

If there is one respect in which acquisitions work is more challenging and rewarding at the university library than at smaller academic libraries, it would be in the area of bibliographic searching. Preorder searching and verification in the large research library is necessarily more complex than at a smaller library for a number of reasons: first, the large volume of current orders and the size of the card catalog and other files increase the danger of unwanted duplicate purchases and call for a greater ability to discriminate between similar-seeming records. Often local cataloging policies will have changed substantially over the years, and with retrospective conversion of all the "old" records being impractical in a large collection considerable sophistication is required of searchers in locating and interpreting all pertinent records despite changes evolving over the history of the catalog. In addition, university library systems usually include numerous divisional libraries that may do their own ordering and cataloging but whose holdings must be taken into account by the searcher, and this can present special problems. Serial records at a large institution are another formidable challenge--they seem to increase in size and complexity at a trigonometric rate. Finally, the university collection will tend to contain a much higher proportion of foreign-language works and esoteric research materials that are difficult to search. As a result, bibliographic works that the college library could not afford and would seldom use (e.g., national bibliographies of foreign countries) must regularly be consulted by university library searchers. These employees must at least be well-trained paraprofessionals and are often graduate students in library science.

By contrast, in the college library much of the searching can be performed by clerks and students; and trade bibliographies, mainly <u>Books in Print</u>, are the primary source of preorder information. In the college library it is generally not necessary to retrieve catalog copy at the preorder stage, as must be done at the university level. For example, in a large collection all of the series tracings on every incoming order must be searched in the library's catalog, and in standing order and serial records, to make sure that the item is not expected to arrive as a continuation. Accurate verification of series entries can only be accomplished by examining catalog copy via Library of Congress bibliographies and OCLC or other source of MARC tapes. A very different situation prevails at the college library having only one or two hundred standing orders on file, most of them for standard items (e.g., <u>World Almanac</u>, <u>ALA Directory</u>,

Europa Yearbook, etc.) which are well known to the acquisitions staff. In such a small library it is not necessary to pursue painstaking series identification for acquisitions purposes. Doubtless some small academic libraries have elected to perform thorough series and main-entry verification at the preorder stage, especially if they have combined their acquisitions and catalog services into a single technical services unit. Such efforts at the preorder stage in a small library, however, are not necessary for ordering and can only be justifiable for cataloging purposes. It is also true that some small libraries maintain high standards for bibliographic searching, while some university libraries may experience deficiencies in this area. Nevertheless, it seems evident that bibliographic searching is one acquisitions-related activity that tends to be more demanding and more intellectually satisfying in direct proportion to the size and complexity of the collection for which the work is performed.

Bureaucracy and the Single Librarian

While university librarians are able to avail themselves of greater material resources, as well as the expertise of numerous professional colleagues and skilled technicians, college librarians may have the advantage of actual working involvement in a wider variety of operations. Often one professional with the help of a few clerks and students can perform a range of tasks that in the university library might be divided among eight or more administratively distinct units-- selection, ordering, payments, searching, continuations, gifts and exchange, bindery, and receiving. Some of these units might be subdivided further, for instance into English-language and foreign sections. The autonomy of divisional libraries in some or all of these categories results in further stratification.

Such an elaborate bureaucratic structure, however necessary and functional, embodies obvious limitations for university librarians in terms of their professional development. Working within a narrowly defined area of responsibility, they lack opportunities to experience the integrated wholeness of their libraries' purpose, particularly the relationships between the technical and public services. Furthermore, few university librarians have frequent opportunity to confer with top library administrators or to influence policy decisions. This can foster a fatalistic attitude toward the goals and direction of the organization, which can hardly be beneficial to morale and productivity. Librarians may become frustrated by decisions of others that have a negative impact upon their own operation, but they are often prevented by the bureaucratic structure from effecting any change. For example, a librarian who is only responsible for ordering books, and who has no selection input, may become unhappy with what he considers to be misguided selections by the library's subject bibliographers. This acquisitions librarian might well experience difficulty in maintaining enthusiasm for his work if it involves primarily the ordering of materials that he feels are less than ideally chosen for the collection. Selection is none of his business, however, and any effort he makes to express his concern is likely to be perceived by those who specialize in this task as a hostile political act.

This contrasts with the situation of the typical college acquisitions librarian. She not only has some involvement with selection, and with those faculty members who are active in ordering, but also takes a turn at the reference desk, conducts bibliographic instruction and library tours, and in general, has more frequent and regular contact with patrons--even in the most casual sense of being recognized as a librarian and thus being available to patrons throughout the working day.

The university technical services librarian is likely to have little working contact with anyone outside the library; those faculty members who order books communicate only with certain bibliographers, and students rarely encounter any librarian other than those assigned to service desks. Employees of the acquisitions department of a university library not only experience this lack of contact with faculty and patrons, but also have less contact with the materials being ordered; often librarians or searchers never see the book for which they have conducted a preorder search. Their only involvement may be with pieces of paper--order cards, catalog copy, card files, etc. They do not know whether the books they have searched will arrive, what they look like, or whether anyone will ever read them. They simply move bits of paper from one location to another (or, in an automated system, push a few buttons), comparing order requests with the card catalog and other files.

This distance from the material being acquired is also felt at the payments end of a university library's acquisitions process. In a small operation ledgers relating

each item ordered to an encumbrance and payment can easily be scanned. But in a very large library--even one with
an automated system that can link bibliographic records to
payment records--the sheer volume of ordering reduces the
attention that can be paid to individual orders. There one
must conceptualize large amounts of money and plan for
broad budgetary trends, rarely focusing upon single orders.

In sum, university acquisitions librarians are removed
from much of the material evidence that their departments
are continuously functioning as integral parts of organisms
whose purpose is the retrieval and dissemination of scholarly
information to interested human beings. However, the potential for joyless paper-shuffling and a sense of alienation must
be balanced against the many advantages of working in a
large organization.

As for college librarians, we have seen that they are
offered the possibility of becoming involved with the total
range of their libraries' services. They are in a position
to make many ordering and selection decisions that have a
major effect upon the quality of their libraries' collections.
Clearly, this is a responsibility as well as an opportunity:
failure to evolve optimal acquisitions strategies and to develop a working commitment to the prosperity of the library
and college at which they are employed will indeed cause the
situation of college acquisitions librarians to compare un-
favorably with their counterparts in universities.

Notes

[1]Evan I. Farber, "College Librarians and the University-
Library Syndrome," in The Academic Library: Essays in
Honor of Guy R. Lyle, ed. Evan I. Farber and Ruth Walling
(Metuchen, N.J.: Scarecrow, 1974).

[2]Several excellent essays on this topic may be found in
Farewell to Alexandria, ed. Daniel Gore (Westport, Conn.:
Greenwood, 1976).

[3]Robert R. Hellinga, in "Departmental Acquisitions
Policies for Small College Libraries," Library Acquisitions:
Practice and Theory 3 (1979): 81-84, recently noted that
while research institutions can acquire materials according
to broad "levels of support," or "levels of collection density"
for the various disciplines and special collections, the small

college library must pick and choose specific titles from
among the many available: "In the one case, the decision
to order a book (or not to order it) is based on the kind of
book it is; in the other case, the decision is based on the
book's relative merits among other books of its own kind. ...
The small college library can build strong collections only
by being highly selective at every 'level.' It cannot afford
to purchase a second-rate book simply because said book is
on a particular level."

THE CHALLENGE OF CATALOGING
IN THE COLLEGE ENVIRONMENT

Marian Bishop

Libraries have catalogers for two main reasons. Obviously, since the books are meant to be used, returned, and reused, they must be labeled with some identification and a location marker so they can easily be found when needed. But more importantly, a permanent description needs to be prepared for the patron's help in selecting books, and, to further simplify selection, appropriate topics need to be assigned under which the description is duplicated in a catalog of some type.

Theoretically, the job should be similar in all libraries--especially in two such closely related types of library as those of colleges and universities. Any good cataloger will do the same quality of work, regardless of the size of the library, and the written codes of rules for classification and for descriptive cataloging should minimize cataloging variation from one academic library to another. Yet there is some difference; when the program chairperson at a 1961 ALA Resources and Technical Services symposium was asked to define "technical services," the response was, and still is, that "the specific library or situation dictates the answer."[1] This is certainly true with the cataloging part of technical services. Each library has its own clientele, and it is the job of the cataloger to describe and classify in a manner that will meet the needs of this unique group.

But, even though each library is unique, there are

164

obvious similarities in the needs of the patrons of academic
libraries. Will cataloging, therefore, be much the same in
college libraries as it is in university libraries, or do the
patron's needs differ in some way? In his article "The
Undergraduate Library; Is It Obsolete?" Henry Wingate noted
that universities that set up small undergraduate libraries in
the sixties were closing them in the seventies. These special book collections were set up on the assumption that it
would be possible to select a core library that would adequately serve undergraduate needs. But methods of instruction began to change, and more emphasis was put on assigned readings than on the textbook/lecture format. The
assumption that undergraduate reading interests and needs
are quite limited in scope became difficult to defend. 2   In
other words, college patrons have many of the same basic
needs, or at least the same demands, as university patrons.
It follows that cataloging should not differ greatly.

Conceding that their reading interests and needs are
similar, is the level of sophistication of the library users
the same in both situations? I don't find it so. The college library is used largely by undergraduate students who
lean heavily on the subject entries in the catalog. They use
natural language rather than technical terms. They are not
apt to look for books under series entries. By the time
they receive their Bachelor's degrees we hope they know
how to research a subject in some depth, but we have to
start with freshmen. The catalog we provide (card, book,
COM, or otherwise) must therefore include adequate subject
coverage for the beginner. If time, money, or space are
lacking, a cataloger for this group may need to eliminate
the complicated series entry in favor of an extra subject
heading. (How many undergraduate students do you know
who will look for a book under the heading: "California.
University. University at Los Angeles. Housing, Real
Estate, and Urban Land Studies Program. UCLA Housing,
Real Estate, and Urban Land Studies Program Series"?
And how many freshmen will be looking under "castoridae"
for "beavers"?) Conversely, the faculty and graduate students at a large university library may find these entries
useful.

I mentioned time, money, and space. Here college
and university libraries do differ. Money usually dictates
how many people can be assigned to cataloging. A major
difference between cataloging in a small college library and
in a large university library is the size of the staff.

In a large university there are numbers of trained professionals working in one department, usually with areas of specialization. Most college libraries have only one cataloger who must specialize in everything. In the smaller college libraries this cataloger is sometimes a nonprofessional, largely untrained in the niceties of descriptive cataloging and classification. This one cataloger, trained or untrained, is responsible for all languages, all subject areas, all types of materials (books, serials, microforms, audiovisuals, etc.). In addition, this one cataloger normally has duties outside the catalog office, such as reference-desk work and faculty responsibilities. In some small colleges the cataloger must also handle acquisitions.

And now we have OCLC computer systems in a large number of college libraries. This is both good and bad. Original cataloging is reduced, but "the original cataloging which is necessary is complicated and tends to create anxiety from threat of error reports and possible sanctions."[3]

The computer is a great leveler. It used to be that the cataloger in a small college library could do descriptive cataloging in any convenient way, so long as it seemed to meet the needs of the patrons and satisfied the head librarian. Obsolete or local forms of subject headings caused no big problems. Incomplete collations were purely optional. But not so with OCLC. Rigid standards must be met, and these standards are not only required for all libraries, regardless of size or amount of use, but also are continually changing. Therefore The cataloger must learn computer coding for a constantly increasing number of formats as well as changes in existing formats, regardless of the infrequency with which he or she catalogs various types of materials.

Keeping up with all the paper output from both OCLC and local network offices is time-consuming. In larger university libraries several trained catalogers can share the load. They can not only concentrate on changes and additions in the field of their particular expertise, but can also work out together the application of rulings that are vague or confusing. Unfortunately, The cataloger in a small college library must absorb and interpret the avalanche alone. Head librarians, reference librarians, etc. usually care not at all about fixed fields, subfield codes, and slashes.

The cataloger must not only keep up with the paperwork engendered by the system but should also attend numerous meetings and workshops. In many small colleges, however, travel funds are not available. The professionally minded cataloger may wish to participate, but finds the personal financing prohibitive. In large universities it is more likely that funds will be available, and, with a larger staff, it is also easier for some of the catalogers to leave the office without interrupting the work flow. Moreover, specialists at the large university can concentrate on the sessions appropriate to their cataloging areas, while The lone cataloger from a small college must manage to cover them all, or at least be responsible for the material covered in all areas.

Peter Spyers-Duran has noted that automation also puts a lot of pressure on the head cataloger, who "is constantly challenged by the system's potential." Besides such day-to-day concerns as hit-rate and potential down time, the average head cataloger at a university must look ahead to such questions as local use of archival tapes, closing the card catalog, and public acceptance of nontraditional systems.[4] For the small college library delete head and we are back to The cataloger.

When OCLC began, many incomplete or poorly cataloged records were fed into the data bank. Each cataloger who subsequently uses one of these for producing card sets must decide how much to add or correct. In large university catalog offices these can easily be brought up to acceptable levels. In small college libraries, however, staff and time limitations may dictate acceptance of these as they are.

When an item that does not appear in the data bank is to be processed original cataloging must be fed in. In large university libraries there are usually trained personnel to handle this. In actual practice many libraries hold books for some time before taking this step, hoping that with a little bit of luck someone else will do the bloomin' work. I suspect that the smaller college libraries may hold them longer than large university catalog offices because of the time required to add material to the bank, though I have no solid information to support this, and in fact have known catalogers in very small college libraries who enjoyed the challenge of being the first to add an item to the system. According to a study of OCLC users done by Barbara Moore at the University of Wisconsin, Whitewater, nearly 60 percent of the time participating OCLC librarians delay processing books that do not appear in the

data bank before inputting original cataloging. In an average
of over 16 percent of these cases the materials were held
until a record appeared. In less than 15 percent of the sample original cataloging was input immediately. [5] There is,
however, nothing in the study to indicate the size of the libraries making up these percentage groups.

The trained personnel in large universities who add
records to the computer data bank usually work full time at
the job and are so at home with the rules and formats that
they readily recognize possible errors. On the other hand,
small college libraries often have the work done by clerks
who also have other duties, and their work must be proofread in great detail by The cataloger in order to cut down
on errors. With his or her attention divided as it normally
is by other duties, it is easy to overlook a period at the
end of a series sentence, or a 1 where a 2 should be in a
string of numbers. These things look normal, but constitute
errors according to cataloging rules and OCLC standards,
and they adversely affect all subsequent users of the record.

The original intent of installing the OCLC system was
to cut down on the number of employees required for cataloging. In discussion with librarians from other colleges I
find that university libraries have indeed cut staffs, but in
most smaller colleges this is not true. College cataloging
staffs were minimal even before OCLC, and even though the
computer does do some work for the cataloger, the cataloger
also works for the computer. The computer certainly saves
processing time by cutting down on original cataloging, typing headings, and alphabetizing cards. Much of the time
saved, however, is lost because of the rigorous requirements
of computer cataloging. For example, under nonterminal
conditions the cataloger found it unnecessary to track down
exact formats for main entries or for series not used in the
local catalog. If a subject heading changed slightly in the
latest supplement to the LC list of subject headings, who
cared, as long as the form used worked with the local system? Computer standards now require that the latest correct format always be identified and used.

In the small college library all these complications
caused by automation lead to the lowering of standards for
descriptive cataloging when not prescribed by the system.
OCLC standards are only set for what you put into the data
bank, not what you choose to take out. For instance, the
prepublication records provided by Library of Congress do

not complete the collation, and in many of these same records the title is incomplete or is worded differently from
the printed title page. Most catalogers have the terminal
operator correct these fields before ordering cards, but if
he or she doesn't have the time, or doesn't care, the cards
can be produced without making any changes. In smaller
college libraries this does happen. Again, undergraduate
students will not be as concerned with these omissions as
the serious researcher.

Obviously, not all libraries use OCLC or other automated systems. The very small college libraries find it
prohibitively expensive for the low number of items handled.
This means that we are really talking about three kinds of
libraries instead of two: university, college with OCLC, and
college without automation. For cataloging purposes I think
we can assume that the standards and methods in large university libraries must be similar, regardless of OCLC or
no OCLC. They are dealing with large numbers of materials and large cataloging staffs. They are preparing materials for patrons ranging from beginners to those doing advanced research. Their clientele are knowing and exacting.
Procedures must be well planned and documented or large-
scale mayhem would result. Ergo, there is fairly strict
adherence to the accepted rules and standards.

The cataloger at the small college library is free
from many of these restraints. Since he or she is closely
associated with all the work being done, cataloging decisions
can be made that favor local usage, and changes can be
made without long planning periods. If a geology professor
complains every time a book on minerals is put in TN instead of QE with the majority of the geology books, the cataloger can shift the books in question into the Q's without
repercussions. If the head librarian wants all subject headings typed in capital letters, the change can be made right
away.

The cataloger at a non-OCLC library has even fewer
restrictions. Nobody "up there" will know or care what
rules you follow. If students can find information on the
subjects in which they are interested, or can find the books
their professors have assigned, their needs have been met.
Many non-OCLC libraries still get their catalog cards from
Library of Congress. Others get proof slips from the same
source and reproduce them. Sometimes copy is received
for the correct author and title, but for a completely different

edition from the book in hand. The copy may be for a two-volume edition, with notes and glossary, when the book being cataloged is a single volume, with nothing but the original text. Nevertheless, in many cases the copy is used "as is." It saves time and money to do so and affects very few people.

There are some other ways in which the size of the library, with or without automation, affects the descriptive cataloging done in academic libraries. The smaller the library, and the smaller the collection, the more necessary it becomes to make the best use of the books available. In some cases The cataloger is called upon to cover the bare spots with analytics, and these are particularly appropriate for the college library with its more limited book collection. In our particular library we have very few play scripts in a complete form, but we have numerous questions about plays. Therefore we make analytics on such annual series as Best Plays. This provides the student with authors, lyricists, dates, and access to some of the script. In large university libraries they undoubtedly have enough of the original material that such tactics are unnecessary. Analytics, however, can be carried to extremes. We recently had occasion to reclass a book on literary criticism that contained fewer than 700 pages. The busy typists who originally processed the volume made over 120 analytics. Unfortunately, they had not bothered to use the same wording on the card headings as they had used on the contents note. Ridding the catalog of the cards with the old call number was like trying to rid the lawn of crabgrass.

In addition to differences in their descriptive cataloging practices, college and university libraries very often differ in their choice of classification schemes. Virtually all university libraries use Library of Congress call numbers, while thirty-eight out of eighty-two colleges polled in 1975 still used the Dewey decimal system. [6] The OCLC system, which has become such an important factor in college cataloging, is programmed to favor the Library of Congress classification. All Dewey numbers must be recoded and completed for use, while LC call numbers print on the cards without corrections. This fact should increase the number of college libraries using the LC classification scheme in the future. On the other hand, changing from one classification system to another is expensive and irritating to patrons, and the number of libraries changing from Dewey to LC has slowed considerably since the sixties, when many libraries were making the switch.

Nevertheless, the trend toward LC cannot obscure the fact that Dewey has its advantages. It is used almost exclusively in secondary schools, and students are thus familiar with it when they arrive on campus. Also, in the opinion of many librarians and patrons, the Dewey system is easier to comprehend. Thus some schools, especially those too small to join OCLC profitably, will continue to classify books according to the decimal system.

Nonbook materials pose problems for catalogers in both college and university libraries. Although audiovisuals are rapidly assuming a more important role in academic libraries, they have traditionally been largely ignored. In some libraries they are cataloged and classified according to the same standards and class schedules as book materials, but more often they are unclassed or arranged according to a local system that "jest growed" like Topsy. (Any attempt to come up with a definitive work on classification schemes used for sound recordings in libraries would quite likely drive a researcher berserk.) Here again, the larger the library and the greater the number of nonbook materials used, the greater the likelihood of a standard cataloging procedure. In small college libraries, however, the number of nonbook items regularly handled is often too small to warrant full cataloging treatment.

Two things are causing this situation to change: the Library of Congress is now producing cataloging copy for more of these items, and cards can now be ordered from OCLC for most of them. Increased standardization in this area may make it difficult to pin down any great differences between the cataloging of audiovisuals in college libraries and that done in the large universities.

By and large, cataloging in college and university libraries is becoming more uniform. Some small college libraries not able to afford OCLC are trying to cope with substandard practices by banding together into cooperatives as many public libraries and school libraries are doing. Some accept the work of job-order houses for cards, spine labels, etc. Currently much planning is being done in academic libraries to cope with the coming change to AACR II; the great number of college catalogers who are finding the new rules required reading certainly underlines the general trend toward standardization in cataloging procedures.

This trend is a positive development. It should not,

however, be allowed to obscure the cataloger's primary obligation to make the collection accessible to its users. College catalogers working in a less structured environment than their university counterparts can, and should, tailor their output to the needs of their patrons. Since most small college libraries do not have formal written cataloging policies, and the cataloger is in touch with the clientele, more creative cataloging can be done. This "freewheeling" environment makes cataloging in a college library more of an art than a science, but also makes it more enjoyable.

No cataloger going into another library will find all cataloging done the same, regardless of size. Patrons vary. Administration varies. Head librarians vary. Money spent on library services varies. And last but not least, catalogers vary. Some see the whole woods, and others see only the tree in front of them. But with automation, more and more of us are being forced to look at the whole scene. As automation increases college cataloging will become more standardized, but it will never lose the individuality that makes it such a challenge.

Notes

1Helen W. Tuttle, "From Cutter to Computer: Technical Services in Academic and Research Libraries, 1876-1976," College & Research Libraries 37 (September 1976): 425.
2Henry W. Wingate, "The Undergraduate Library: Is It Obsolete?" College & Research Libraries 39 (January 1978): 31.
3Diane Murray, Cataloger at Hope College, to William Miller, September 13, 1979.
4"Automated Cataloging: More or Less Staff Needed?" Library Journal 103 (February 1978): 415.
5Barbara Moore, OCLC cataloging use survey results (Whitewater: University of Wisconsin, [1979]), p. 2.
6Tuttle, p. 439.

USER INSTRUCTION IN THE COLLEGE LIBRARY: ORIGINS, PROSPECTS, AND A PRACTICAL PROGRAM

Frances L. Hopkins

The library-instruction movement has clearly outgrown its infancy. The basic questions that first worried us (will faculty and students accept the need for library instruction and can librarians be effective classroom teachers?) have long since been answered affirmatively in principle if not everywhere in fact; instructional responsibilities are regularly specified in job ads for reference librarians; and groups devoted to the development of instruction now have a place in the formal structure of ALA.[1] Jon Lindgren's 1978 survey of small liberal arts college libraries shows that these institutions, the ones least likely to have resources for new programs, are well along in user instruction. Eighty-four percent of the responding libraries (135 of the 220 selected for his survey) had ongoing group instruction programs.[2]

A pervasive theme of the library-instruction movement has been its potential for transforming the academic library's traditional role as scholars' warehouse to one of visible, active participation in the academic process. But although library instruction is widely practiced, in all but a few college libraries it seems to have been absorbed into the general consciousness as an adjunct to, more than a transformation of, conventional reference service. To believers in the potential of the instruction movement, therefore, what has been achieved so far is mainly prologue.

Veterans in the movement seem to share an expectation of imminent breakthroughs in the scope and technique of

173

library instruction. The teaching of basic skills, subject bibliography, and search strategy in support of traditional term-paper assignments has been a broad-gauge approach. Lately the focus has turned to approaches more closely tied to the content and methodologies of the various academic fields and to particular teaching and learning problems that occur within them. As instruction programs expand many see consultative reference service as a natural corollary, with the reference desk becoming more of an information and referral station, particularly in libraries serving small populations of undergraduates.

But conservative forces are still very much in evidence. For many librarians traditional patterns of reference service are sacrosanct, and it tends to be our immediate colleagues, not faculty, who see the increasing intellectualism of library instruction as pretentious. New staff still come from the library schools with little sense of the academic enterprise, naive about the political problems of library instruction, and only superficially informed of what to teach and how to teach it. [3]

Lindgren suggests, and I agree, that what the instruction movement needs to fulfill its promise is a "working tradition" that encompasses both widespread cultural support and a developing theory, methodology, and technique. [4] But proselytizing should begin at home. Instruction librarians must, with sustained and concerted voice, claim from their own professional community--in the library schools and in the field--recognition of library instruction as a serious professional specialty requiring intensive preparation. Beyond that, they should zealously press the claim that the primary end of all that goes into a college library is instruction in how to locate, select, and use library resources in various academic contexts. We instruction librarians say as much to each other and imply it in our work, but we seem diffident about espousing this position unequivocally in public.

As a small first step in strengthening our common ideology I shall begin here with a brief history of library instruction, emphasizing its relation to reference work. I shall then examine the chief objections to the instruction movement that emerge from this history. Finally, I shall describe the kind of comprehensive instruction program that I believe should be our goal and discuss the process of developing such a program in a college library.

User Instruction and Reference Work to 1960:
A Historical Sketch

Although a number of writers have traced its roots to the
1800s, critics and proponents alike often assume that library
instruction is a 1960s outgrowth of reference work with individuals. In fact, personal reference assistance and group
instruction developed concurrently in the nineteenth century as
efforts to help inexperienced users cope with libraries organized for a scholarly clientele. Although implementation of
library instruction burgeoned only after 1965, much of what
exists today was envisioned years ago.

The professionalization of scholarship in the United
States in the latter half of the nineteenth century, with emphasis on specialization and exhaustive research after the
European model, resulted in an extraordinary effort to build
American library collections. Scholars, the dominant clientele of both public and university libraries, regarded librarians as acquirers and custodians of books. The librarians'
concern for improving subject access found expression in
this period mainly through meticulous organization. [5] Subject cataloging, advocated as the ultimate answer to the access problem, was welcomed precisely because it would
minimize staff and user interaction, as the scholar typically
preferred. [6]

Undergraduates, however, needed more guidance in
the use of libraries, and as early as 1820 the Harvard librarian offered lectures on important items in his collection.
By the early 1880s Columbia, Cornell, and the University of
Michigan were all providing lectures on library use. [7] Most
college libraries were rudimentary before World War I and
had no instruction programs. But Azariah Root, librarian
at Oberlin College, conducted a remarkable program from
1899 to 1927 consisting of an introduction to library organization, exercises in use of bibliographic resources, and a
history of the printed book. [8] Academic librarians everywhere also assisted individual students in selecting reading
and finding information. All these activities reflected both
their commitment to a service ideal and their cherished am-
bition of attaining professorial standing. [9]

Although the large public libraries of this period were
also geared to scholarly research, they had another clientele
who could not easily cope with the intricacies of card catalogs or select books knowledgeably. When Samuel Green,

public librarian in Worcester, Massachusetts, pioneered organized personal reference assistance in the 1870s he was
motivated both by the ideal of service and by a desire to
gain the support of the citizenry at large for increasing the
collection.   Reference service there, and a little later at
the Boston Public Library, was provided--and desired--only
in the popular-book area. [10]

Organized reference service spread to academic libraries very gradually before World War II, especially in
the conservative East.   Melvil Dewey soon brought it to
Columbia, but Yale had no reference librarian before 1900
and only a part-timer for a decade afterward.   Dewey's successors at Columbia also promoted reference work, but when
a professor of classics was appointed librarian in 1913, further extension of the service gave way to increasing acquisitions. [11]

In this century the development of both reference work
and library instruction has been closely related to the professional aspirations of librarians and their search for role definition.   At first, in university and public research libraries,
subject specialization seemed an obvious step toward the
elite world of the scholar.   Cornell and Columbia were in
the forefront of this movement.   But in most academic libraries subject collections were departmental enclaves with
no professional staff at all. [12]   Moreover, few librarians
were trained for subject specialization, and those with advanced degrees functioned as reference librarians secondar-
ily to their primary work as bibliographers.   Most regular
reference service, therefore--and all reference service in
small libraries--remained in the hands of generalists.

In many public libraries the general reference librarian, in relation to the less-educated average user, had an
unambiguous role and status.   In the academic setting the
same work was far less gratifying.   Faculty had little need
of help, they themselves fulfilling the main advisory role
toward students, and the librarian's expertise in finding information had low prestige compared with the scholar's
quest for knowledge.   Some head librarians had faculty status in the early 1900s, often by virtue of credentials other
than a library school degree, but lower-level professionals
were treated more like clerks.   In 1922 a reference librarian at the University of California urged librarians to raise
their status by engaging in instruction, earning advanced
degrees, and differentiating themselves clearly from the
clerical staff. [13]

Why, then, did personal reference service eventually take priority over instruction in academic libraries? Economics, the nature of undergraduate education, and attitudes dominant in librarianship all contributed. By 1926 about half the major academic research libraries offered instruction; by 1956 almost a third of all U. S. academic libraries did so. [14] But most gave either a separate course in bibliography to a few students or, more often, merely discussed the mechanics of library use and a few basic reference sources in a session of freshman English. [15]

Extensive course-related instruction in all but the smallest institutions would have required more substantial staff expansion than the simple addition of a reference desk, and diversion of money from acquisitions to such services was unthinkable. Because standard reading lists and assigned paper topics were the norm, few discerned the potential contribution of library instruction to the liberal arts curriculum. Finally, any teaching beyond the basic-skills level invited faculty scrutiny, whereas reference-desk work could be carried out in comparative privacy. For most librarians, imbued with the semiclerical values of the library schools and ALA, [16] the reference desk added sufficiently to their self-image as academic professionals without major budgetary changes and with little risk of exposing their limitations.

Efforts to raise performance standards and achieve a professional identity did not abate, however. Some librarians, primarily attuned to the public library model or impressed by the total service approach of special libraries, [17] gave priority to perfecting reference service. [18] Others, chagrined that their expensive collections and services were disgracefully underused, sought more active involvement with faculty and students.

The reference-oriented literature focused on role analysis. In a 1930 textbook James Wyer labeled as "Conservative" the view that reference librarians should teach clients to find and use materials by themselves and as "Liberal" the view that reference librarians should provide the needed materials and all possible assistance in using them. [19] The latter policy, although economically feasible only in special libraries serving highly paid professionals, has been adopted as an ideal by many general reference librarians as well. This served as reference "theory" into the 1950s. More recent efforts have analyzed question negotiation, [20] categories of questions, and the search process, [21] but these approaches, too, are limited to self-scrutiny within the traditional role definition.

Instruction-oriented literature, on the other hand, looked outward at the librarian's relationship to the larger educational enterprise. In 1934 Louis Shores used the term "library arts college" to denote a visionary concept of educational librarianship as opposed to the prevalent research librarianship. The educational library of the undergraduate institution, he said, should have a highly selective collection limited in size. Its acquisitions and organizational functions should be proceduralized and placed in the hands of semiprofessionals. Its professional staff should become teacher-librarians, teaming up with subject-specialist professors to guide students in independent, interdisciplinary study. [22] Shores has been amply criticized as fuzzy-minded and impractical, [23] but although his library-college has never been implemented in pure form in any lasting way, it is clearly the prototype of contemporary course-related and integrated library instruction.

More conventional proponents of library instruction had limited aspirations for librarians as teachers, although they agreed that undergraduate education should foster independent student use of libraries. In 1940 Harvie Branscomb's Teaching with Books[24] endorsed integration of library and faculty goals, but with librarians teaching only basic, general skills to freshmen. The regular faculty, he believed, could better integrate bibliographic instruction with students' major programs. The notion of librarians as full-fledged teachers was not confined to visionaries, however. In 1946 William Carlson's postwar planning study of academic libraries matter-of-factly proposed "the employment of teacher-librarians ... cooperating with the instructional staff and using classroom assignments as a basis for instruction" even "at the expense of book acquisition in impressive quantities"[25]--an idea not far from the library-college concept.

In the contrast between Branscomb and Carlson, a question emerges that still eludes consensus: not whether instruction is appropriate at all in academic libraries, but whether teaching should ever be a primary role of the academic librarian. In 1954 Jesse Shera stated bluntly that it should not:

> The librarian, though admittedly a part, and a
> very important part, of the total educational

system, is not a teacher.... This does not imply
that the position of the librarian is of either greater or lesser stature than that of the teacher--it is
merely different. [26]

The Role of the Teacher-Librarian

Shera was addressing the questions of why so little progress
had been made in integrating library programs with college
curriculums and how faculty status, enjoyed by more and
more librarians, could be transformed from a nominal into
a truly functional teaching role. [27] His answer was that
these questions arose from a mistaken view of librarianship.
Librarians want to be teachers, he said, because they feel
academically inferior, but they cannot be real teachers because they have no control over curricula or students' intellectual development. The true discipline of librarianship,
he asserted, encompasses the acquisition and organization
of recorded knowledge and, above all, research in "social
epistemology"--the study of "the production, dissemination,
integration, and utilization of all forms of communication
throughout the entirety of society. "[28] The proper concerns
of academic librarianship, therefore, are subject bibliography, advances in organization and access, and the study of
why and how scholars and students use recorded knowledge.

Shera's statement was mainly a call to upgrade the
quality and expand the content of library school programs.
He warned that nothing short of serious intellectual work
could win academic respectability, and he saw correctly that
the library skills instruction prevalent during the 1950s was
no way to win colleagueship with faculty.

The 1960s, however, opened new avenues for library
instruction. The college population expanded and student
academic backgrounds became more varied. Librarians
turned to programmed and audiovisual techniques to individ-
ualize instruction for larger classes. At the same time efforts to liberate students from textbooks and assigned-paper
topics made effective library use more important than ever
before. The bibliographic apparatus was also rapidly expanding on the heels of the knowledge explosion, and no general introduction to the library could begin to cover the
range of important tools now available to undergraduates.
One answer was to teach upper-level students the basic
bibliographic tools of their major disciplines.

But undergraduates do library research for courses in
many fields, and at liberal arts colleges especially there
was widespread development of honors, independent study,
and interdisciplinary programs.   To promote library competence in this context it became necessary to focus on principles of search strategy developed from the basic concept
of the structure of the literature.   The seminal program of
this type was Patricia Knapp's experiment at Monteith College during 1960-61. [29]   Her students carried out guided library research in which they applied practice in library procedures and the use of various types of reference tools and
search strategies to problems significant in the subject matter of their courses, while they were led in small-group discussions to understand these experiences in relation to the
library seen as an intelligible information system.

Knapp's program did not survive, but she did demonstrate that a modified library-college approach was not totally impracticable, and her experience remains a source of
ideas and inspiration even today.   Knapp herself accepted
Branscomb's principle that library instruction should be carried out by faculty, but her view of what library instruction
should be was at least as broad as Carlson's.   She maintained that competence in library use is a genuine liberal
art, "a complex of knowledge, skills, and attitudes not to
be acquired in any one course," that must "be integrated into the total curriculum."[30]   At the start she believed that
librarians would need only to initiate such ventures and encourage faculty to implement them.   By the end of the Monteith experiment, having discovered that "most faculty members simply do not have a systematic view of the library,"
she had come to believe that the librarian must join the professor in the classroom rather than remain in the background. [31]

Shera's opposition to the teacher-librarian had been
that of a library school dean who hoped to define a professional role worthy of academic esteem and develop a training program to meet that standard.   Other doubts, among
those who saw library instruction as a threat to the liberal
reference-service ideal, were activated by rapid expansion
of library instruction in the 1960s and have not abated.

Anita Schiller argued in 1965 that information service
and instruction were no longer complements, but competitors.
She attacked librarians for moralism in promoting instruction for the sake of client self-improvement, and she ques-

tioned the assumption that users cannot clearly articulate
their information needs.   Instead, she claimed, users ask
vague questions because most librarians know too little to
understand specific information requests and, when they do
understand, are unwilling to search out answers.   She argued that special librarians, who find their professional
identity precisely in their ability to provide efficient, comprehensive retrieval, should be the model for all reference
service.   Even in academic libraries, she believed, instruction diverts attention from the primary goal of providing information and thus may hinder, rather than promote, effective library use. [32]

Schiller probably had in mind individual user instruction at public library reference desks and the single freshman instruction session common in academic libraries at the
time.   Thirteen years later, in the 1978 edition of his widely used reference textbook, William Katz accepted the same
models when he cited Schiller in his own argument against
library instruction.   He urged that users be given a genuine
choice, even in academic libraries, between instruction and
total information service, arguing that it is not really possible to develop user independence and that specific goals for
instruction are lacking. [33]   Also in 1978 Millicent Abell, although long a proponent of library instruction, agreed with
Schiller that academic librarians have failed to resolve the
information/instruction issue.   Her reservations about library instruction focused on the hours spent preparing and
teaching credit courses in library use that reach a very
small proportion of university students. [34]

In 1979 Pauline Wilson published a strong statement
reminiscent of Shera's but lacking his commitment to up-
grading librarians' training and performance.   Librarians
claim to be teachers, she said, in order to counter an un-
flattering stereotype, enhance their status, and make their
work intelligible to outsiders.   But academic librarians are
not as well educated as faculty nor, she claims, do they aspire to be.   More importantly, genuine teachers, who disseminate the content of a body of literature, cannot logically
recognize librarians, who disseminate the physical entities
that make up the literature, as members of the same profession.   The librarians' entirely spurious claim, therefore,
makes them vulnerable to social rejection and to performance
evaluation by standards irrelevant to their main responsibilities.   In her view user instruction is primarily a ploy of
strongly career-oriented librarians to attain faculty status.

Although Wilson grants that user instruction is often a legitimate dissemination activity, her perception of such instruction is quite negative--she sees it as a dull repetition of
basic skills that could be taught just as effectively by mechanical methods as by live librarian-teachers. [35]

My quarrel with these four writers is that each of
them, legitimately criticizing one type or one aspect of instruction, illegitimately moves to a blanket indictment of the
instruction movement as a whole. This particularly mis-
leads new librarians who are still largely unaware of the
difference between public and academic, or university and
college, librarianship. Only Katz specifically exempted "the
college library [sic] movement" from his criticism, but he
described that movement in less than a sentence and gave
no supporting references to lead his student readers to further information. [36]

The objections of these writers are largely invalid, I
believe, for programs directed toward the goals of the Monteith model. They nevertheless must be answered if such
instruction is to gain the understanding of the profession as
a whole and attract the committed staff necessary for program expansion and continued conceptual development. From
Shera on, the main objections to library instruction are that
it (1) lacks serious content, (2) detracts from the quality of
reference service, (3) is a ploy for achieving faculty status,
and (4) is, as a primary professional role, incompatible
with the essential nature of librarianship. I shall discuss
these charges here in relation to user instruction in the
college library context.

1. Library instruction lacks serious content. In
Lindgren's survey of college libraries the subject-tailored
classroom presentation was the predominant type of group
instruction reported. [37] The critics' apparent assumption,
therefore, that instruction concentrates on elementary skills
may not hold for college libraries. Katz's complaint that
the objectives of library instruction have not been specified
has perhaps been adequately answered by the publication of
model statements of goals and objectives, [38] although, ad-
mittedly, few college librarians have had the time to develop
comparable statements of their own.

Lindgren's survey provides no specific information on
the content of subject-tailored instruction. Surely it covers
specialized reference and bibliographic sources, but presen-

tations probably range from a dry recitation of facts about specific tools to meticulously planned, illustrated sample subject searches followed up by consultative guidance of students' individual research projects. Although 56 percent of those in Lindgren's sample who give instruction reported that more than half their sessions are "integrated,"[39] that term seems to have been used loosely for instruction related in any way to specific academic courses. But what Katz fails to understand, in castigating all but that truly integrated instruction "where the librarian and the teacher and the student work cooperatively together for independent education,"[40] is that fully integrated instruction can emerge only at an advanced stage of program development unless a massive injection of funds is made to support concentrated planning.

Each course in which library instruction is integrated requires a professor with a sophisticated appreciation of how a carefully guided library experience can enhance students' conceptual development and willing to reorganize the course to accommodate such an experience, as well as a librarian knowledgeable enough to devise library assignments that genuinely contribute to course objectives. Programs that cannot yet move beyond instruction in basic reference tools and library procedures, whether for want of vision or want of financial support, may be lackluster, but they should not be dismissed as useless. They are at least a beginning in which the expectation of student library competence is established, the college becomes aware of the library as a force in the learning situation, and the librarians come to view themselves as active participants in the academic enterprise.

2. Library instruction detracts from the quality of reference service. Katz notwithstanding, it is not the aim of library instruction to make users independent. It is generally accepted, in fact, that instruction increases the number of serious reference questions because instructed students are more aware of possibilities and more trustful of the librarian's expertise and interest.[41] I can only counter the critics' perceptions with my own, but I have found experienced instruction librarians more willing than others to pursue students' specific information requests at length, because they can gauge more accurately what the students are competent to do and where they are likely to flounder. In any case, the request for a definition, quotation, statistic, or fact is generally less frequent in academic than in public libraries, because students engaged in extended research

are mainly in need of fruitful bibliographic leads.   The librarian who is recognized from the classroom as knowledgeable about course requirements and relevant subject bibliography has a clear advantage over one who is not.

In the smaller library that lacks trained subject experts preparation of instruction sessions for various courses is, moreover, the best possible from of continuing staff education.   A librarian who prepares an annotated guide and demonstration literature search for an accounting class, for instance, acquires detailed knowledge about SEC bulletins, accounting standards, and the caliber of professional journals and can relate this knowledge, on demand, to the specific research needs of students in the course.   The same librarian, not involved in class preparation, would be unaware of the range of student research topics and, with no definite expectation of demand, little motivated to study the resources closely.

A final point is that investigations of the quality of traditional reference-desk service tend to support the suspicion that the privacy of the reference transaction, combined with low user expectation, fosters superficial work and protects incompetence. [42]   Classroom instruction exposes librarians' claims of bibliographic expertise to public scrutiny, a situation that motivates all but the most irresponsible to do their homework well.

3.   Library instruction is a ploy for achieving faculty status.   There are two kinds of faculty status to be considered: informal social acceptance by teaching faculty of librarians as fellow educators and formal political recognition of librarians as full citizens in a given academic institution. For many years there were librarians who cherished a genteel hope that by demonstrating intelligence and seriousness they could attain the former and through it, as a matter of justice, the latter.   Against this naive belief Shera argued that only by developing a distinct discipline with its own intellectual core and by raising standards of entry and training could librarians ever attain academic esteem.   But Shera's vision has remained a remote ideal, and contemporary librarians aspire to faculty status in the latter sense primarily for practical reasons--to qualify for collegial staff organization, to participate in institutional governance, and to obtain higher pay scales and such perquisites as sabbaticals and faculty-development funds.

To substantiate their claim to full institutional

citizenship librarians have been obliged to prove not that they are the same as classroom teachers but that they can contribute equally as professionals to the total educational enterprise and are willing to live up to standards broader than possession of technical skills. They have used library instruction programs to demonstrate active interest in the academic program, but they have as often shown their professionalism through publishing, campus committee and professional association work, competition for outside grants, and pursuit of advanced degrees. The teaching role, therefore, is neither crucial to faculty status nor motivated chiefly by the drive for faculty status, although the two may coincide. The fact is that library instruction is of intrinsic interest because it is so obviously a neglected aspect of higher education that does not fall within the purview or expertise of any academic department. In a field all too constricted by rules and procedures it offers rare scope for individual achievement to the librarian who develops content relevant to different fields of study and appropriate strategies for teaching it.

4. Library instruction, as a primary professional role, is incompatible with the essential nature of librarianship. I do not oppose Wilson's view that the librarian's function is to match the user's need with relevant portions of the graphic record. But her general definition obscures an important aspect of the librarian-student transaction. The reference librarian who is not actively engaged in instruction is a blind intermediary between the student doing research and the professor whose requirements the student has to satisfy. Students often misunderstand professors' expectations; professors cannot guard against all student research problems because the range of possible topics is often far broader than the specialized literatures they control. The librarian, therefore, needs to know firsthand something of the professor's approach and standards in order to match the student's expressed need with resources both relevant to the topic and appropriate for the course. Otherwise, reference "help" may mislead the student. I can best explain this by example.

A student came to me about a paper on how the thalidomide incident influenced the tightening of drug laws in the United States. After I had helped her locate congressional hearings, medical and newspaper reports, and commentary in various serious journals of opinion, she had the makings of a well-documented account. The resulting paper, prepared for a history of medicine course, was criticized for over-reliance on "popular" sources because students were expected to base their papers on the sort of historical analysis found in the pages of ISIS or Bulletin of the History of Medicine. At the time no such literature was available on the thalidomide tragedy, but the student might have been helped by reading scholarly treatments of similar events as models for her own analysis of the primary source materials she had found. Alternatively, she might have been led to another topic of interest for which scholarly secondary sources were ample.

Subsequent discussion with the student and the professor revealed that the latter had never explicitly told the class what types of sources were acceptable, for she had assumed that any student in a history course would consult mainstream historical scholarship. Nor had she discussed with them the distinction between primary and secondary sources and their appropriate uses in historical writing. Unaware of the professor's rigorous expectations, I failed to lead the student to sources that would take her beyond factual reportage. Other students without prior research experience in the field suffered the same disadvantage.

The following semester, I prepared a library instruction session, for all history of science classes, that introduced the concepts of primary and secondary literature and compared popular journals, journals of opinion, professional scientific journals, and scholarly journals relevant to the field. Each student then derived three tentative paper topics--one from readings in the course, one from recent issues of recommended journals, and one from a comprehensive classified bibliography--and took them through a guided search to obtain background information, assess the range and availability of relevant literature, and focus the topics accordingly. At the end each student was expected to turn in a concise statement of the one topic selected for the actual paper with a brief preliminary bibliography and a plan for further research. In this one exercise the students were introduced to important reference sources in the field, practiced using a systematic search process in the light of certain structural features of the literature, and got a firm grasp on a research assignment that had at first seemed daunting.

This instruction session and exercise, simple as they were, illustrate an approach to library instruction compatible with Shera's view that librarianship should incorporate the discipline of "social epistemology"--the study of the production, communication, and use of recorded knowledge. Ideally, the academic instruction librarian should keep abreast of research in the structure of the substantive and bibliographic literatures of the disciplines; provide faculty with this perspective so they can better understand their own tacit assumptions and the problems of novice researchers; teach students the use of specialized reference sources in the context of the structure of the literature and in relation to concrete problems in their courses; and, through observing teachers and students in their research activities, contribute to an understanding of the uses of recorded knowledge in the teaching-learning process. A cogent argument for library instruction based on the study of the growth and structure of recorded knowledge has been made by Raymond McInnis, who uses citation diagrams to teach undergraduates how to search the social-sciences literature effectively. [43]

A Comprehensive User Instruction Program

I would argue that integrated bibliographic instruction, as pioneered by Knapp, is the mode that can best enhance course content, raise the quality of reference service, and provide an intellectual focus for the college librarian. But integrated instruction is the culmination, not the starting point, of an instruction program. It will be useful now to describe the various modes of library instruction in the context of a comprehensive program such as that outlined here:

Introduction to Library Use

1. Orientation
2. Library Skills Assessment Test and Remedial Tutorials
3. Basic Skills Instruction

Bibliographic Instruction

4. Course-related and Special-Purpose Instruction
5. Course-integrated Instruction
6. Curriculum-integrated Instruction

1. Orientation, a brief A/V show, should be entirely attitude-directed. It should impress upon new students that in college they will learn to use a bibliographic system, more complex than they ever knew existed, to do a level of research not before required of them. It should make them

aware that, although bibliographic expertise used to be expected only of graduate students in their specialties, undergraduates now need to develop a respectable level of research
competence in a wide range of disciplines. In this context
librarians should be introduced as both organizers of the bibliographic system and guides to its use through a library instruction program closely coordinated with the academic curriculum. Examples of students satisfying three or four different kinds of information need related to actual courses
should be included to illustrate the kind of library competency that will one day be theirs. Brevity and wit are, of
course, essential. But the presentation should unabashedly
insist that, in a community of budding scholars and professionals, research proficiency is a part of savoir faire.

2. The library skills assessment test should cover
at least the elements on a catalog card, citations in a periodical index and Essay and General Literature Index, and
basic library terminology. Its main function is to screen
out students needing remedial instruction, [44] but the test
should be rigorous enough to show that the competency standard can be derived from written library program objectives
of the better high schools the college draws from. These
are usually much more ambitious than one would guess from
incoming college freshmen. If the college tests the writing
competency of new students, giving the library test at the
same time will enhance its academic aura. The library's
best upper-level student assistants, with special training,
may be entrusted to conduct remedial tutorials. However,
librarians should do it themselves for the first year or two
to get a feel for what the problems are.

3. Basic skills instruction unavoidably includes information about the library's buildings, hours, procedures,
and services. Details are best covered in a handbook, perhaps a collection of simple leaflets on circulation or interlibrary loan that are also available separately at points of use.
The real focus of skills instruction should be on information
and literature searching in the context of an intelligible bibliographic system. This is the time to explain the nature of
a scholarly discipline and to introduce schematically the concept of the structure of the literature of a discipline and its
corresponding bibliographic apparatus. Differences between
the structures of science and humanities disciplines should
be emphasized, and their different concepts of primary and
secondary sources should be clearly distinguished. The
main categories of reference sources, both informational and

bibliographic, should be specified in relation to this scheme, and a simple subject search on a familiar topic should be demonstrated, using an example of each type. The card catalog and periodical record should be tied in at appropriate points to locate a particular book and article found in the demonstrated search. Conceptual continuity should be carefully articulated and not obscured by procedural detail. Filing rules, for example, can best be imparted by posting graphically simple reminders at the card catalog itself and merely calling attention to the posters during class.

An exercise following the instruction sessions should take the students through a simple information and literature search. Meticulous planning to avoid blind alleys is important; the object is not to display quirks of library organization but to familiarize students with a basic model search procedure and a few reference sources they are likely to find recurrently useful. To ensure that students absorb the concepts and procedures a test should be given later in the first semester if logistics can be worked out.

It is crucial to find a means of imposing sanctions so students will have to take this skills instruction seriously. Obviously, all freshmen should complete it before they receive bibliographic instruction, which assumes a working knowledge of basic tools and procedures. Requirements can be instituted in several ways. A required freshman course, if the college has one, may be the perfect vehicle, especially if its professors are earnestly willing to integrate library components into appropriate units of the course and give them weight in testing and grading. In the absence of an all-freshmen course basic library instruction cannot be integrated with other academic work and is not likely to be retained as well. Second choice would be a formal college requirement that freshmen attend several separate skills sessions and pass the library exercise and final test in order to qualify for sophomore standing. A first step in this direction might be to persuade a few professors who teach courses taken by many freshmen to treat the skills sessions and exercise as graded assignments in these courses and to incorporate the final test questions into their exams.

It is wise to have an expanded instruction program in mind from the start. Terminology to be used at all levels should be standardized at the earliest possible stage. The imprecise usage of librarians--for example, in distinguishing primary from secondary sources in the sciences and humanities, substantive from bibliographic information sources, [45] and scholarly from professional or clinical literature-- confuses students. Lacking consensus in the field, we can at least strive for consistency within each program. [46] With the help of published guidelines for instruction[47] the terminology, search steps, and library procedures to be covered in the skills sessions should be specified in writing, not left to the discretion of individual librarians. These written objectives will be useful, also, in preparing the introductory reviews that should tie later bibliographic instruction sessions to what the students have previously learned.

4. Course-related instruction has been defined by Thomas Kirk as "instruction in the use of a library and the literature, in relation to an academic program, be it a single course or a discipline. The instruction is given in the context of a subject and in relation to a specific assignment."[48] In the comprehensive program I am proposing here I would confine the term "course-related" to instruction designed to support an assignment predetermined by the professor. For example, called on to prepare students to write term papers on the Romantic poets, the librarian would organize a coherent presentation of selected journals and bibliographies specific to the poets and the period; relevant LC subject headings; literature indexes, abstract services, and on-line data-bases; poetry dictionaries and concordances; and perhaps relevant special collections at nearby research libraries. For economics majors in a senior seminar on economics and women the librarian might be able to assume the students' familiarity with the main resources of their own discipline and could concentrate on resources in women's studies and related social-science disciplines.

Special-purpose instruction, like course-related instruction, also answers a pre-existing need, but it may apply to more than one course or to several user groups. Economics and marketing students may both need a workshop on census publications, or humanities faculty and majors may benefit from an introduction to on-line literature searching and the new data-bases in their disciplines.

Because course-related and special-purpose instruction are offered in self-contained units, each session can be added or dropped according to need and workload. However, integrated instruction, as described below, requires a prolonged commitment.

5. In course-integrated, as distinct from course-

related, instruction, library research assignments are planned by professor and librarian together to expand course goals or enhance understanding of course content, usually in connection with a specific pedagogical problem. In the example given above, in connection with history of science courses, the prepaper instruction and exercise were deemed necessary because most students' knowledge of the field is too unsophisticated for them to be able to think up topics of interest early in the term, and much of the literature of the field is in foreign languages or available only in research collections. They must, therefore, delve into the bibliographic tools for a panorama of possible topics and then compare the accessibility of resources relevant to several of their interests.

Virginia Parr has reported a more advanced example of integrated instruction. Beginning psychology majors are given short statements on current issues involving popular psychological assumptions (e.g., whether homosexuals should be permitted to teach in the public schools). They analyze the statements into researchable concepts and, using reference tools and search strategies taught previously in the classroom, find scholarly or clinical literature to support, discredit, or reinterpret the assumptions in the statements. This assignment demonstrates to new psychology majors that an untutored approach to psychology is vastly different from a disciplined approach, trains them to read the popular press critically, and introduces them to reference sources they will use throughout their program. [49]

6. Curriculum-integrated instruction is the most difficult to achieve and is not suitable for all academic disciplines. It requires that an academic department, in cooperation with a teaching librarian, establish library competency goals for majors and plan its curriculum so that every major's program includes the required levels of library research experience. A religious studies department may want to work first with the specialized reference sources useful for identifying concepts, persons, events, and places, and later with religion periodical indexes to access information on religions and social issues. In other courses students might make a comparative study of the popular and scholarly publications issued by major religious groups, trace the development of western notions of eastern meditation through a succession of widely used reference books, or compare treatments of the same concept or event in the publications of different contemporary religious groups. Probably the department would want to introduce students

to biographical tools and major bibliographic tools in history, sociology, and anthropology. At some point a research exercise modeled on Parr's psychology assignment would be eminently suitable. Professors and librarian together should evaluate such possibilities and translate the most promising into exercises for appropriate courses so that they cumulate into a coherent library program.

Building the User Instruction Program

Logically, an instruction program should be initiated with basic skills instruction, but there may be good reasons for starting with course-related sessions. An inexperienced instruction librarian cannot usually prepare a skills session that holds the interest of students not motivated by an immediate paper assignment. To do such a session well requires a massive investment of time preparing visuals, lecture, and coordinated handbook, all of which may seem exorbitant for the sake of a few students. Yet it is rarely possible to require basic instruction for all freshmen at the start, and few faculty will readily recognize it as a worthwhile assignment for their students until they themselves have had considerable exposure to the idea of library instruction.

A low-risk approach to skills instruction is to direct it first to the training of student assistants, perfecting it on this captive audience, and later extend it to selected freshman courses. Once perfected, it is infinitely repeatable, readily updated and expanded, and easily taught by other librarians, to whom the content is simple and familiar.

If course-related instruction is chosen to begin with, candidate courses can be identified from reference-desk encounters with floundering students, and faculty can be solicited for as many courses as workload permits. Course-related instruction has more appeal for faculty than skills instruction because it meets their immediate needs. Moreover, students are motivated by an impending course assignment, the librarian's knowledge of subject bibliography is sharpened, and gaps in the reference collection and a host of remediable access problems (e. g., needed catalog cross-references) are brought to light. However, the less the students know of basic skills, the more carefully these must be woven into each presentation, stealing time from more advanced material. At some point it becomes desirable to break out the basic skills content and teach it separately.

As a course-related program grows deeper problems appear. Faculty typically think only of the term paper as a means of getting students to the library, unaware that a shorter research assignment may be equally valuable and more suitable for the level and content of a given course. But fruitful discussion on this point with professors used to assigning papers develops only gradually with those whose courses become library instruction "regulars." Those who do not want full-fledged term papers but are unaware of alternatives may shun library instruction altogether.

A more difficult problem is the cost-effectiveness of course-related instruction. If each session includes an annotated guide, a lecture with an illustrated sample subject search, and sometimes hands-on practice with the more complicated reference tools, preparation will be very time-consuming. At the start of a program, before efficient techniques are developed, one can easily spend fifty or sixty hours preparing a new instruction session. This is worthwhile for courses frequently repeated; it is extravagant for one-time classes with a handful of students, yet the majors in such seminars deserve well-planned instruction, too.

An obvious way to avoid full-scale instruction for many one-time courses is to provide broad, discipline-oriented instruction for all beginning majors. But in most liberal arts colleges relatively unstructured curricula in the humanities and social sciences make it difficult to reach beginning majors altogether. Even when a department does have a required introductory course its content may not lend itself to such broad-gauge library instruction. Also, library work may be acceptable in some sections but not in others, according to the preferences of individual professors. Where majors can be reached together in a required course, usually in the sciences, faculty may expect you to cram into a single lab period all the reference tools and search techniques students will need for the totality of their undergraduate research. This is a marathon for librarian and students, ineffective pedagogically.

As the program grows, therefore, the instruction librarian will want to work with faculty at the departmental, as well as individual, level. With an initial investment of planning time, long sessions that would be required for adequate instruction of majors can be broken into small components--some live, some self-instructional--each with a corresponding research assignment, to be spread through several courses. In departments with less structured curricula group goal-setting may motivate several professors to incorporate brief library work into their courses for the common good, even though their personal goals may not require it. Thus, course-related instruction leads inevitably to course-integrated instruction, which in turn, given a receptive climate and enterprising librarians, leads ultimately to a curriculum-integrated approach.

The program described here is ambitious--not only beyond the resources of most college libraries now but, many would argue, in the foreseeable future as well. In the beginning, library instruction is in effect free. In many colleges it is started by an individual who sees an interesting job that needs to be done and is willing to invest considerable personal time in doing it. But library instruction cannot be long sustained or expanded on the strength of a single enthusiast with other duties. Although administrators are often lavish with moral support, they will resist financial commitment to library instruction until they are convinced of its worth and assured that the library is able and willing to guarantee a long-range program. Libraries that hope to institute more than a superficial teaching program, therefore, must first commit themselves to reordering their priorities, reapportioning staff responsibilities, and establishing supportive hiring practices.

This commitment typically is made little by little. The first step is usually increased involvement of other library departments in reference duty to give the reference librarian free hours for planning and class preparation. Gradually other librarians begin sharing the instruction load. A cataloger with a subject specialty may want to prepare and deliver course-related instruction in that area. Others may take on instruction sessions that have already been developed, undertaking merely to learn the material and update it, thus freeing the initiator for new planning efforts. Librarians who are reluctant to enter the classroom can contribute by writing bibliography annotations slanted toward specific student needs or by preparing visual aids. As positions become vacant recruitment for all departments should emphasize participation in the instruction program.

Such nonfinancial support for the developing program will, however, generate conflicts. As more librarians become involved in teaching their contributions may at first be offset by the complications of having too many cooks. For the sake of coordination, quality control, and a unified

approach, clear lines of authority must be established.
Time-consuming policy and training meetings will be necessary, creating further tensions for librarians who feel their
primary responsibilities lie elsewhere.

In addition to increasing workload, a developing instruction program makes new qualitative demands. Librarians must begin to think more like academics in order to
articulate the links between their technical knowledge and
the actual problems for which students need to use library
resources. They must make a continuing effort to become
acquainted with course content and objectives, to the point
of specializing as far as staff size permits, taking courses
to fill in needed subject background, and auditing others to
find out where, intellectually, the students are.

Instruction invites students' confidence in librarians'
expertise, but that confidence can be quickly undermined.
As soon as most freshmen begin to get systematic basic-
skills instruction simple questions no longer dominate at the
reference desk. The more serious research questions that
supplant them may be welcome to experienced reference librarians, but they tax the knowledge of those whose brief
stints of reference duty afford only cursory acquaintance
with the reference collection. When course-related instruction is introduced students want and deserve consultative reference follow-up from the same librarians who have taught
their classes. Although attendance at each other's sessions
and review of handouts can superficially familiarize every
librarian with subject bibliography, the one who has worked
through the preparation can best recognize and unravel
quirky research problems. As specialization and instruction experience increase, this becomes more and more the
case. Librarians should therefore be on call during the assignment periods following their instruction sessions. Those
who are pressured by other work will resent the interrup-
tions; at the same time they will be appalled at the inept
responses of less knowledgeable librarians to students from
their classes. [50]

These obstacles are not insurmountable. Library
instruction has grown from nothing in countless colleges
within a decade, and the need for comprehensive programs
has been recognized for years. At least two genuine examples of the teaching library already exist--at Earlham College and Sangamon State University.

At Earlham the teaching library has been slowly

developing for about fifteen years. The philosophy and content of the Earlham program has been thoroughly reported, but background conditions that have helped it flourish are less well known. [51] Evan Farber, Earlham's head librarian, credits staff commitment, a faculty devoted to good teaching and open to working with librarians, and an administration willing to accept the library's priorities. [52] But that is hardly an accidental constellation. First, Farber himself has been both initiator and guiding force of the program. The burden of convincing an uncommitted director has not fallen to a librarian lower on the organization chart, and the authority to establish necessary work priorities and performance standards has resided in the person most knowledgeable about program needs. Second, Farber has taken the unequivocal position that the primary goal of a college library is to promote proficient student use, not to acquire and service a little-used research collection. The technical workload has thus been kept at a manageable level. Third, Evan Farber, reference librarian James Kennedy, and science librarian Thomas Kirk together nurtured the program through its formative years. A coherent philosophy has been maintained, work has been cumulative, and highly efficient preparation methods have been worked out. Although staff changes can bring new ideas and fresh commitment to an established program like Earlham's, frequent turnover in key positions would be crippling at an early stage. Strong and consistent leadership, both conceptual and administrative, are essential.

Sangamon State, in contrast, is an upper division and graduate institution that opened in 1970. The president, convinced by Patricia Knapp's work at Monteith of the importance of a teaching library in a liberal arts institution, authorized a department of teaching librarians responsible for expanded reference activities, collection development, and classroom teaching of library use, but not for administrative functions. The librarians began by organizing the usual library operations, but as these became stabilized, they transferred all technical functions to high-level support staff skilled in office management. The latter may call on the library faculty as consultants, but they report directly to the university librarian. A Library Program Committee, comprised of library faculty, other faculty, and students, sets goals and policy relating to the library's educational activities. [53] An entirely fresh start with no entrenched old guard, an initial 11-percent share of the university budget, [54] and a radical pro-library policy decreed by the institution's chief administrator are, for most of us, unimaginable advantages. Sangamon

State is nevertheless part of the real world and perhaps an exemplar of things to come.

Obviously, establishment of a well-conceived instruction program requires a shift of resources from other departments into public services and, almost certainly, longer work hours for those involved in teaching, even with reduction of their noninstructional responsibilities. Although computerized cataloging has released some professional time, the changeover to AACR II and new types of public catalog threaten to reabsorb it for a while. Strict control of collection growth and transfer of more technical and office-management responsibilities to nonprofessionals should gain something for instruction, but time, attitude, and ability requirements combine to make it preferable to hire specifically for full-time instruction positions. [55] Such fundamental restructuring of the staff, in any organization and for any purpose, takes patience, sensitivity, and well-planned staff re-education.

Earlham and Sangamon State present two models for the administration of an instruction program. At Earlham a strong tradition has been established by a director who subordinates technical operations to teaching. At Sangamon State the teaching librarians have been freed from the tension between operational duties and academic concerns by their formal separation from the library's administrative hierarchy. [56] These are difficult models to replicate because the first is so dependent on an individual's personality and the second is a radical departure from traditional library organization. A more conservative approach, recommended by Givens, is the division of instruction from general reference service and from collection-housing and care. [57] The important thing is that bibliographic instruction be given autonomy in some form that gives it a fair claim to resources and ensures at least one librarian's undivided commitment to purely academic goals. Separation from general reference need not entail any loss. Instruction would, of course, include follow-up consultations with individual students, while general reference should include regular desk service in response to requests not directly generated by instruction. Such a reference desk would not have to be staffed by professionals as long as a librarian was on call for difficult questions. [58]

The time has come for instruction librarians to relinquish the self-limiting principle that library instruction, because it concerns every academic discipline, has no subject matter to call its own. The same can be said of logic, which enjoys a rather high status, and composition, which is only now freeing itself from subservience to the study of literature. Lindgren has suggested that we look to the teaching of composition for a model. [59] If we do so, we find that composition teachers claim to own a discipline by virtue of three things: they have a teachable content beyond simple performance rules, they conduct research in writing behavior and attempt rigorous definition of their domain, and they have begun to influence the job market and professional education. [60] There could be no closer parallel to the present state of library instruction.

For more than a century we academic librarians have looked hopefully to some form of user instruction to bridge the gap between the library's complex mishmash of organizational principles and a multiplicity of student needs--the latter obscured from us by our traditional isolation from the classroom. Creating our own separate classes to teach procedures, specific sources, and techniques is not enough. Only in the aftermath of Monteith have a significant number of us begun to learn that technical library knowledge, although necessary, is insufficient for research proficiency. Today investigation of the scholarly communication patterns that produce the literatures of the different disciplines and examination of the related bibliographic apparatuses appear to provide the most fruitful approach to understanding library research. Leaders in the instruction movement are using our growing understanding of the structures of literatures to help students relate their specific problems to aspects of recorded knowledge. Close communication with students engaged in library research in turn reveals new areas for analysis and investigation. Faculty have begun to see that their discipline-bound research methods, idiosyncratic and based on tacit knowledge, are inappropriate for novices; they are turning to librarians on their students' behalf for teachable concepts and procedures. As interaction between instruction librarians and regular faculty increases, new possibilities emerge for using library work to teach aspects of subject content that have eluded verbal explication. Academic libraries of all sizes are seeking staff who can establish or participate in instruction programs, and the growing number of instruction workshops attests to the zeal of librarians already so engaged. Library schools are beginning to offer credit courses in instruction, although they are hampered by the fact that the real experts are not on their faculties but are practitioners in the field.

The logical, eventual outcome of the library instruction movement will undoubtedly be the establishment of the teacher-librarian as an acknowledged specialist quite different from the traditional public service librarian. Conventional reference-desk service, relatively passive and uneven in quality, will be seriously challenged. The bureaucratic work styles and clerical hours of traditional librarianship are already suffering comparison with the greater individual autonomy and more intense commitment of the instruction librarian. Educational requirements will continue to rise, pushing up the caliber of individuals attracted to the field. Of course, economic obstacles, entrenched conservatism within librarianship, and the poor quality of much instruction during the transition period will slow these reforms, but it appears that library instruction is now here to stay. The earliest and greatest benefits should be in the colleges, where small size and commitment to close teacher-student relationships provide the most hospitable environment for the teaching librarian.

Notes

[1] These include: the ALA standing committee on Instruction in the Use of Libraries; in the ACRL Division, the Bibliographic Instruction Section, the Community and Junior College Libraries Section ad hoc Instructional Development Committee, and the Education and Behavior Science Section Committee on Bibliographic Instruction for Educators; and the Library Instruction Round Table (LIRT).

[2] Jon Lindgren, "Seeking a Useful Tradition for Library User Instruction in the College Library," in Progress in Educating the Library User, ed. John Lubans, Jr. (New York: Bowker, 1978), p. 82.

[3] Concerning the failure of library schools to train instruction librarians see Anne Beaubien, Mary George, and Sharon Hogan, "Things We Weren't Taught in Library School: Some Thoughts to Take Home," in Putting Library Instruction in Its Place: In the Library and in the Library School, Papers Presented at the Seventh Annual Conference on Library Orientation for Academic Librarians, Eastern Michigan University, May 12-13, 1977, ed. Carolyn A. Kirkendall (Ann Arbor: Pierian, 1978), pp. 71-84; and Vida Stanton, "The Library School: Its Role in Teaching the Use of the Library," in Progress in Educating the Library User, ed. John Lubans, Jr. (New York: Bowker, 1978), pp. 139-46.

200 ● College Librarianship

⁴Lindgren, "Seeking a Useful Tradition," pp. 74-75.
⁵For a fuller treatment of the development of U.S. libraries in the 19th century see Samuel Rothstein, The Development of Reference Services Through Academic Traditions, Public Library Practice and Special Librarianship (Chicago: Association of College and Reference Libraries, June 1955), from which much of my historical sketch was drawn.
⁶Ibid., p. 17.
⁷Examples of library instruction in nineteenth-century university libraries are given in Kenneth Brough, Scholar's Workshop: Evolving Concepts of Library Service (Urbana: University of Illinois, 1953), pp. 152-55; and George S. Bonn, "Training Laymen in the Use of the Library," in The State of the Library Art, 5 vols., ed. Ralph Shaw (New Brunswick, N.J.: Rutgers University Graduate School of Library Service, 1960), vol. 2, pt. 1, p. 28.
⁸Richard Rubin, "Azariah Smith Root and Library Instruction at Oberlin College," Journal of Library History, Philosophy and Comparative Librarianship 12 (Summer 1977): 250-61.
⁹Concerning the history of academic librarians' yearning for faculty status see Robert B. Downs, "The Role of the Academic Librarian, 1876-1976," College & Research Libraries 37 (November 1976): 491-502.
¹⁰Rothstein, p. 22.
¹¹Ibid., p. 36.
¹²Ibid., p. 51.
¹³Downs, p. 496.
¹⁴Bonn, p. 28.
¹⁵Johnnie Givens, "The Use of Resources in the Learning Experience," in Advances in Librarianship, vol. 4 (New York: Academic, 1974), pp. 156, 158.
¹⁶A documented history of the anti-intellectualism of the library education establishment and ALA is given in Lloyd J. Houser and Alvin M. Schrader, The Search for a Scientific Profession: Library Science Education in the U.S. and Canada (Metuchen, N.J.: Scarecrow, 1978).
¹⁷For the development of special library reference service see Rothstein, pp. 53-61.
¹⁸Kenneth Whittaker, "Towards a Theory for Reference and Information Service," Journal of Librarianship 9 (January 1977): 49-63, traces the development of concepts of reference work, arguing that effective service depends on theoretical understanding of the nature of the work.
¹⁹James I. Wyer, Reference Work: A Text-book for Students of Library Work and Librarians (Chicago: American Library Association, 1930).

[20]For example, Robert S. Taylor, "The Process of Asking Questions," American Documentation 13 (October 1962): 391-96, and his "Question-Negotiation and Information Seeking in Libraries," College & Research Libraries 29 (May 1968): 178-94.

[21]F. W. Lancaster, The Measurement and Evaluation of Library Services (Washington, D.C.: Information Resources, 1977), discusses evaluation of reference services by categorizing questions, pp. 75-76, and by analysis of reference procedures, including flow charting of search behavior, pp. 109-32.

[22]Louis Shores, "The Library Arts College, a Possibility in 1954?" a speech delivered at the Chicago Century of Progress Exposition, 1934, and later published in School and Society 4 (January 26, 1935): 110-14.

[23]There is an extensive literature on the library-college movement. For a brief history and criticism see Fay M. Blake, "The Library-College Movement," Drexel Library Quarterly 7 (July-October 1971): 175-88. See also Robert S. Taylor, The Making of a Library: The Academic Library in Transition (New York: Becker and Hayes, 1972), pp. 224-26.

[24]Harvie Branscomb, Teaching with Books: A Study of College Libraries (Chicago: Association of American Colleges, American Library Association, 1940).

[25]William H. Carlson, College and University Libraries and Librarianship: An Examination of Their Present Status and Some Proposals for Their Future Development (Chicago: American Library Association, 1946).

[26]Jesse Shera, "The Role of the College Librarian--a Reappraisal," in The Role of the College Library--a Reappraisal in Library-Instructional Integration at the College Level, Report of the 40th Conference of Eastern College Librarians (Chicago: Association of College and Reference Librarians, 1955), p. 7.

[27]Role of the College Library--a Reappraisal, p. 5.

[28]Shera, p. 10.

[29]Patricia Knapp, The Monteith College Library Experiment (New York: Scarecrow, 1966).

[30]Patricia Knapp, "A Suggested Program of College Instruction in the Use of the Library," Library Quarterly 26 (July 1956), p. 230.

[31]Knapp, Monteith, p. 107.

[32]Anita R. Schiller, "Reference Service: Instruction or Information," Library Quarterly 35 (January 1965): 52-60.

[33]William A. Katz, Introduction to Reference Work, 3d ed. (New York: McGraw-Hill, 1978), p. 260-65.

[34]Millicent D. Abell, "The Changing Role of the Academic Librarian: Drift and Mastery," College & Research Libraries 40 (March 1979): 154-64, discusses reference and instruction in relation to changing professional roles on pp. 158-63.

[35]Pauline Wilson, "Librarians as Teachers: The Study of an Organization Fiction," Library Quarterly 49 (April 1979): 146-62.

[36]Katz, p. 264.

[37]Lindgren, p. 83.

[38]Several model statements have been published, most recently, "Objectives: A Model Statement," in Bibliographic Instruction Handbook, Policy and Planning Committee, ACRL Bibliographic Instruction Section (Chicago: Association of College and Research Libraries, 1979), pp. 35-45.

[39]Lindgren, p. 84.

[40]Katz, p. 264.

[41]Benita J. Howell, Edward Reeves, and John Van Willigen, "Fleeting Encounters--A Role Analysis of Reference Librarian-Patron Interaction," RQ 16 (Winter 1976): 124-29, presents evidence that reference librarians are more effective in academic libraries when they are perceived as teachers.

[42]Lancaster, Measurement and Evaluation, discusses unobtrusive studies of correct and incorrect answers to information-type questions, which have been carried out mainly in public libraries, pp. 91-109. Marcia Myers, Miami-Dade Community College, Florida, reported a similar study of academic libraries at a program of the Reference and Adult Services Division, annual meeting of the American Library Association, Dallas, Texas, June 26, 1979.

[43]Raymond G. McInnis, New Perspectives for Reference Service in Academic Libraries (Westport, Conn.: Greenwood, 1978).

[44]For a discussion of a screening test used by Earlham College Library see James Kennedy, Jr., Thomas G. Kirk, and Gwendolyn A. Weaver, "Course-Related Library Instruction; A Case Study of the English and Biology Departments at Earlham College," Drexel Library Quarterly 7 (July-October 1971), pp. 283-84.

[45]McInnis, pp. 135-42.

[46]There is a glossary of instruction terms in the ACRL Bibliographic Instruction Handbook, pp. 57-60, but it does not provide terminology relating to the structure of literature. Two good sources of analysis and terminology are McInnis, New Perspectives, and Thelma Freides, Literature and Bibliography of the Social Sciences (Los Angeles: Melville, 1973).

47ACRL Bibliographic Instruction Handbook, pp. 35-45.
48Thomas Kirk, "Course-Related Instruction in the '70s," in Library Instruction in the Seventies: The State of the Art, Papers Presented at the Sixth Annual Conference on Library Orientation for Academic Librarians, Eastern Michigan University, May 13-14, 1976, ed. Hannelore B. Rader (Ann Arbor: Pierian, 1977), p. 35. Course-related and course-integrated instruction are also defined in the ACRL Bibliographic Instruction Handbook, p. 58.
49Virginia H. Parr, "Faculty Liaison: A Departmental Model in Psychology," paper presented at the program of the ACRL Education and Behavioral Sciences Section, annual meeting of the American Library Association, Dallas, Texas, June 25, 1979. See also Parr, "Course-Related Library Instruction for Psychology Students," Teaching of Psychology 5 (April 1978): 101-02.
50Mary Mancuso Biggs, "The Perils of Library Instruction," Journal of Academic Librarianship 5 (July 1979): 155, 162, is outspoken about the problem of reference service that is unequal to the expectations created by an instruction program.
51Evan Ira Farber, "Library Instruction Throughout the Curriculum: Earlham College Program," in Educating the Library User, ed. John Lubans, Jr., (New York: Bowker, 1974), pp. 145-62, discusses the institutional context and gives an overview of the program.
52Evan Ira Farber, letter to the author, December 6, 1979.
53For descriptions of the philosophy and organization of the Sangamon State University Library see: Howard W. Dillon, "Organizing the Academic Library for Instruction," Journal of Academic Librarianship 1 (March 1975): 4-7; Joyce A. Bennett, "The Sangamon State Experience," in Putting Library Instruction in Its Place: In the Library and in the Library School, Papers Presented at the Seventh Annual Conference on Library Orientation for Academic Librarians, Eastern Michigan University, May 12-13, 1977, ed. Carolyn A. Kirkendall (Ann Arbor: Pierian, 1978), pp. 13-21; Robert C. Spencer, "The Teaching Library," Library Journal 103 (May 15, 1978): 1021-24; and Patricia Senn Breivik, "Leadership, Management, and the Teaching Library," Library Journal 103 (October 15, 1978), 2045-48.
54Bennett, p. 19.
55Breivik discusses the implications of an expanding instruction program for staff organization and for the qualifications of teaching librarians.
56Patricia Senn Breivik, "A Model for Library Management," LJ Special Report 10 (New York: Library Journal,

(1979), pp. 4-9, provides an organizational chart of the
Sangamon State Library and discusses its problems and advantages as the library ends its first decade.

[57]Givens, pp. 167-68.

[58]Fred E. Smith, Assistant Professor and Coordinator
of the Library/Bibliographic Instruction Center at Shippens-
burg State College in Pennsylvania, has been compiling statistics on the effects of library instruction on the volume and
type of questions asked at the reference desk. According to
a personal communication from him, January 9, 1980, within the coming year that library will replace the professionally staffed reference desk with an information desk staffed by
clerical employees, and instruction librarians will provide
consultative reference service.

[59]Lindgren, pp. 75-77.

[60]Robert M. Gorrell, "Like a Crab Backward: Has the
CCCC Been Worth It?" College Composition and Communication 30 (February 1979): 32-36.

MEDIA RESOURCES IN COLLEGE LIBRARIES
AS FACILITATORS OF HIGHER LEARNING

Dana E. Smith

Nonprint curricular material has traditionally been associated with secondary and junior college education. In recent years the response to nonprint curriculum development by college libraries has meant the establishment of new facilities or the restructuring of old facilities to make room for media centers within the library. Technological advances have changed some libraries from traditional book-oriented, one-medium depositories to highly complex multimedia communication centers. Progress has been slow and frustrating, because many libraries have not kept pace with technological advances, while the transition from library to multimedia learning center has prompted considerable controversy and debate over which media (16mm film, videocassette, videodisc, etc.) are best for curriculum support. Nearly everyone now agrees, however, that the academic library of the 1980s should acquire some multimedia resources. Information transfer cannot be relegated solely to one format, and libraries have traditionally acquired and stored information, regardless of format, on the premise that information is the prime ingredient to facilitate learning.

College libraries exist, of course, to support the parent institution's objectives. Any resource, print or otherwise, that might expedite student learning and faculty research has legitimate potential for inclusion in a college collection. This is fundamental and is the basis of the traditional approach to collection development in all areas including media resources. However, there have been major problems in carrying out this seemingly fundamental approach to collection of nonprint resources.

The underlying problem with the "instructional/support" approach to collection development of audiovisual materials is that it increases the library's tendency simply to store such materials in a warehouse-like fashion rather than to facilitate their use. To an extent, librarians through bibliographic-instruction programs have alleviated some of the barriers between students and information and have had a marked impact on improving the effectiveness of the library user, but BI programs generally focus on the standard print resource and mention nonprint resource materials as only a part of the larger "store." Thus the tendency remains to acquire A/V materials and to honor them in the breach in a multitude of formats, but the library has not effectively been able to facilitate use of its nonprint sources. There are many reasons for this.

It has always been difficult to work library nonprint resources into college curricula. Many instructors, administrators, and librarians have never really taken such materials seriously. Some people despair about even being able to work media into the curriculum in traditional, conservative college programs. It would be well to reexamine why such media are indeed worth acquiring and integrating into college curricula.

The importance of using nonprint materials in educational activities has long been recognized, at least in theory, by many educators and librarians alike. Certain subject areas (e. g. , cinema, literature, theater) are most effectively presented when visual or audio formats are incorporated to convey or support an instructor's classroom lecture. In addition, students at all educational levels are used to a variety of formats and have become progressively more oriented toward interaction with audiovisual materials. The gradual recognition of the impact of visual literacy has even prompted some colleges to take a serious look at the use of audiovisual materials as a viable alternative to more traditional teaching methodologies.

Why, then, have not college libraries better adapted themselves to nonprint materials? Traditionally the college library routinely adjusted to individual or group requests for expansion of the collection into existing or new subject disciplines. But nonprint materials represent a complex of physical and organizational problems of such magnitude that college libraries have resisted their inclusion and use. Selection guidelines generally reflected the institution's teaching and research objectives. However, when it became apparent that nonprint materials should in some way be included in the curriculum and would require attention equal to that given traditional print items, the routine adjustment of the acquisition profile was not that easily accomplished. Although a few institutions were successful at acquisition, organization, and dissemination of nonprint resources, with a reasonable level of uniformity with traditional print materials, others found their efforts frustrated by numerous complications and considerable diversity of opinion on the matter. Thus, unable to borrow from past experience when making important decisions, conflicting interests erupted, and soon a professional resistance to nonprint material emerged throughout the academic community.

It is not too difficult to ascertain why professional resistance to the acquisition and use of nonprint materials evolved as it did. When college and library administrators were faced with the development of an effective curricular media philosophy they justifiably envisioned significant, and costly, facility and equipment overhauls. Nonprint packages and supporting hardware simply do not conform to the standard, conventional space appropriated for print-material growth and development. In addition, nonprint materials are expensive and require special handling and equipment. Library budgetary support would have to be justified and increased to initiate, maintain, and acquire additional materials in this area. Library staff quite often were not qualified or were not able to divert the necessary space and staff from other library activities. Also, there is considerable technical difficulty with this new medium. Description and cataloging rules are neither well defined nor consistently applied, while selection and reviewing aids were, initially, virtually nonexistent. For the teaching faculty the use of nonprint materials in the classroom meant considerable adjustment in instructional design and presentation format. Equipment had to be scheduled, available, and working at the desired time. Not all classrooms were equipped for multimedia presentations, so the effectiveness of media varied with the environment available for viewing. In some cases supplemental viewing of an item by individuals outside the classroom was desirable but not possible due to time constraints. One cannot expect an instructor to assign

208 ● College Librarianship

eighty students to watch the same film or videocassette in a week's time. With this as the backdrop, one could wonder where the initial concern for the development of nonprint as an alternative resource in the academic community had its real origins, and why, encountering so many insurmountable problems, colleges continued to endeavor to offer this alternative with such a seemingly high priority.

To a large extent it was the students, not the educators and librarians, who mandated the inclusion of alternative media resources in higher education. The many divergent social, political, and economic forces of the 1960s had a pronounced and sudden impact on teaching methodologies, course content, and ultimately on supporting curriculum resources. The campus demands for relevance in instruction produced reforms in the American college environment that were swift and far-reaching. Prepared or not, the college library was faced with the immediate challenge of providing curricular support for a multimedia, multifaceted approach to higher education. Amidst all this turmoil many media resource programs were implemented as a reaction to demands and not as well-defined responses to the basic and long-range need, interest, budget, space, and staff capabilities of the parent institution. On the one hand, students pressed for alternatives to the standard approach to higher education, while on the other hand, administrators, teaching faculty, and library staff wrestled with the methods and means whereby this curricular challenge could be met. For many institutions all these problems combined had to be remedied before the serious business of implementing an effective, responsive curricular media program could begin to grow and develop.

Nevertheless, there are college media programs, though they have not been in existence long enough to be evaluated comparatively, nor can we yet say with certainty what will make a college library media program successful. There are, however, some indicators that would suggest in which cases college libraries have been able to accommodate nonprint demands with less overall difficulty and at a level compatible with the recognizable immediate and long-range information needs of the parent institution.

If the success of a media resource program can be measured in terms of the degree of support it receives from administrators, faculty, and students, then we can determine a successful media program by measuring the size of its budget, total circulation or use of nonprint items, total hours of operation for the media resource center, size of professional and support staff, and the number and type of existing media hardware. This would seem to indicate that the most successful centers are those that took considerable care to plan a program that would have overall support and acceptance within the library, in other audiovisual centers on campus, and by faculty and students, who were involved in the routine operation and long-range planning of this support activity. Most studies made in this regard point out that without administrative backing (financial support) many media resource programs have fallen onto difficult times, as budget officers attempt to reduce the "frill" spending in campus programs. This would also indicate that the program really could not have had a very significant impact upon the teaching faculty or students. Had they realized the potential learning benefits of a comprehensive media program, it would have been possible for their interests and continued pressure on campus administrators to guarantee this approach as an alternative to the standard curriculum. It would appear that the successful media program is that program which initially and throughout its development had the support and understanding critical to its existence at all levels of the campus community.

The size of a program is one determinant of success, but there are also others. If the audiovisual material does not have a significant impact on the learning objectives of the parent institution, the size or cost of the collection means little. In this respect, no matter what level of planning, development, operation, and evaluation of a media program is undertaken, the real success of the impact of nonprint resources on the undergraduate curriculum lies in that resource being made available whenever necessary to facilitate, enhance, and support learning. This brings us back to the original problems of instruction and collection development.

Throughout the academic community there are some pervasive media-use patterns that have developed as a result of nonprint items being acquired and managed along principles that pertain primarily to traditional print items. In most cases these use patterns were determined when the type and scope of the intended nonprint resource program did not realistically reflect the need, interest, availability, budget, space, or staff capabilities of the parent institution. For example, many college libraries are housed in older buildings designed during the founding years of the college. Therefore, space considerations necessary for the inclusion of a comprehensive media resource center in this type of a facility are made particularly difficult. As newer facilities have appeared, new design concepts have emerged that have facilitated the use of multimedia programs, but it is still common to find that these facilities have cordoned off their media resource centers for whatever reasons. A few colleges that have adopted the learning-resource-center philosophy have attempted to integrate nonprint materials in that environment; most libraries, however, still keep these items separate from the main collection. This suggests that libraries, new or old, recognize the need for some type of nonprint representation, but, when confronted with the expense and unique handling problems characteristic of nonprint items, decided to treat them as separate from the bulk of the collection to monitor their use and ensure their security.

A number of other problems in the use and handling of nonprint items make the accessibility of the information contained within difficult to retrieve. These same problems also account for the vast majority of media-resource-center materials being controlled and stored separate from the main circulating collection. Some of the problems that have determined the current media-use patterns and limited the development of this resource as an alternative instructional resource in higher education include the following:

1. Some materials require rigid temperature controls (filmstrips and slides, as well as videocassettes and 16mm films), and it is usually less expensive to install such temperature controls (if they do not already exist) in a separate room rather than throughout older buildings. This would need to be done in some locations if nonprint resources are interfiled with print materials in existing shelving facilities.

2. Most nonprint items are easily damaged if not carefully controlled by trained library personnel. It is easier and less expensive, in the long run, to keep such items secured in one staffed area than interfile them with print materials that are less fragile. For example, many nonprint items are sets (e.g., one filmstrip and a cassette cartridge stored in one box and both part of an automatic sound-filmstrip instructional unit to be used in conjunction on one machine specifically designed for sound-filmstrip units).

3. Replacement, loss, and damage to fragile non-print items are less if they are housed in a separate room or area where staffing, storage, and constant checking can be the rule.

4. Whenever one interfiles nonprint items with print items on open shelves the storage equipment costs (cabinets, etc.) are less, but there is a loss of protection and security.

5. If one separates such nonprint collections and houses them separately from print materials, one needs more staff and additional storage facilities (cabinets and the like), and in-house circulation costs are higher. In addition, most media or nonprint centers do not circulate these items outside of the building, room, or area, limiting the circulation to in-house users. This may extend the life of the item and increase the number of users to which the item is made available.

6. Expense of nonprint resources varies from one format to another and even within the same format, from one publisher or distributor to another. Thus even though an item may not receive high use (and would indeed be used more if one could charge it out for home or classroom use), the library may feel obligated to limit all nonprint to in-house use to eliminate expense of replacement copies.

7. When relying solely on in-house use classroom instructors may be less likely to encourage use of these items for their students; or they may assign heavier use knowing the item will be available in-house. However, there have been no major studies comparing either interfiling and shelving of print and nonprint versus housing them separately; nor have there been studies comparing the circulation and damage or loss of in-house versus out-of-the-building use for extended time periods. Such studies are desperately needed, so that more effective management decisions can be made prior to the acquisition and housing, as well as circulation, noncirculation, or limited circulation of these items.

If the concept of the college library collection is to support the instructional objectives of the parent institution, then, regardless of format, those resources should be made available to the student or faculty on an equal basis with the overall objective of ease in facilitating higher learning. Obviously, within the confines of some of the problems facing the total implementation of nonprint materials in the college curriculum this cannot be accomplished overnight. But there are some approaches that could be utilized now so that an effective, responsive curricular media program would be a realistic alternative in higher education for the future.

Essentially, what is needed to allow nonprint resources to transcend some of their current use limitations is an overall national re-evaluation of the purported development, management, and use of nonprint materials in higher education. Until national standards involving the acquisition, cataloging, and retrieval of nonprint information are established each institution will be obliged to act independently in this area, thus causing further confusion. If the academic community would solicit its respective national professional organizations to consider the need for standardization in this area, many of the suggested problems encountered in the use of nonprint resources in higher education today could be alleviated.

We are at a point technologically where the supporting nonprint industries could make available durable, circulatable materials for instructional use. As a large community, educational institutions at all levels should be sharing information with regard to technological improvements and their impact on nonprint use, attempting to acquire proven, high-quality equipment in a standard format so that resource sharing could occur. Creation of union catalogs for nonprint materials could serve many useful purposes. They would be indispensible not only as aids in resource sharing, but they might also provide some indication as to the proliferation of nonprint materials and prompt the nonprint industry to accommodate our pre-established format and content needs and not vice versa. In addition, we should also urge distributors to supply scripts and relevant review citations whenever necessary (so that the citing of relevant materials from nonprint packages can be facilitated).

In all, we should be doing whatever is necessary to bring this valuable learning resource into the curriculum of the academic community. If libraries do not respond effectively to the demands for nonprint storage and retrieval systems, outside organizations can expect to become the intermediaries in this area of information transfer. To some extent this is already occurring, and we should not allow our currently imposed limits on the management and development of nonprint materials to reduce the status and effectiveness of the library as the primary ingredient in the facilitation of learning.

Bibliography

Bissmeyer, Ollie E. "Managing Non-Print Media Programs in Higher Education." Catholic Library World 48 (1977): 387-89.

Boss, Richard W. "Audio Materials in Academic Research Libraries." College & Research Libraries 33 (1972): 464-66.

Brong, Gerald R. "Media Programs and Their Management." Catholic Library World 48 (1977): 382-86.

Burlingame, Dwight F. "Them's Fightin Words: Media in the Library." Audio-Visual Instruction 21 (October 1976): 25-26.

Burlingame, Dwight F., Dennis C. Fields, and Anthony C. Schulzentenberg. The College Learning Resource Center. Littleton, Colo.: Libraries Unlimited, 1978.

Colby, Edmund K. "Is the Academic Library's Non-Print Collection Incidental to Learning?" Catholic Library World 49 (1978): 335-37.

Hart, Thomas L. "Dare to Integrate." Audio-Visual Instruction 21 (October 1976): 18-19.

LeClercq, Anne. "Organizing and Collecting Non-Print Materials in Academic Libraries." North Carolina Libraries 33 (Spring 1975): 21-28.

Sive, Mary Robinson. Selecting Instructional Media: A Guide to Audiovisual and Other Instructional Media Lists. Littleton, Colo.: Libraries Unlimited, 1978.

Teo, Elizabeth A. "Audiovisual Materials in the College and Community College Library: The Basics of Collection Building." Choice 14 (1977): 487-501.

GOVERNMENT DOCUMENTS IN THE COLLEGE
LIBRARY: THE STATE OF THE ART

Kathleen Heim and Marilyn Moody

Introduction

There have been no studies that focus on the college library
and its role in the servicing of government publications.
This article reviews the literature of documents librarianship that is pertinent to the college library and reports on a
small pilot study of the provision of government publications
in college libraries.

Government publications are generally perceived as a
special resource, requiring specific skills and expertise for
provision of their use, when in fact a great number of these
publications are used by all types of librarians, even in the
smallest working reference collection. The Budget of the
U.S., Catalog of Federal Domestic Assistance, Census of
Population, Congressional Directory, County-City Data Book,
Statutes at Large, and U.S. Government Manual are all U.S.
government publications that present no particular problem
to the librarian who works with them. When accepted as
discrete items that provide answers to frequently asked
questions documents are not considered an isolated resource.
It is only when they are seen as a resource set apart, usually in connection with the depository library system, that
they are considered difficult to deal with. Why then do we
wish to isolate documents and discuss their special role in
the college collection?

There has been a change in the emphasis of college library collection development from a traditional model based on the idea that the collection should replicate the university collection in miniature to a more dynamic model of a student-focused, working collection.[1] This ideal should also extend to the provision of government publications. College librarians who work in facilities that are designated depositories must face the problem of selecting from a bounty of materials; librarians in nondepositories must struggle to obtain the critical working items. In either case college librarians looking to the literature of documents librarianship will find little to guide them in their evaluation of government publications as a resource for the college collection.

Documents in the Seventies

Before we discuss the role of documents in the college collection some general remarks about documents need to be made. As we enter the 1980s documents librarianship has become an important specialization in library work. More than 1,150 librarians presently belong to the Government Documents Round Table (GODORT) of the American Library Association, indicating a high level of professional commitment to documents as a resource.[2] A prominent documents librarian has written:

> In the last decade, a revolution has taken place in the whole field of government publications. At no time in the history of American libraries has there been such a groundswell of support and concern for government publications by as large a group of librarians and publishers as at the present time.[3]

The interest in and relative success of documents librarianship in the United States is the result of many factors. The Depository Library Program under Chapter 19 in Title 44 of the United States Code makes U.S. government publications available without cost to designated depository libraries throughout the country. There were 1,312 designated depository libraries as of May 1979, including 770 academic libraries.[4] Most of these are "Selective Depositories," which choose in advance, by category or series, documents most suitable for their clientele. As a backup to these Selective Depositories, two libraries in each state are designated "Regional Depositories," which receive and permanently retain all publications distributed through the depository program.

Although the depository program has been in effect since the nineteenth century, it is only in the last decade that real progress has been made toward full exploitation of this resource. [5] A major factor has been the provision by U. S. commercial publishers of indexing and abstracting tools that fill in where government-issued indexes, such as the Monthly Catalog, leave off. A documents scholar notes, "Never has the rectification of shortcomings in the several guides noted above (government-issued indexes) been more diligently pursued than in the last few years. Commercial firms and their publications demonstrate significantly, and indeed in some cases spectacularly, the bibliographic endeavors toward that end."[6] Publications of the Carrollton Press, Congressional Information Service, Andriot, Pierian Press, and Libraries Unlimited have expanded the bibliographic control of government publications. Better retrieval of discrete bits of information from the mass of government data allows librarians far better access to government information than ever before.

Librarian involvement has expanded beyond the maintenance of documents collections to input at the policy-making level, via ALA's Government Documents Round Table. Through its major publication, Documents to the People (DTTP), its excellent programs at ALA conferences, and its task forces and committees, GODORT has been crucial in creating an intensified documents awareness among U. S. librarians. The formal mechanism for an ongoing dialogue between librarians and government is the Depository Library Council to the Public Printer, made up of librarians appointed by professional associations, which meets twice a year to solve mutual problems. A major achievement of the council was the issuance of Guidelines for the Depository Library System, which sets up standards for the maintenance, evaluation, and organization of depository libraries. [7] These synergistic forces--the depository library program, growing bibliographic control, and a highly developed professional commitment with formalized input to government policy makers--have provided librarians with a solid basis on which to provide access to government publications.

Underutilization of Documents

It is somewhat ironic that although documents librarianship has developed a more refined capability for the retrieval of documents and their contents, we do not in fact use documents sufficiently in the college libraries and elsewhere. An NCLIS report, <u>Government Publications: Their Role in the National Program for Library and Information Services,</u> has just been issued that has as its main theme the need to develop, strengthen, organize, and make available government publications at all levels to the maximum degree possible in the public interest. [8] Indeed, the underutilization of documents has been a recurrent theme in the literature of documents librarianship. Whitbeck and Hernon, who review this situation, point out that

> the literature of librarianship is filled with statements bemoaning the lack of use of government publications. All concede that publications from all levels of government offer invaluable information to patrons of libraries and information centers. However, most also point to a pronounced underutilization of these valuable resources. [9]

Reasons for underutilization of documents include that they are often classified in a manner unfamiliar to library users; that librarians may actually discourage use of documents through ignorance of government structure or publishing, bibliographic tools, and accessing methods; that library administrators may discriminate against documents; that documents may be isolated in relatively inaccessible special collections; and that many librarians share the fear of the unknown and unfamiliar organization of documents so often displayed by users. [10]

Before college librarians can begin to remedy the problem of underutilization of documents in the college library information is needed on the actual use of documents in this setting. However, little information about the provision of documents exists. The NCLIS report notes:

> Previous attempts at comprehensive studies of the basic issues affecting public availability and access to government publications have been few in number and inconclusive of results because of the complexity and scope of the problems encountered. The paucity of quantitative, summary documentation has proved a formidable, but not insurmountable, barrier to the development of needed conceptual overviews. [11]

In discussing documents, therefore, we are operating in a

relatively unknown area, where almost any basic information would be welcome.

Documents in College Libraries

Perhaps a good way to start discussing documents in college libraries is to focus upon their distribution. The best figures available that break down institutions of higher education by enrollment indicate that there are 1,277 four-year institutions that serve 2,500 students or fewer. [12] Of these 1,277 libraries 186, or 14.6 percent, are government-document depositories. [13] These libraries account for 24.2 percent of all academic depositories and 14.2 percent of all depositories. Clearly, college libraries compose a significant portion of the depository library system. However, their particular role in the provision of government publications has not been explored either from the viewpoint of service to the college or participation in the proposed national network for documents provision.

When we speak of documents in the college library we are actually discussing two very distinct types of institutions: those 14.6 percent that are depositories and the 84.4 percent that are not. A major problem in the literature dealing with documents is the focus on documents provision at institutions that are depositories. We must also consider to what degree the very presence of a resource, be it documents, a strong media center, or an archival collection, affects service. Is it used because it is inherently important or because it is there?

Methodology

College librarianship needs a comprehensive study of documents provision in the 186 college libraries holding depository status. A model for such a study would be Edsall's survey of community college library depositories, supported by the Council on Library Resources. [14] Such a study would provide information on administrative practices, use, and collection development in the college environment. Until such a study is undertaken we have only subjective impressions of what is particular to the college depository library.

In lieu of a comprehensive report we decided to do a telephone interview of a sample of college libraries holding depository status and an equal sample of college libraries that do not. After pinpointing the 186 libraries of four-year institutions with depository status we selected every ninth library and then matched these twenty with twenty nondepository libraries of similar size and geographic dispersion. This provided us with a base of similar institutions to query concerning attitudes and practices toward government publications.

Development of the Interview Instrument

The interview schedules were devised by perusing surveys of documents collections, such as Edsall's, with an eye to attitudinal rather than quantitative information. Other pieces of research that added areas for further consideration included a descriptive analysis of the depository system by Whitbeck, Hernon, and Richardson. [15] This analysis provides a panoramic view of the depository-system libraries as to type of primary public served, date achieving depository status, classification scheme used for documents, arrangement of collection, size of library, and percentage of depository items received. Their survey does provide some information about specific subgroups of depositories. The researchers broke out data for academic libraries and then analyzed these data by highest degree granted. One hundred and seventy-nine institutions granting the Bachelor's as the highest degree (which tallies well with our count of 186 institutions falling into the college category) held depository status. The researchers also looked at percentage of depository items received in relationship to enrollment and found that the higher the enrollment and the higher the degree offered, the greater the percentage of depository items received.

Whitbeck and Hernon also conducted an attitudinal survey of midwestern federal depositories. [16] Although the data gathered therein are not broken out by any type of library, they do provide a core of central questions of importance to us here. Their aim was to determine reasons for underutilization of documents as a resource. They found that although there was a generally positive attitude toward documents, there was a great need for further education in order to provide better service, and that collection building seemed unsystematic.

Of special consideration to academic libraries and

useful in devising our interview schedule was Whitbeck and
Hernon's survey of bibliographic instruction for documents. [17]
Working from the unstated assumption that government publications are a grossly underutilized resource, the investi-
gators felt that special training of users would be needed for
effective use of documents collections. They surveyed academic libraries to discover the scope of bibliographic instruction and provision for its evaluation. Focusing on those libraries that used the lecture as a means of bibliographic instruction, the researchers drew a profile of the use of this
method. They found that documents librarians most often
handled these lectures with frequent assistance from the reference staff; that lectures were given in both the classroom
and the library; that most librarians taught twenty or fewer
sessions per year; that libraries giving greater numbers of
sessions had a documents specialist; and that librarians were
interested in the development of techniques to evaluate these
sessions.

Two articles, by McCaghy and Purcell[18] and by Hernon and Williams, [19] investigated academic faculty's use of
government publications. Both of these looked at one university faculty's pattern of use--McCaghy and Purcell at
Case Western Reserve and Hernon and Williams at the University of Nebraska at Omaha. Although Hernon and Williams found a greater use of documents by faculty than did
the earlier study by McCaghy and Purcell, they still con-
cluded that documents use in academic libraries is not keeping pace with the increasing emphasis given documents by
librarians and publishers. [20]

From these surveys and studies we identified major
areas of concern to those doing research in the use of government publications. For the sake of comparability with
these earlier studies we have asked similar questions of our
sample of depository college libraries. Because none of the
studies considered the nondepository library, we have had to
devise a related set of questions without benefit of earlier
work on which to build. The results are presented in summary form, since our sample was too small for any conclusions of statistical significance. The two sets of questions
are included in an appendix at the conclusion of this article.

Characteristics of Depository College Libraries

Description of Collections

The general trend for federal publications is toward a separate collection with an average size of 80,000 documents arranged in Superintendent of Documents (SUDOC) classification. Basic reference tools, such as the Statistical Abstract
and Government Manual, are pulled out and placed in the
reference department. Other heavily used items, such as
area handbooks, may be pulled out and cataloged, but a very
small percentage of items are treated in this way. Periodicals are usually cataloged or placed in the general periodicals collection.

Other categories of documents collected include:

State documents: Half of the libraries collected documents of their home state on a regular basis using either a
classification system devised by their own state library or
cataloging their documents as they would any other item.
Some were depositories for state documents; in general,
however, state documents were not collected on a large
scale, nor did libraries systematically collect documents
from any other states. While a few such documents might
be obtained, these were only as a result of specific requests
and were accessioned and cataloged as any other item in the
collection would be.

Municipal or local: College libraries virtually ignore
these documents. The city directory was the only item collected by most libraries, and no systematic collecting of
municipal documents was carried out. Three libraries noted
that they relied on the local public library's municipal collection. Any municipal documents collected were cataloged.

Other (such as UN): Most of the libraries obtained
the basic United Nations reference tools. Three were partial depositories for UN materials. The libraries that were
not depositories cataloged their UN documents. Other types
of international documents were not collected. There was
little acquisition of UN materials beyond basic sources and
sale items.

Staffing and Services

The amount of staffing devoted to documents varied. The

general pattern of professional staffing was a reference librarian who devoted approximately 50 percent of his or her time to documents. The professional was usually supported by a half-time clerk and five to twenty hours of student help.

Only one professional counted himself as a full-time documents librarian. The rest reported varying percentages of time devoted to documents, ranging from 10 to 75 percent. The professional's time was mainly spent with the selection of and reference services for documents. Some librarians took care of check-in procedures, but support staff were usually responsible for that time-consuming duty.

Documents questions usually come to the general-reference desk (most libraries do not have a separate documents desk), where questions are handled by the reference librarian, with referral to the documents librarian if necessary. Since the documents librarian is usually also a reference librarian, the patron often finds the documents librarian at the desk. Reference service for documents is usually handled in the same way as all other reference services.

When asked if other staff members have documents expertise, the libraries generally responded, "Yes, a general knowledge." Many of the librarians were not satisfied with their coworkers' handling of documents. This is especially crucial, since most of the document questions are fielded through the reference desk. Two librarians held seminars to train other librarians in document use. Most of the documents librarians felt that the other librarians could handle the basic tools, such as Monthly Catalog, but were less confident about their handling of more complex questions.

Bibliographic instruction, when conducted at all, is primarily for upper-level classes in subject areas that use documents heavily and is tailored to the specific needs of the individual class. Some instruction is also done in freshman orientation or rhetoric classes, but that is usually very cursory. Most librarians mentioned one-on-one instruction as their main form of bibliographic instruction.

When we asked about faculty awareness of government publications we received very mixed reactions. Most of the librarians saw faculty use and awareness as critical in promoting student use. Faculty awareness was seen as high in such subject areas as political science, history,

economics, and government programs. But faculty interest
in documents is for class assignments rather than faculty
research. Some librarians reported frustration in attempting to increase faculty awareness of documents. Overall,
individual faculty members' awareness that documents are
important was seen as the key to high use by students.

User aids addressing documents per se are not used
very much in college libraries; one-page handouts on the use
of specific tools or indexes, such as Research in Education,
were common. Some librarians developed bibliographies of
documents for specific classes in order to demonstrate the
potential of documents for research, and others used
bulletin-board displays. All too often, however, librarians
have made no real effort either to publicize documents or to
facilitate their use.

Collection Development and Use

Support of the curriculum was mentioned by all librarians as
the main factor in selection policy. One library did have a
profile of areas it wished to collect, in a variety of genres,
such as statistical materials. Special areas of collection for
specific classes or departments included geology, American
history, energy, sociology, political science, census materials, economics, anthropology, business, HEW--for social
sciences, labor materials, demographic materials, State Department materials, Department of Justice materials, biology,
and psychology. For the most part, however, few libraries
have conducted formal evaluations of their collections, and
weeding has become, by default, the primary means of evaluation.

Students were perceived as the biggest users overall,
while faculty use was variable. Most libraries reported
somewhere between little and moderate use, with only two
libraries reporting heavy use. One library reported that it
used documents to answer 40 to 45 percent of its reference
questions, while another reported using documents to answer
one-third of its reference questions. Librarians at this institution seemed highly committed to integrating documents
into their reference process. A prominent physical location
and closeness of documents to the reference desk seemed to
promote document use. All libraries felt that the full potential of their collection was not being exploited.

Particular materials mentioned as heavily used were

publications related to the census, Congressional Record, Congressional hearings, committee prints, statistical materials, Presidential Commission materials, State, Interior, and Labor Department materials, and Supreme Court opinions. This is a very subjective conclusion, however, since most libraries do not keep any statistics on document use. While they may keep some circulation statistics, this reflects a small percentage of the documents actually used. Some libraries lack even this measure of use, since they do not allow documents to circulate. One library with 90,000 documents estimated that its annual circulation of documents was 1,000, with room use of 3,000--this was compared with a general circulation of 60,000 items. The librarian saw this as low use because documents took up one-eighth of the available floor space of the library.

General Impressions

The degree to which librarians feel positive about the potential of documents as a resource for the college community is related to the level of documents use. Since students seldom access documents on their own, the librarian is a crucial link between this resource and the user. The librarian's energy in informing faculty, who then promote documents for class assignments, provides a cumulative positive effect on the better exploitation of the depository collection. Faculty involvement is very important. Faculty were often involved with selection, and selection centered around faculty requests. Most libraries reported growing cooperation between faculty and the library.

Cooperation with other libraries was often mentioned. The libraries might not select an item because they knew that a nearby library would obtain it. This was especially true for technical literature, which was often mentioned as an item that the libraries did not collect. The librarians stressed that since their colleges did not have graduate programs, they did not support research.

Libraries also cooperated with nearby public libraries. One library had a program of conducting seminars in document use at the public library. Two libraries said that they tried to select items that the general public would use, but this was not the general trend.

There was not much interest in bibliographic instruction or in user aids. The librarians felt the lack of user aids more than the lack of instruction, perhaps because the librarians stressed one-on-one instruction, which is probably easier in a small college than in a large university.

Colleges Without Depository Collections

Attitudes toward documents were strikingly different in the nondepository libraries surveyed than they were at the depository libraries. Nondepository libraries were reluctant to discuss documents and felt that documents were not especially important. These librarians reported little faculty or student demand for more documents and contended that, while becoming a depository would increase their resources, they could not justify the increased expenses associated with depository collections.

All of the nondepository libraries did receive some documents. Of the items recommended for a basic collection by the Depository Council to the Public Printer these libraries generally obtained the Congressional Record, the Monthly Catalog, the Government Manual, the Statistical Abstract, and the Congressional Directory. They also selectively acquired census tracts and committee hearings. The acquisition of those latter items often grew out of faculty requests.

A primary cause of the paucity of documents in these nondepository libraries is the difficulty of selection. Lacking any formal selection policy, they relied on faculty requests, reviews, and a skimming of the Monthly Catalog or Selected List for ideas. Many of the librarians felt the need for a published list of recommended documents for small colleges.

All of those libraries report a low level of documents use. This problem is apparently caused by an amalgam of circumstances. First, the small number of documents in the collection makes it difficult for the librarians to arouse student and faculty interest in documents. The patrons' apathy seems to have led to apathy on the part of the librarians. Thus they did not conduct bibliographic-instruction programs on documents and failed to provide user aids for their patrons. The one librarian who had initiated a trial program to acquaint faculty members with documents reported a complete lack of success. It thus seems probable that these libraries lack the critical mass of documents needed

to mount a successful program, and, in conscious or uncon-
scious recognition of this fact, the librarians are making
little effort to expand documents use.

The handling of documents is also different at nondepository libraries. All of those surveyed integrated documents into the general collection, although one library had
tried, and had abandoned, a separate collection. Most patrons' requests for documents were handled either through
interlibrary loan or by referring the patron to a depository
library. To facilitate these processes most of the libraries
had a cooperative arrangement with a library offering depository service. The librarians involved seemed to feel that
these arrangements were satisfactory for their needs.

Nondepository librarians seem to have a dualistic
view of documents. On the one hand, they see documents
as a separate and unique resource that is somehow beyond
their needs and means. On the other hand, however, they
acquire and handle documents just as they would any other
items. This means that since no one person is really responsible for selecting documents or for becoming familiar
with them, documents are a largely neglected area.

Conclusion

The findings of our survey indicate that there is a great
deal of difference between college libraries with depository
status and those without. There is a greater tendency on
the part of librarians with depository status to feel that
documents are underused. Ironically, librarians in institutions without depository status did not generally seem to feel
this was a problem, even though documents at their institutions are barely used at all.

A follow-up telephone interview to one documents librarian in the sample (selected because of her positive attitude toward documents), who served a college of 1,870 students, was conducted to obtain some information about the
value of the depository collection.[22] She calculated the cost
of subscribing to serials obtained via depository status at
her library as $3,472.15. This included some items that
the library might not obtain if it did not have depository
status, but most college librarians would agree from the
partial list of serials obtained by this library that these
items are critical to a working college collection.[23] The

interviewee also noted that the many monographs and valuable pamphlet materials obtained on deposit enabled her to serve her faculty in a much more sophisticated way than if she did not enjoy depository status. Her selection policy focused on material of use to a college collection and did not replicate the research holdings of a university. She noted that "although staff time is costly, the benefit of documents, even outside of the substantial savings in serials and monographs, inheres in large part simply in current awareness of government that we can provide to our faculty and student body."[24]

This pilot study has underscored the paradoxical nature of documents as a resource for college libraries. While we assert that documents are really no different from any other resource, the very real problems of special acquisitions procedures, special selection tools, lack of reviewing media, and high costs make them different for the nondepository library.

The depository librarians in our sample, like depository librarians studied in previous research, are striving to make documents an integral part of the college collection. They do this by fostering an attitude that providing information, wherever it is found, is part of the service of their library. Like other depository librarians, they feel that documents are underused.

The nondepository librarians in our sample do not generally perceive documents as a major resource. The financial burdens and lack of staff that beset small colleges militate against staff time being assigned to pursue documents in the rather roundabout way that they must be pursued when libraries do not have depository status.

This survey points to several things that must be done to maximize government publications as a resource for college libraries. First, a full-scale study of college libraries holding depository status should be undertaken to provide us with data to develop guidelines and standards. Second, those libraries with depository status must work to achieve full integration of documents into the information services of their institutions. Documents should not be housed in dusty basements and accessed only when specifically requested. They should be a regular part of the information resources of the library. Third, some vehicle must be developed to enable college libraries without depository status to begin to acquire documents in a workable manner.

College library collections are special in their close attention to the needs of the curriculum and their students. This specialness can be enhanced if documents are seen as a major resource and selected as are monographs and serials--with particular attention to the demands of the community. Failure to incorporate documents into the selection policies of college libraries can only result in a lowering of the quality of the college collection. Many college librarians are now struggling to develop superior collections that do incorporate documents. We commend their efforts and hope that this article points out the importance of government publications and the great need for attention to this source of information.

Notes

[1]William Miller and D. Stephen Rockwood, "Collection Development from a College Perspective," College & Research Libraries 40 (July 1979): 318-24, also reprinted in this volume.

[2]"GODORT Membership as of April 30, 1979," DTTP 7 (July 1979): 139.

[3]Yuri Nakata, From Press to People: Collecting and Using U. S. Government Publications (Chicago: American Library Association, 1979), p. vii.

[4]U. S. Congressional Joint Committee on Printing, Federal Government Printing and Publishing: Policy Issues, Report of the Ad Hoc Advisory Committee on Revision of Title 44 to the Joint Committee on Printing (Washington, D. C.: Government Printing Office, 1979), p. 41.

[5]The first depository library was designated in 1814; the General Printing Act of 1895 systematized the depository library system, as described by Nakata, pp. 9-11.

[6]Joe Morehead, Introduction to United States Public Documents, 2nd ed. (Littleton, Colo.: Libraries Unlimited, 1978), p. 138.

[7]Guidelines for the Depository Library System (as adopted by the Depository Library Council to the Public Printer, October 18, 1977) (Washington, D. C.: Government Printing Office, 1977).

[8]Bernard M. Fry, Government Publications: Their Role in the National Program for Library and Information Services (Washington, D. C.: National Commission on Libraries and Information Science, 1979), p. 46.

9George W. Whitbeck and Peter Hernon, "The Attitudes of Librarians Toward the Servicing of and Use of Government Publications; A Survey of Federal Depositories in Four Midwestern States," Government Publications Review 4 (1977): 183.

10Ibid., pp. 183-84.

11Fry, pp. vi-vii.

12"Number of Institutions of Higher Education and Branches, by Type, Control, and Size of Enrollment: United States, Fall 1975," in Yearbook of Higher Education: 1977-78 (Chicago: Marquis Academic Media, 1977), p. 612. The next breakdown goes from 2,499 to 4,999 and adds 218 institutions to the 2,499 figures. For our purposes here we take the lower figure as more typical of the universe of college libraries.

13This information is not readily available. We determined this by checking the enrollment of every academic library with depository status (770) against the College Bluebook.

14Shirley Edsall, A Study of the Administration, Utilization, and Collection Development Policies of Government Document Collections in Community College Libraries Which Have Been Designated as Depositories (Arlington, Va.: ERIC Document Reproduction Service, ED 146 954, 1977).

15George W. Whitbeck, Peter Hernon, and John Richardson, Jr., "The Federal Depository System: A Descriptive Analysis," Government Publications Review 5 (1978): 253-67.

16Whitbeck and Hernon, "Attitudes of Librarians."

17George W. Whitbeck and Peter Hernon, "Bibliographic Instruction in Government Publications: Lecture Programs and Their Evaluation in American Academic Library Depositories," Government Publications Review 4 (1977): 1-11.

18Dawn McCaghy and Gary R. Purcell, "Faculty Use of Government Publications," College & Research Libraries 32 (January 1972): 7-12.

19Peter Hernon and Sara Lou Williams, "University Faculty and Federal Documents: Use Patterns," Government Publications Review 3 (1976): 93-108.

20Ibid., p. 103.

21Guidelines for the Depository Library System, "Appendix A," p. 10.

22Joan Hopkins, interview held at Illinois Benedictine College, Theodore F. Lownik Library, Lisle, Illinois, August 28, 1979.

23Items Hopkins obtained via the depository system that she indicated were critical to good service include: Monthly Catalog; Congressional Record; Research in Education; Busi-

ness Conditions Digest; Catalog of Federal Domestic Assistance; Children Today; Aging; Code of Federal Regulations; Federal Register; Abridged Index Medicus; Background Notes; Commerce Business Daily; Consumer Price Index; Department of State Bulletin; Department of State Newsletter; Digest of Public Bills and Resolutions; Energy Research Abstracts; FDA Consumer; Foreign Economic Trends and Their Implications for the U.S.; Internal Revenue Bulletin; Monthly Checklist of State Publications; Monthly Labor Review; NASA Activities; Nuclear Safety; Occupational Outlook Quarterly; Overseas Business Reports; Public Laws; Social Security Bulletin; Slip Opinions of the Supreme Court; Survey of Current Business; Treasury Bulletins; Treaties and Other International Acts; Weekly Compilation of Presidential Documents.
24Interview.

APPENDIX:
QUESTIONNAIRE FOR DEPOSITORY LIBRARIES

Description of Collection

1. How is your collection organized?
    ___separate   ___integrated   ___mixed

2. How large is your collection?

3. What other categories of documents do you collect?
    Home state___   How classified?

    other states___

    municipal or local___   How classified?

    other (such as UN)___

4. What level of staff supports the documents collection?

Services Provided

5. What happens when someone asks a document question?
    Does anyone else other than the documents librarian
    provide service?

6. Do other librarians have a general knowledge of documents?

7. What type of bibliographic instruction is done with documents?

8. How would you rate the faculty's awareness of documents as a resource?

9. What types of user aids have you developed?

Collection Development

10. How do you decide what items to select? Do you have any form of a selection policy?

11. Do you collect in any special areas for specific classes or departments?

Use of Collection

12. Who uses your collection?
    ___students   ___faculty   ___outside college

13. Level of use.
    ___little used   ___moderately used   ___heavily used

14. Does there seem to be any specific type of material that is heavily used?

Evaluation of Use

15. Do you keep any statistics on document usage?

16. Have you ever done any type of evaluation of your collection, or the use of your collection?

Questionnaire for Non-Depository Libraries

1. Most libraries that are not depositories integrate their documents into their general collection. Is that the case in your library?

2. As a library that is not a depository, how do you go about obtaining documents? Do you use any of the following?

___ Selected List   ___ Monthly Catalog

___ jobber for documents

3. Do you obtain any of the following items?

___ Congressional Record   ___ Monthly Catalog

___ Government Manual   ___ Statistical Abstract

___ Congressional Directory   ___ Census Tracts

___ Committee Hearings

4. If a patron comes in with an exact citation to a government document, what happens?

5. Is there any faculty demand for documents? Do faculty require documents for any of their classes or for their own research?

6. Is there any involvement of documents in a general bibliographic instruction program?

7. Have you developed any user aids for government documents?

8. Can you recall any specific documents or group of documents that are heavily used in your library?

9. Do you cooperate with any other library that does have a depository program?

10. In a college library, there seems to be two views of documents. In a college library with a depository collection, much time and money is spent on the collection, so that the staff may try to use documents more, in order to justify the expenditure. In a library without a depository program, the same level of service may be reached by using other resources, without spending the time and money on a depository program. Could you comment on these two views, and how they relate to your situation?

PLANNING THE COLLEGE LIBRARY BUILDING: PROCESS AND PROBLEMS

Frazer G. Poole

Introduction

It has now been a little more than a decade since the general availability of federal funds gave rise to the biggest building boom in academic library construction ever experienced in the United States. During that period, which lasted from about 1965 to 1975, more than 650 new college and university libraries were constructed. Today, with the drying up of government funding, the building boom has subsided and new college library construction is at a low ebb. There will always be, however, a need for some new library facilities-- whether these be new buildings, remodeling projects, or additions--and this article is intended to provide insight and guidance into the planning process for those to whom the responsibility for such projects may fall. It is not intended to provide detailed technical information on building planning. For this the reader's attention is directed to the selected bibliography at the end of the article.

During the period when academic library construction was at its height there appeared a number of articles, all written to assist librarians in planning their new buildings. It would be interesting to know how successful these efforts may have been. The evidence, if one is to judge from the limited number of really first-class academic libraries constructed during this period, and those that continue to be built, suggests that too often this advice goes unheeded, or, largely for reasons beyond librarians' control, is ignored.

233

Metcalf's definitive volume, Planning Academic and Research Library Buildings, has been the library planner's bible since it was published in 1965. Although out of date in some respects, and with omissions of some topics of major interest in library planning today, this is being corrected in a revised edition now in preparation by the American Library Association. Other library consultants, such as Mason, Ellsworth, Rohlf, Thompson, and McAdams, made significant contributions to the literature of library planning. With few exceptions their recommendations and guidelines are as applicable today as they were a decade ago, and librarians faced with the task of planning a new college library should not ignore this earlier literature.

Initiating the Planning Process

Planning the new building usually begins with the realization by the librarian and the staff that the existing facility is overcrowded and too small--too small for the book collection, or too small for the number of readers who wish to use it, or too small to permit the introduction of new services not planned when the building was designed, or perhaps all three. Communication of these deficiencies to the administration generally elicits the response that funds for a new building are not available. There then follows a period of constant effort to identify and use every possible square foot of space in the building.

Eventually, if the director makes a strong case and makes it often enough, there will be high-level recognition of the problem and some degree of approval for initiation of the planning process. In most instances the librarian will have anticipated such approval and will have already begun to gather data and outline the building program. Whenever possible, the director should visit a number of new libraries, libraries comparable to the one he or she envisions, to compare notes with colleagues, identify problem areas, and gather ideas to be incorporated in the director's own plans.

In most situations the librarian will be asked to document the need and to demonstrate the inadequacies of the existing building in terms either of some recognized standard or of other comparable institutions. One librarian mounted a successful campaign for the approval of a new library building when he compared his insitution with several others, all of which were academic competitors. He was able to demonstrate that these libraries had less library use and more seating, more square feet, newer buildings, and larger book budgets. The inadequacies of his own building and budget made a glaring contrast with those of his colleagues and led eventually to the approval of a new library building.

Although generally of somewhat limited usefulness, Formula C of ACRL's "Standards for College Libraries" may occasionally be used to advantage in convincing a college administration of the inadequacy of an existing library.

In addition to such comparative statistics, the director can effectively use data from his or her own library, e. g., the linear feet of unused shelf space, the number of books sent to storage because of lack of shelf space, the inadequacy of certain library activities resulting from lack of space, or the inadequacy of seating at peak periods. Other measures of inadequate facilities or shortage of space may be useful in particular situations.

After receiving the necessary approvals the librarian can turn to the detailed task of planning; but before doing so it will be useful to discuss a major problem area that usually manifests itself early in the planning process.

The Politics of Planning

The librarian planning a new building should realize early on that the planning of the new library and, in the end, the building itself will be subject to a variety of pressures that can only be described as political, i. e., there will be pressures dictated not by considerations of function, economy, student convenience, or staff efficiency but by the personal likes and dislikes of superiors and colleagues, the plans and ambitions of other academic units, and the degree to which the architect is willing to listen and learn about the functional requirements of the library.

Recognition, at the earliest stages of planning, of the importance of these factors is essential in overcoming them, although there will be situations that the librarian must accept if planning is to go forward, even though this may mean a less-than-successful building.

In one instance the library that should have faced a

main campus thoroughfare, where it would have provided the most convenient access for hundreds of students and permitted a building with only one entrance, had to be oriented ninety degrees from the street, with the result that two entrances were required and access for students made significantly more inconvenient, solely because the administrative official in charge of campus planning lived across the street from the proposed site and did not want to "face the mass of a large building."

In another instance a college administration, which objected to obstructing one end of the campus quadrangle, almost forced a college library to go underground, increasing costs and effectively eliminating the possibility of later expansion. Only the last-minute discovery, after working drawings were nearly completed, that the water table was so close to the surface that an underground structure was impossible led to approval of the far more appropriate and convenient site--above ground at the end of the quadrangle.

Delegation of responsibility for oversight of library planning not to the librarian but to a campus planning officer who would much prefer to use the library building funds for construction of a new field house; selection by the college president of an architect who also happens to be a relative-- or, in one case, a golfing partner--but may have few other qualifications for designing the new library; or an arbitrary decision that only so much money can be allocated to the proposed building--all these are among the "political problems" that often affect the planning process.

In many such instances there will be little or nothing the librarian can do to change the situation. At the same time "forewarned is forearmed," and the librarian should be aware that such situations can and do occur. Thus it is important to reach an understanding (with the college president if possible) about the librarian's authority and responsibility at the earliest possible moment in the planning process.

Delegation by the president to an administrative assistant, rather than to the librarian, of authority to communicate with the architect and to make major building decisions almost always works to the detriment of the new building. Whenever possible the librarian should try to obtain such authority, with major problems to be resolved by the president, not by an administrative assistant. Lacking such authority, the librarian should seek approval to bring such matters to the attention of the president for final resolution, if there is reason to believe that any decision at a lower level is seriously inimical to the proper design and functioning of the new building.

In many instances, either because of a lack of the required experience or because professional support in a situation with political overtones will apparently be needed, the librarian is well advised to obtain the services of a library building consultant. Often the consultant has access to a higher level in the administrative hierarchy than the librarian, although this is not always true. Often, too, it is the familiar situation of prophets in their own country--the outsider has more influence than the person on the scene.

The Library Building Program

A carefully prepared, detailed, written building program is the foundation stone of a good building. This is not to say that such a program will guarantee a good library, but it is always the most effective means of communicating to the architect the basic criteria to be used in designing the building. The writer knows of a library that was designed on the basis of a one-page program. A few have been constructed without any written programs. Such buildings are rarely successful. Those that do achieve some limited degree of success are due more to architects who are willing to take on the librarian's work, or to good luck, than they are to good planning.

In summary, a good building program is essential to a good building, and it is not overstating the case to say that it may well be the most important document that many librarians will ever write.

Functions of the Building Program

A written building program serves four basic purposes:

1. It gives necessary guidance to the architect and the architect's staff. Not only is the program the architect's bible in the design process, it is also the librarian's basic "contract" with the architect. The librarian can make no greater mistake than to assume the architect is clairvoyant or omniscient and thus will instinctively know the require-

ments of a new library. Such basic data as the required
book capacity, the number and type of reader seats to be
provided, the space required for staff work areas and offices, and the details of other essential features constitute
the information needed by the architect.

2. It demands detailed consideration and analysis of
the library's present and future organizational structure, library services, growth of collection and staff, technological
developments, and other factors that may influence building
design. Prepared in advance of the initial meeting with the
architect, the librarian and staff have time to think through
such problems in an orderly and systematic fashion and thus
reach viable conclusions.

If the required decisions are postponed, they can only
be resolved after the architect's work begins, usually around
a conference table, when the need for immediate information
and quick decisions effectively prevents the careful, logical
thinking and analysis good planning requires.

3. It provides a record of the decisions made and,
if properly documented, the reasons behind such decisions.
Every decision in the program should be documented, i.e.,
the rationale should be recorded for future reference. More
than once the librarian will wish to look back at the reason
for a particular decision. Such a record can be very helpful. Thus, for example, the seating capacity of a new building should be based on the official enrollment projections of
the institution, and such projections should be incorporated
in the program. Similarly, staff work-space requirements
in the program should be based not upon some rule-of-thumb
percentage but upon a carefully developed organization chart,
a detailed analysis of the staff required to operate the new
building, and a careful appraisal of the work space needed.

4. Finally, a written building program provides an
opportunity for the librarian to submit the document to the
administration for official approval before transmittal to the
architect. There are certain obvious advantages to such a
procedure, not the least of which is that it eliminates the
need for the architect to seek administrative approval for
every proposed feature of the new building. Submission of
the written program for official approval also provides an
opportunity for the administration to make any recommendations it thinks appropriate. The librarian may or may not
agree, but it is far better to resolve the question of a snack

bar, of faculty offices, or of some other special facility desired by the administration, at the outset than after the
building is under design.

Preparation of the Building Program

A library building program is a written document setting
forth the background, purpose, scope, and functions of the
proposed new building.   There is no standard pattern for
these statements and no two programs are precisely the
same.   The organization, the depth of coverage, and the
degree of detail vary with the author.   Unfortunately, but
not infrequently, the length and depth of coverage will depend upon the time schedule, although a good program requires at least three months to prepare.

Where planning begins well in advance of selection
of the architect or the availability of funds, there is normally ample opportunity for the librarian to devote the necessary
time to the thinking and staff discussion that should precede
the preparation of a written statement.   Adequate planning
time also allows opportunity for consultation with faculty,
for visits to other libraries, for correspondence with colleagues on points that may pose special problems, and,
finally, for the careful writing of a program that will cover
clearly and fully all those aspects of the new library that
the architect will need to know in order to design a successful building.

In the ideal situation the building program should be
prepared by the librarian.   In others, especially in those
situations where the librarian is inexperienced or does not
have time to write the program, a library building consultant
may be brought in.   In some instances the consultant may
write the entire program.   Less frequently an architect as-
sists in preparing the program.   In most instances, however,
this is an undesirable practice, for the simple reason that
architects lack the necessary in-depth knowledge of library
operations.   Architect-prepared building programs concentrate on architectural matters and may set forth the architect's viewpoint at the expense of the library's functional
requirements.   Unless the librarian feels fully qualified by
reason of long experience, the work of writing the program
should be assigned to a building consultant who has dealt
with a dozen or more library buildings and will probably
have prepared several building programs as well.

Whether the librarian or a consultant prepares the
program, however, it is essential that library staff members be involved in the planning, not only for the ideas and
assistance they can contribute but, of almost equal importance, as a means of developing a spirit of cooperation and
a feeling of participation in the project.

A consultant will wish to review the first draft of
the program, if it has reached this stage, or will want to
discuss the broader aspects of the program with the librarian to get a firsthand idea of the librarian's goals and objectives as these relate to the building.   The consultant will
also want to meet with the librarian and staff and with members of the library building committee, if there is one.

Even an experienced librarian will find it helpful to
visit a selected number of new libraries of the approximate
size of the proposed new building.   Although situations will
vary, libraries selected for such a tour should normally
have been operating for at least six months.   This will have
given the librarians involved an opportunity to have lived
with their buildings long enough to see where mistakes were
made or where one or more aspects of the planning could
have been improved.

We can now turn to the specific nature of the building
program, remembering that the architect will depend upon
this written statement for explanation of the building and its
functions.   Every detail that will give the architect more insight into the operation of the library and the needs of the
new building should be included in the program.

General Form of the Building Program

The following outline for a building program and the topics
to be included should be regarded only as suggestive.   What
is important, however, is that each and every area or function that requires space in the new building be mentioned
and discussed.   To omit any essential function from the
written program is to risk its omission from the ultimate
building.   It should never be assumed that the architect will
think of things the librarian has forgotten.   More than one
building has been completed without adequate storage space,
janitor closets, or librarians' conference room, simply because these essential spaces were not mentioned in the program.   In two recent cases multistory library buildings were

planned without elevators. Had these essential facilities been mentioned in the program it is unlikely they would have been forgotten. Fortunately, in one case, this serious omission was discovered in the final stages of planning, when a building consultant critiqued the architect's drawings. The other library was less fortunate--the four-story building was constructed without elevators, and staff members carry all the books up the stairs in their arms.

Introduction. The introduction should cover, as applicable, the following topics:

- Purpose of the program.

- Special comments about the planning schedule.

- Earlier programs, revisions, etc.

- Identification of those responsible for the program.

- Role of the library committee (if there is one).

- Acknowledgment of special help and assistance (e. g., support of the president, role of the library staff, etc.).

Institutional Background. This section should include a comprehensive statement describing the institution the library serves. This is the place to discuss the background and educational philosophy of the college, the academic future of the college, and present and projected enrollments. If a chart of the expected growth of the institution is available, it should be included here. Mention should be made of any unique or special features about the institution that may affect the new building or that distinguish it from other, similar institutions. Expansion of the curriculum, the addition of graduate programs, and service to users outside the college are among the factors that may warrant inclusion in the program.

Library Background. This section should discuss the important background aspects of library service. Usually included here are such elements as the following:

- Brief statement covering history of the library--if this is pertinent in later discussion of future plans.

- Present library situation--present building, location of parts of the collection, unusual or undesirable conditions that require solution.

- Administrative policy as regards centralization or decentralization of library services.

- Library policies--present and future as these are expected to affect library administration and services.

- Present size of the collection and future growth based upon present and projected budgets.

- Staff size and projected growth of staff.

- Special collections--rare books, etc.

- Departmental collections or libraries.

Architectural Considerations. Usually the librarian has arrived at some general conclusions about certain architectural matters. He or she may wish to emphasize the need for flexibility, to point out the importance of designing the building for later expansion, to discuss possible problems, such as entrances from two directions, special problems caused by a proposed site, the importance of good lighting, the need for environmental controls and the temperature and humidity parameters required, the general problem of fenestration, the need for acoustic control, the use of carpeting, the importance of color, special electrical problems (e.g., the need for underfloor ducts), and similar matters.

The librarian should never try, however, to play architect, but rather should state the problems to be solved and leave it to the architect to solve them. This is, of course, what the architect is paid to do. At the same time, most librarians will have certain ideas about the design of the new building. Within limits, there is no reason why these cannot be expressed in the program. Thus, while not presuming to suggest the structural system to be used in the building, if the librarian wants to indicate general objections to glass-box buildings, to great focal-point stairways, or to open light wells running from ground to skylight, there is no reason not to do so.

It should be remembered, too, that the librarian's successors must be able to operate the building after he or she has moved on to greener fields; the librarian should try to leave a building that will function under a new administration as well as under the old.

One of the more important architectural considerations is the site of the new building. In some instances the

librarian, the faculty library committee, and possibly the
consultant, will have given this extended consideration before
the architect is engaged. In a few cases no final solution
may be possible unless a master plan for the campus has
been developed. If no such plan is available, the architect
may suggest--and rightly so--that it be developed before
making a final decision on the site for the library. No extended discussion of this matter is necessary in the program,
but a paragraph noting the problem and the status of a solution will be helpful to the architect and possibly to others.

Functional Areas of the Building. Having covered the
introductory aspects and general background of the new building, the writer of the program is now in a position to discuss the functional elements or areas that must make up the
new building. Different writers organize this detailed material in different ways. The present writer has generally
found it useful to describe the library in terms of four major categories of space. These are not strictly logical in
all instances, and circumstances sometimes suggest a different arrangement, but they are applicable to most college library building programs.

● The service center (exit control, lobby, circulation
  desk, card catalog, bibliographic collection, reference collection, etc.).

● The subject reading areas (reader facilities, stack
  areas, newspaper and periodical collections, study
  rooms, etc.).

● Special collections and services (audiovisual, maps,
  documents, microtext facilities, copying services,
  archives, curriculum laboratory, reserved-book services, rare books, etc.).

● Staff work areas (administrative offices, acquisitions,
  and cataloging space, staff room, loading dock and
  receiving room, storage space, etc.).

The above list is only indicative. In a small library the
reserved-book collection may be handled by circulation-desk
attendants and discussed under the heading of "Service Center. " If larger, and not part of the service center, it might
be discussed under the heading "Special Collections and Services"; or, if sufficiently large, it could be discussed under
a separate heading.

Few architects, unless they have had significant

---

previous experience, have any real knowledge of the kinds of activities that take place in a library. Thus, in order to give the architect a clear understanding of these activities and of the physical requirements of the areas in which these activities occur, they need to be described in some detail.

One effective way of communicating this information to the architect is to provide a written description of the basic functions of each activity. This should be followed by a page (or pages) showing in detail, the number of square feet required for each function; the number of staff members (or reader stations) each area should accommodate; and the number of desks, tables, chairs, filing cabinets, computer terminals, typewriters, telephones, and other furniture and equipment items requiring either floor space or electrical/ telephone connections. This "inventory" helps the architect to visualize the functions and physical requirements of each area and prevents such instances as the one in which the architect's interior designer showed half of the furniture in technical services as lounge chairs.

Such data can be developed and presented in a standard format, one example of which is shown after the "Topical Outline and Checklist. "

Space Requirements and Space Summary. It is essential for the program to contain an estimate of the number of square feet required for each facility discussed in the program. Thus, for example, the description of an audiovisual service area might conclude with a statement of the space required as follows:

Audio-Visual Space Requirements	Assignable Square Feet
Earphone-listening facilities for 30 @ 25 sq. feet per station	750
Group-listening room for 20 @ 15 sq. feet per station	300
Service and storage areas	500
Film and preview facilities for 4 @ 90 sq. feet each	360
Total net sq. feet	1,910

At the conclusion of the program it is useful to include a summary of the space requirements for the individual areas.

In compiling this Space Summary one should remember that estimates of the space required for library functions are normally given as "assignable" square feet. That is to say, these figures represent the amount of square footage required for, or assigned to, library functions. The difference between the assignable square feet, as set forth in the program, and the total or "gross" square feet in the building, includes space for stairways, toilets, elevators, mechanical rooms, air shafts, janitor's closets, etc.

A good building will have about 70 percent of the gross space usable for library purposes. The remaining 30 percent is required for nonlibrary purposes. Such a building is said to be 70 percent efficient. Occasionally an architect may be able to arrange space so well that only 25 percent is required for nonlibrary purposes, but it is better to estimate on the basis of 70-percent efficiency. Focal-point stairways, open light wells, and similar architectural features significantly reduce this efficiency and seriously inhibit the proper functioning of the building.

At some point in the program the librarian should make clear that he or she is not trying to do the architect's work but is only attempting to develop a clear statement of the problems the architect must solve. The librarian's basic task in writing the program is to outline the requirements of each element of the building and to set forth the necessary relationships of these elements in order that the architect may arrive at a clear understanding of the overall problem.

The following outline is suggestive of the topics that should be covered in the program. It can also serve as a checklist for the later reviews and critiques of the architectural drawings.

Topical Outline and Checklist

SERVICE CENTER

Foyer or vestibule

Lobby

Exit control

Exhibit facilities--wall cases, movable cases, etc.

Bulletin boards--built-in, movable, etc.

Director of library offices

Hours of service

Telephones

Circulation services

Service counter--special requirements, number of staff to be accommodated

Reserved books--if included in circulation services

Work space for discharging books--special requirements for present and future charging systems

Telephone requirements

Book lift, if required, or need for proximity to service elevator

Central lighting control

Office space for circulation head

Book-truck storage space

Staging area (or proximity to adjacent shelving) for organizing books to be shelved

Locker or coat-rack facilities for staff

Time-clock location if required for student assistants

Book drops--service-counter drops, after-hours return facilities, special requirements

Reference facilities

Type of counter or desk, possibility of combining with circulation desk

Shelving for special reference collection

Telephone requirements

Office space--location and amount

Special requirements

Periodicals and periodical records

Periodical indexes--location

Central serials record--where located, how serviced

Visible record files for public use

Location and display of:

Unbound general periodicals

Unbound periodicals in subject fields--shelved by broad subject groups in stacks, displayed in single large periodical section or room, etc.

Bound general periodicals

Bound periodicals in subject fields--classified, filed with monographic materials, filed in single large periodical section

New book display

Paperback book display

Newspaper display and reading

Card catalog (or COM CAT, or on-line terminals)

Number of units required

Size of units required (60 vs. 72 tray)

Catalog reference tables

Type of catalog--dictionary or divided

Space required for catalog expansion

Lighting requirements for card-catalog area

Location of card catalog as related to use by technical services and reference staff

Traffic flow around card catalog

SUBJECT READING AREAS (BOOKS AND READERS)

Book stacks--type, arrangement, special units

Reading facilities--types of equipment, general arrangement

Individual study tables

Individual study carrels

Multiplace tables

Multiplace electronic carrels

Enclosed carrels

Lighting

Acoustical control

Lounge or informal reading areas

Browsing room--if any

Group Studies

Seminar room

Faculty studies

Smoking rooms

SPECIAL COLLECTIONS AND SERVICES

Microtext reading facilities

Audiovisual or media facilities

Rare books

Archives

Maps

Government documents

Copying and reproduction services

Typing rooms

STAFF WORK AREAS

Administration
Librarian's office
Secretary's office
Other administrative offices
Conference room
Office-supplies storage
Staff restrooms

Loading dock and receiving room--general location and arrangement, relationship to technical services

Book storage facilities

General storage facilities

Technical Services

Acquisitions and cataloging department--arrangement and workflow, location of shelf list, location of trade bibliographies, relationship to bibliographic materials, relationship to card catalog, storage for books in-process, design of work stations, special files and equipment, computer terminals

Book processing area--facilities

Serials and government documents processing--if separate

Mending and binding

Storage for books awaiting processing

Other work areas not covered above or in other sections

Alphabetical Checklist

This is the place for a number of items that have not been discussed elsewhere. A partial list of such items is given below, but each library will have a somewhat different list.

Acoustics
Air-conditioning
Auditoria
Bells
Book-return chutes
Bulletin boards
Coat-room space
Clocks
Computer terminals
Doors
Drinking fountains
Electrical outlets
Elevators
Emergency exits
Fire-detection and -control systems
Janitor's storage
Keys and locks

Lighting
Machine room
Pencil sharpeners
Signs
Telephones
Toilets and quiet rooms

Space Requirements

Space Designation: _____

Assignable Square Feet: _____

Function or Use: _____

Relationship to Other Spaces: _____

_____

Number of Persons to be Accommodated: _____

_____

Number of Volumes to be Accommodated: _____

_____

Furniture and Equipment Required:

    Shelving _____

    Desks _____

    Files _____

    Tables _____

    Individual Study Carrels _____

    Etc.

Special Facilities Required:

    Air-conditioning _____

    Booklifts _____

    Drinking fountains _____

    Ducts for computer cables _____

Electrical _____

Elevators _____

Service Desk _____

Telephones _____

Work counter with sinks _____

Etc.

The Planning Team

Every good building is the result of a team effort. Libraries are no exception, although the team will vary from institution to institution. Ideally, perhaps, the team will consist
of the architect, the librarian, a consultant, and an interior
designer. To this will be added, in some situations, a member of the president's office, or the chair of a campus building committee, or some other representative of the administration.

The Architect

The architect, of course, is the first essential member of
the team; although the architect's role in the planning would
seem clear enough, several problems should be noted. It is
a common practice among architects to send a principal of
the firm to make the first presentations to the board of
trustees, or to whatever body has the authority to make final
decisions in this matter. This same principal may also attend the first few meetings with the librarian and other members of the team. Thereafter a subordinate member, often
with limited experience, may attend such meetings, often to
the detriment of the planning process. Insofar as is possible the college should have a clear understanding, written
into the contract, as to which member of the architect's
staff will represent the firm and be responsible for the basic
design of the building. As an example--in one recent situation the layout of space in a moderately large library was
assigned to a young and inexperienced member of the architect's staff. The architect brought to a meeting of the planning team plans that he himself had never reviewed. It was
left for the consultant to point out to the architect that the
only route by means of which two major departments could
reach other offices of the library, other than by going up
two floors, across the building and down two floors, was to
cross the large loading dock.

Another common practice is for the architect to assign a well-qualified staff member to begin the design work, then, when the work is underway, but far from finished, to assign the person to a new project and substitute a junior architect with less general experience and with no background in the library project. Such situations are not uncommon, and the librarian and the administration should make certain: (1) that the architect clearly accepts responsibility for the design work, and (2) that the staff member assigned to the library project will stay with the project.

The Librarian

The librarian is, or should be, the second essential member of the planning team. Unfortunately, this is not always true. There are, and probably will continue to be, a number of situations in which the librarian is removed from the planning process. In one library, later cited as one of the three or four worst-designed buildings in the United States, the librarian, by administrative fiat, was permitted no part in the planning process.

There have been a number of other, similar situations. Campus politics being what they are, there is no way in which such situations can be avoided in all cases. Nevertheless, it is clear that the librarian should, in nearly every case, be the representative of the college to the planning team. When lacking the necessary experience, the librarian should seek the approval of the administration to retain an experienced library building consultant. By the same token, if the college administration thinks that the librarian is not qualified because of a lack of experience, or for other reasons needs assistance, a consultant should be employed. It is a frequent but mistaken assumption for the administration to believe that the design of the building can safely be left to the architect.

Assuming, however, that the librarian is assigned adequate authority, it will be his or her task to work with the architect on a day-to-day basis and to carry the major weight of the decision-making process, backed by the consultant, if one is employed. In addition to a day-to-day association with the architect, the librarian is also the member of the team who should coordinate the roles of the library staff and other campus groups in the planning process.

Probably no two institutions assign responsibilities for

planning a new library to the same group or groups. Here again, politics often play a major role. The president may appoint a library building committee of which the librarian is only one member or may delegate the appointment of such a committee to the librarian. On some campuses the regular faculty library committee may serve as a faculty building committee. In such cases the librarian may also wish to appoint a building committee composed of members of the library staff. In any case, the librarian should be, if at all possible, the chairperson of such committee or committees and should be fully authorized to deal with the architect and make all final decisions related to the functioning of the building.

The Consultant

Already noted is the fact that unless the librarian has had previous experience in planning a library, in working with architects, in reading blueprints, in developing space requirements, and in the other tasks related to planning a new building, an experienced building consultant can be of invaluable assistance as the third member of the planning team.

The role of the consultant will vary from situation to situation. In far too many instances the consultant is called in only after problems have arisen and, with no previous exposure to the project, is then expected to review the plans and resolve the difficulties in a single meeting or possibly two meetings. In many, perhaps most, such cases the consultant is often forced into suggesting compromise solutions that still leave much to be desired. Some consultants are reluctant to accept these one-time "hand-holding" assignments because they are at an immediate disadvantage and in no position to use their experience properly. Others may accept such short assignments with the rationale that being of some help is better than being of no help at all.

In an excellent paper, most of it as valid today as when it was prepared twelve years ago, Rohlf[1] distinguishes between the "critic," engaged on a short-term, often one-meeting basis, and the "consultant," retained on a long-term basis, often for the duration of the project. Rohlf believes that "when a consultant is engaged on a full-project basis, he has the best opportunity to perform the greatest service for the money received."[2]

The present writer can add to Rohlf's pertinent

remarks on the subject the fact that consultants are often reluctant to accept the role of critic simply because after a one- or two-day exposure to the project they are all too frequently labeled as consultants to the project and charged with the mistakes that may have occurred in the planning but over which they had no control.

If the consultant's experience is to be fully utilized, he or she should be retained on a full-project basis, that is, should be employed at the very beginning of the planning process so as to have the opportunity to bring to bear the full weight of this experience. The consultant cannot be expected to solve, in the course of a single meeting, all the problems that may have arisen in the planning.

The question often arises as to whether the building consultant should be employed by the college or by the architect. Frequently the administration assigns responsibility for the consultant to the architect, along with engineering, lighting, and acoustical consultants. Such reasoning overlooks the important fact that the building consultant's primary contribution to the project lies in a knowledge of library space requirements, functional relationships, library administrative and organizational problems, and library technical services, as well as furnishings and equipment. The consultant should be available to assist and advise the librarian, not the architect. In a few instances architects may be unwilling for library consultants even to speak with the librarians unless the architect is present. Thus the experience of the building consultant is unavailable for use by the librarian except under the most formalized and structured conditions.

This situation becomes more serious when the consultant is employed by the architect and there arise differences of opinion as to the solution of a particular problem. In many such instances the consultant--who should always strive for total objectivity and impartiality--must in all conscience remember that basic loyalty must be to the institution. In most instances, but certainly not in all, the consultant's viewpoint on a controversial problem will coincide with that of the librarian; when it does not the obligation to the institution must be paramount.

When architects expect the total support of their consultants and this is not forthcoming in every instance, a strained relationship can develop. It is fortunate that such situations occur infrequently. Nevertheless, there is always

enough conflict of interest in these arrangements to suggest
strongly that the building consultant should be retained by
the college as adviser to the librarian and the institution.

One or two further comments about the role of the
consultant may be noted here.   Neither the librarian nor the
administration should feel any embarrassment about seeking
the aid of a building consultant.   In a day of increasing
technological development and specialization the person who
has had experience in planning fifteen, thirty, or more buildings can bring a great deal of valuable experience to bear on
a project, as compared with the librarian or architect who
may have worked on one library or on none.   There is as
much reason for the college to employ a building consultant
as for the architect to employ a lighting consultant.

Administrators may ask about the duties of the building consultant.   Space does not permit a detailed discussion
of such duties, but they may be outlined as follows.   Initially the consultant can assist the librarian in preparing the
building program, and in many instances may actually write
the program or a large portion of it.   The consultant's experience will be particularly valuable in calculating space requirements for book collections, seating, and staff work
areas.   A knowledge of the functional relationships of various
areas and of the environmental conditions desirable for the
preservation of the collections, a background in the various
architectural problems of special concern to libraries, and
a familiarity with the problems of other library buildings all
give the consultant a unique opportunity to contribute to the
design of the new building.

Once planning gets underway the building consultant
should review and critique the plans.   Such review may be
expected to range from recommendations for a better arrangement of functional areas, to questions about the adequacy of the space allocated to functional areas, to the
fenestration pattern, in the earlier stages of planning, to a
review of telephone and power outlets, the location of ducts
and water pipes, and similar matters, in the near-final
drawings.

Unless the librarian is adept at reading blueprints
such assistance will be invaluable.   Nor should it be expected that the architect will catch all of these problems,
omissions, or mistakes.   Indeed, long experience suggests
otherwise.   The library that found a six-inch water main

running through a rare-map vault housing millions of dollars worth of rare maps (fortunately discovered before it was too late), the multistory library built without elevators, the library with no drinking fountains, and the library that found a large air shaft running vertically through the circulation desk when the building was finished, could well have used a consultant to review and critique the drawings before it was too late.

Beyond that, the consultant should be available, as one member of the planning team, to advise the librarian, to meet with the architect and the librarian as requested, and to offer opinions and recommendations whenever they may be requested.

The Interior Designer

Also essential to the planning of a good building is the interior designer. In many instances there may be a competent design group on the architect's own staff; in others the architect may recommend or use an independent firm for this work. In still others the library (the college) may select and employ the interior designer. In many instances the third alternative is preferable. Certainly the librarian should beware of the architect who has a relatively inexperienced interior designer on the staff, a person who may have designed a few commercial offices or a motel lobby but has had no experience with libraries. It is this lack of experience that leads to such situations as occurred recently at a college library in which long rows of single-faced bookstacks (which are not and cannot be free-standing) were used as room dividers or as "walls" fitted with doors; all the lounge chairs in the library were placed side-by-side in a long row with their backs to the window wall that formed the front of the building; and the index tables were standing height (forty-two inches) but had flat rather than sloping tops and were equipped with stools of sitting height instead of high-chair height. In another instance the architect's interior-design team proposed to install a large lounge chair for each staff member in the Technical Services Department. Few such ridiculous proposals are ever carried out, but the librarian should not have to educate the interior designer.

It will repay the investment many times over for the library to retain a qualified interior design group with experience in equipping and furnishing libraries. There are a number of such firms or individuals working in this field, and all can provide expertise that will help make the new building successful from the viewpoints of both function and appearance.

The question is often asked: how soon should the interior designer enter the picture? The answer is: at the very beginning. A good interior designer is also a competent space planner, whose input is a valuable adjunct to the team effort. Indeed the work of interior design should go hand-in-hand with the development of the building plans.

These four, then, form the basic planning team: the architect, the librarian, the library building consultant, and the interior designer. Employing a good building consultant and a qualified interior designer will add only a small percentage to the total building cost. It is a fully justifiable price for a successful library.

Basic Building Considerations

The Site

Perhaps no problem is more difficult to solve in many situations than the site of a new library on an existing college campus. If the trite saying that the "library is the heart of the campus" bears any truth, then in theory the new building should be so located that it is equally convenient of access for all students and faculty--from classrooms, dormitories, parking lots, and the student union.

Desirable though this may be, in most cases it is impossible. On some campuses the original library building stands in the location where the new library ought to be. In other situations the most convenient site is occupied by some other building. If the old library stands on the best site for the new library, then it is necessary to face the problem of tearing it down and building on the old site. In the great majority of instances this is a totally impracticable solution-- first, because there is unlikely to be any place to house the library during the process of demolition and new construction, to say nothing of the cost involved, and second, because space that might be converted to some other useful purpose will be lost to the college.

Thus it becomes necessary to find a new site that

still has a high degree of convenience. Such a decision cannot be made without consideration of the master plan for the campus. Somewhat surprising is the fact that many colleges lack master plans, reacting primarily to the requirements of the moment. On occasion the approval of a new library building triggers the development of a master plan. If begun in time, this may be highly desirable, but if done under the threat of delay to a new library, such a master plan may be worse than no master plan.

Where no master plan exists the librarian can only look at the direction of campus growth, try to obtain some idea of where the next academic buildings are likely to be located, and discuss the problem with the administration and the architect.

Wherever the building is located, it should provide the following essential features:

1. Enough vacant land to accommodate the proposed building with enough remaining land for a substantial addition to the building fifteen to twenty years hence. (Vertical additions, although possible, are costly and often impractical.)

This suggests that the exact size and shape of the new building should be known before the site is selected. In practice this is rarely possible. At the same time, careful analysis by the architect will usually indicate whether the proposed site is likely to be adequate. What sometimes happens is that the site is selected for political reasons, i. e., reasons that have nothing to do with the needs of the building. Thus the site for one library was chosen solely because of its historical associations. As a result, the building was forced to assume an "L" shape that was completely at odds with the functional requirements of the library. To make the situation worse, it was necessary to create two pedestrian walkways through the building at ground level, thus forcing a design in three segments, the legs forming two segments and the juncture of the two legs a third.

In other, less extreme, cases there may be no viable alternatives. On one metropolitan campus the only available open land dictated a design that was too shallow and too elongated for maximum efficiency. In such instances there is, of course, no choice except to use the space available as effectively as possible.

Libraries included as part of a much larger building

designed primarily for other purposes are always at a disadvantage for two major reasons: (a) the requirements of
the other functions nearly always dictate the shape and size
of the library portion of the building, and (b) there is rarely any opportunity for expansion of the library in a combination structure. Thus one recent college library occupying
the lower floor of a multistory campus building and placed
immediately adjacent to the student union in the same structure encountered problems in the initial design and will face
even larger problems when it outgrows its present facilities.

Sometimes (not always) the consultant can be helpful
in convincing college administrations of the impractical nature of such plans. Lacking the moral support and technical
expertise of a consultant, the librarian can only discuss with
the administration the long-range implications for the library
of a site selected solely for political reasons.

2. Reasonably convenient access from classrooms,
dormitories, and parking lots for the greatest number of
students. "Convenient access" is susceptible to different
interpretations, but a reasonable definition suggests that
students wishing to use the library between class periods
should not require more than five minutes to reach the library after a class is dismissed or more than that time to
get to their next class from the library. Sites that can be
reached in this time are more likely to be identifiable on a
college campus than on a large university campus.

Convenient access also suggests that students should
be able to reach the library at night without walking through
dark areas of the campus in going to and from the dormitories.

3. Access for trucks delivering mail and equipment,
and for other vehicles, including private automobiles carrying the physically handicapped. This requirement needs little explanation. Nevertheless, it is worth noting that the ·
increased emphasis society places on the provision of facilities for the physically handicapped has clear implications
for library design. This emphasis suggests the importance
of selecting a site readily accessible to those in wheelchairs
or on crutches, either by automobile or by pedestrian traffic
routes.

In addition, a good site should make it possible:
(a) to orient the building properly with respect to roads,
campus traffic patterns, and other buildings, and (b) to

introduce a lower or basement level if the requirements of
the building make this desirable.

Although it may appear to be a reminder of the obvious, these matters should be examined at the earliest possible time in the planning process.   It is an enormous and
wholly unjustified waste of college money to proceed to the
working-drawing stage before it is known whether soil conditions will permit construction of the proposed building, as
happened in the situation referred to earlier.

Expansibility

Expansibility is a basic concept in library design.   Despite
the prophesies of the few who believe that the printed page
will become obsolete by the year 2000, there is no supporting evidence to indicate that their crystal balls are any more
accurate than those who made essentially the same prophecies
in the 1950s.   The fact is that the book remains one of the
most convenient and practical artifacts for the transmission
of knowledge and is not likely to be superseded within the
next century, if then.

Weber[3] has forecast that by the year 2030

> Huge collections of film, fiche, videodiscs, and
> data sets will supplement books, journals, and re-
> ports.   These new formats will provide important
> new dimensions to library services, but most will
> be additions rather than replacements for printed
> works. ...   Extensive collections of published ma-
> terials on specific topics will remain the heart of
> the academic library.

Thus it is likely that the proportion of materials in micro-
formats to those in traditional book form will increase during the next half-century and that the rate of expansion of
academic libraries will be reduced somewhat as a result.
Nevertheless, it seems certain that libraries will continue
to grow, although probably at a slower rate.   Weber's remarks were developed in the context of research libraries,
but there is no reason to think that the situation in the undergraduate college library will be significantly different.
It is important now, as well as in the future, that librarians plan for reasonable growth and expansion, just as they
have in the past.

It is perhaps well to emphasize this latter point, since some administrators have read so much about the increasing use of microforms that they have come to believe that present-day library design is archaic and that planning libraries for the continued use of bound books is a waste of college money. The college library in a shoe box full of microfiche is as far from reality today as it was when it was first seriously proposed two decades ago. The present writer is willing to prophesy that no readers of this chapter will live to see the paperless library any more than they will live to see the paperless office, about which so much is being written today.

Future library expansion requires more than the setting aside of the necessary land. It involves a conscious design effort on the part of the architect. Unfortunately, too few architects seem able to view their present work in this light. Instead, they tend to see the new library as a complete entity in its first phase and are often unwilling to consider the possibility of expansion. It is, in fact, surprising to note how few libraries of the past quarter-century can be easily and effectively expanded.

One way to help ensure an adequate expansion is to require the architect, as part of the contract, to present a reasonably well-developed schematic drawing showing how and in what direction expansion could occur and to provide basic data on the book capacity, seating, and staff work spaces such an addition could provide.

Flexibility

Flexibility is a design concept that has received more attention in recent years than in the past, yet it remains a concept too often ignored. Complete flexibility is probably neither desirable nor attainable because of the high costs and complexities involved, but certain key principles should be observed. Thus in any college library the minimum elements of flexibility should include the following:

1. Self-supporting floors and free-standing bookstacks. All floors in the building should be self-supporting and capable of holding bookstacks arranged on conventional fifty-four-inch centers. This requires that all floors be capable of supporting a live load of 150 pounds per square foot.

More than one college library now faces the need to

expand its bookstack area, only to find that the architect
allocated one area of a given floor to bookstacks and designed the other areas of the same floor for office use or
seating space, but not for loaded bookstacks.

As serious as this failure to provide floors strong
enough to support bookstacks at any point is the college library designed with multitier stacks in which each level of
bookstacks supports the stacks above. If it ever becomes
necessary to use these stack areas for some other purpose
or to move some portion of the book collection, the librarian is faced with a veritable forest of steel columns, usually
arranged three feet on centers in one direction and four and
a half feet on centers in the other. Such problems are all
too common. Whether it be in the Thomas Jefferson Building of the Library of Congress, constructed in 1936, where
it is now desirable to convert one-time stack space to people
space, or in the small Midwest college library where central, multitier stacks in a library poorly designed in the beginning prevent reconfiguration of space for more effective
library operations, this lack of basic flexibility poses insurmountable barriers to the effective reassignment of library
functions.

2. Uniform, high-quality, glare-free lighting. The
lighting system should serve equally well in offices, bookstacks, and reading areas. This is not to suggest that all
lighting in the building should be of identical design and in-
tensity. Such a sameness in all areas would be both monot-
onous and unnecessary. It should, however, be possible to
move bookstacks and replace them with seating, or vice
versa, without any significant modification of the lighting
fixtures. Office areas, too, should be interchangeable with
both seating and bookstacks.

This subject raises the question of the use of general
overhead lighting versus the use of task/ambient lighting.
Space does not permit a full review of the pros and cons of
such lighting, but it should be noted that those consultants
with whom the present writer has discussed the subject are
in agreement that task/ambient lighting has not yet proved
itself in libraries. As one consultant phrased it: "I know
of no way in which one can design task/ambient lighting to
be sure of obtaining an even distribution of high-quality,
nonglare lighting on library working surfaces. " This is not
to say that fill-in light for office desks with service mod-
ules, for individual study carrels, and for some similar

situations is not desirable or necessary. In fact, such
auxiliary or supplemental lighting has been used in libraries
for a long time. Further, considerable research in this
field is currently underway, and better task/ambient systems may well be developed in the future. Nevertheless,
at this time, and in the present writer's opinion, the best
library lighting remains a well-designed general, overhead
lighting system.

Some engineers are now experimenting with indirect
overhead lighting for libraries. Such systems can offer
high-quality lighting, but in at least one installation there
were objectionable dead spots where unacceptable shadows
made seeing difficult. Whether these installations will provide energy-saving advantages and/or can provide superior
lighting remains to be seen.

3. Uniform environmental conditions that meet program criteria. Although surprisingly few heating, ventilat-
ing, and air-conditioning systems (HVAC) meet this basic
requirement, the written building program should make clear
what is expected of the system.

HVAC systems are often deficient in three major respects: (a) they are unable to maintain uniform conditions
throughout the building, (b) they are unable to maintain design parameters with regard to permissible fluctuations in
the temperature and humidity, and (c) they are unable to
maintain the conditions necessary to provide suitable temperatures and humidities in the rare-book room and different
temperatures and humidities in the rest of the library. In
one building recently visited by the writer winter humidities
in the rare-book and special-collections area ranged between
20 and 25 percent, while summer humidities are often 75
percent or higher. One area of the building was too warm
for comfort, another area too cool. This problem is discussed in greater detail in another section.

4. Other factors in flexibility. The use of underfloor ducts or other cable-carrying systems in technical
services, general offices, and other areas of the building
to provide for telephone, electrical, and computer cables;
reduction in the use of permanent walls in favor of movable
partitions; the use of modular design to achieve the maximum amount of open, usable floor space; and the avoidance
of focal-point stairways and large open wells running through
one or more floors--all are important in achieving desirable
flexibility.

264 • College Librarianship

Some additional comments may be useful here. The writer does not suggest that a college library ought to install an expensive underfloor duct system in all areas of a new building. He does suggest that the ability to provide telephone, electrical, and computer-terminal services in many areas of the building adds highly desirable flexibility to the future operation of any library. For this reason the several alternative methods of routing cables should be carefully considered during the planning process.

The advantages of modular design are so universally recognized that practically all libraries built during the past twenty years have been based on this concept. Occasionally, however, one sees a recently constructed nonmodular building. Without exception these have proved inflexible and inefficient.

Libraries with large focal-point stairways or with hundreds of square feet of floor space lost to open light wells are similarly wasteful, inefficient, and inflexible. Architects tend to point with pride to the "feeling of openness" such architectural features create. Librarians, on the other hand, decry the lost space, the inconvenience of walking around them to reach the other side, the degree to which noise on one floor is heard on other floors, and the extent to which they restrict or prevent adjustments in operational functions. One library of medium size, built over the librarian's protests, contained six such openings in the second floor and cost the library several hundred square feet of floor space. Recently, after spending thousands of dollars over a ten-year period, the library filled in the last of these wells and recouped the lost space. There may be instances in which such openings have advantages, but in most cases librarians would do well to resist these wasteful designs.

Simplicity of Design

The importance of simplicity in building design is less often considered in relation to library planning than it ought to be. Thus one sees library buildings that are overelaborate, complex, and clearly difficult for students to use easily or effectively. Good design locates the principal areas of the library where they are conveniently accessible. Interior layouts should permit students to orient themselves quickly and easily. Key areas of the building repeated on different floors should be arranged vertically in order to permit quick orientation. These are basic principles, but they are not always observed. Some examples will illustrate. In one college library the architect's first design included a reference collection of some 5,000 volumes located on a raised podium six feet above the level of the ground floor and without any seating accommodations. There was seemingly no understanding of the need for simplicity or flexibility, and no realization of the extra steps and time that such a scheme would have entailed for both reference librarians and students. Even more elaborate and complex was the college library design of one architect who proposed to make every bay a separate room. Such a scheme would have resulted in total frustration for students and librarians alike. In another instance the architect proposed a building with five floors of bookstacks and no elevators. The only access was via circular stairways in each of the four corners of the building. All seating was on the first floor. No more inconvenient design can be imagined. In another plan the restrooms were in different areas on each floor, an arrangement both inefficient and expensive. Fortunately, none of these plans was ever developed beyond the drawing stage because the clients involved made it clear that such schemes were unacceptable.

Complex building plans in which simplicity is too often overlooked tend to be more characteristic of large buildings than of the usual college library. Nevertheless, simplicity, convenience, and a straightforward approach to building design are essential characteristics of any good library. It is this type of complex design against which the librarian must be on guard and which suggests that the importance of simplicity and convenience be emphasized in the building program.

Economy and Efficiency

These attributes of a good building usually go hand-in-hand. In an era when budgets grow ever tighter, when book prices and subscription costs increase each year, and when staff salaries rise to keep pace with inflation, few librarians have the funds to support inefficient buildings, i.e., those that require an excessive number of staff to operate or in which the relationship of the various elements is inefficient and staff time is wasted in excessive travel time.

Most librarians and consultants are keenly aware of the effect of building designs that require additional staff to

operate. Indeed, it is because of the significantly greater
staffing costs that the subject-division arrangement, once
favored by many larger academic libraries, has been generally abandoned over the past two decades. The infrequent
building design that requires two entrances on the same level also adds to operating costs. More frequently seen is the
building that, because of the slope or contour of the site,
has an entrance/exit on each of two levels and thus two
staffing points. Such situations as this are sometimes un-
avoidable, but there is no excuse for the two exits necessi-
tated by the reorientation of the building for political reasons, as in the example noted earlier.

Some college libraries will wish to consider combining the reserved-book collection with the circulation desk in
order to reduce staff costs. In the small college library
aligning the circulation or loan desk and the reference desk
so that one person can service both points permits more effective use of staff at slack periods. Larger libraries, on
the other hand, usually should not attempt such economies,
since they are likely to result in reduced service to students
or may result in an undesirable concentration of traffic at
one point, as can happen when a very active reserved-book
collection is combined with the circulation or loan desk.

In most libraries some 85 percent of the microform
collection consists of periodical or serial-type materials.
For this reason locating the microform collection and reading facilities adjacent to or near the periodical collection
makes for greater student and staff convenience.

Before computer-output microforms resulted in the
COM catalog it was considered essential that the card catalog be located where it was conveniently accessible to students, reference staff, and technical services. Today libraries that have converted to COM catalogs find that it is
no longer important to locate the catalog near technical
services. In the future, when the college library has its
catalog on-line to the computer, the catalog will not necessarily be restricted to a particular location but can have
terminals placed where they can be most effective. This
suggests, of course, that the plans for a new building should
determine in advance where computer terminals may be
needed in order that necessary ducts or conduits can be provided.

Environmental Control

Effective environmental control has become increasingly important for research libraries, as librarians become aware
of the extent to which such factors as improperly controlled
temperature, humidity, and gaseous pollutants, as well as
dust and other particulate matter, affect the useful life of
their collections. Although the college library does not have
the same degree of justification for maintaining rigid environmental controls as does the research library, it is well to
realize that most modern library materials have a useful life
of less than fifty years unless the above factors are held
within reasonable limits. Moreover, most college libraries
have rare-books and special-collections departments, some
with holdings of substantial rarity and value. Here, temperature and humidity controls should be of even greater concern.

The importance of such controls should be noted and
emphasized in the building program since many architects
are unaware of them. Achieving some reasonable degree of
control of these environmental parameters is not only a matter of air-conditioning system design but of building design
as well. The rare-book room in one college library recently visited by the writer had large windows on the south and
west sides. Although the space was air-conditioned, it reg-
istered a heat gain of more than ten degrees each day--a
condition that the air-conditioning system was unable to control. There was virtually no humidity control in the room
(or in the library), and the collection was subject to humidities as low as 20 percent in winter and as high as 75 percent in the summer. On one wall of the rare-book reading
room in another library two large built-in bookcases were
exposed to the western sun for two hours each afternoon.
As a result, the bindings of the rare, leather-bound volumes housed here were seriously faded and the paper was
embrittled. In other libraries, supposedly air-conditioned
but with large window areas, heat gains of twenty or more
degrees have been observed.

Control of heat gain can be achieved by the use of
roof overhangs, heavily tinted or reflective windows, or by
omitting windows altogether in such areas as rare-book
rooms. It should be noted that internal blinds and draperies
will not provide the necessary degree of control and should
not be accepted as substitutes for more basic control measures. These are, of course, architectural problems to be
solved by the architect. In too many instances, however,

the architect must not only be alerted to the problem, but
the building design must be checked to make certain that it
will, in fact, provide the environmental control required.
In far too many instances the architect's desire to follow
some particular architectural design overrides the functional
requirements of the building.

Reducing heat gain (and controlling light) is only one
facet of environmental control, however. More important is
the proper design of the air-conditioning system. Again,
this is a problem for the architect and engineers. The librarian is responsible only for establishing the criteria to
be met by the system. Unfortunately, not all air-conditioning
systems are properly designed and thus capable of functioning
as they should. Here, the librarian is at a disadvantage, as
is the consultant, in not being in a position to evaluate the
air-conditioning design. A few consultants have, on occasion,
recommended that an independent engineer review the HVAC
design or have taken it on themselves to have such a review
made. Although a somewhat unusual procedure, this is a
wise precaution if there is any question about the effectiveness of the design.

Another difficulty in achieving adequate environmental
control is that of proper operation after the building has been
turned over to the college. In too many instances the campus engineer has simply not had the training to operate a
new air-conditioning system at maximum efficiency. The
tendency is to think that if it is reasonably cool in the summer and hot enough in the winter, no other criteria are
needed. Even a well-designed HVAC system will not provide
a stable, carefully monitored environment unless it is properly operated. Proper operation of the system depends on
the work of a qualified engineer who has complete understanding of the importance of environmental control.

In establishing appropriate criteria for the air-
conditioning system it is important to remember that there
are two essential aspects of environmental control: (a) the
maintenance of appropriate limits for temperature, humidity,
gaseous pollutants, and dust, and (2) the maintenance of a
stable, or nonfluctuating, environment. It is generally accepted by conservation scientists that a major factor in the
deterioration of paper is acid. Such acid may be built into
the paper as a result of the sizing used; may result from
the degradation of impurities, usually lignins; or may be the
result of absorption of such gaseous compounds as sulfur

dioxide, nitrous oxide, ozone, and other constituents of the atmosphere. In many cases all three causes are involved. Whatever the source, the acid results in a chemical reaction termed acid hydrolysis, which weakens or breaks the paper fibers and eventually results in severe embrittlement. As with all chemical reactions, the rate is accelerated at high temperatures and retarded at low temperatures. Extremely low temperatures are, of course, not practical in the ordinary library, but a reasonably constant temperature of 68° F will add many years of usable life to a research collection, as opposed to a temperature of 78° F, for example.

Without going further into the details, it is recommended that a well-designed HVAC system for a college library should be able to maintain a temperature range of 68° ± 2° F and a relative humidity of 45% ± 5% in the collection areas day in and day out throughout the year. Special-collections and rare-book departments should be able to maintain a temperature of 65° ± 2° F and a humidity of 50% ± 5% in the collection area.

In this connection it should be noted that repositories of cultural materials, including libraries, are eligible for exemption from the "Mandatory Thermostat Controls, Final Regulations" issued by the Department of Energy. Details will be found in The Federal Register of July 5, 1979, pp. 39354-69. Securing an exemption under these regulations is a matter of self-certification. The owner of the building must complete and post a "Certificate of Building Compliance" and must also file a "Building Compliance Information Form" with DOE. Forms are available from the Director, Office of Building and Community Systems, DOE, Office of Conservation and Solar Applications, 20 Massachusetts Avenue, N.W., Room 2221C, Washington, DC, 20585, Attn: Building Compliance.

Filtering both the incoming air and the recirculated air of the HVAC system is also important in maintaining a suitable environment for the long-range preservation of library materials. Since this is a matter architects sometimes ignore, it should be discussed in the building program, where reasonable standards should be established for the filtering system.

In general, three types of filters are used by mechanical engineers: (1) viscous impingement or oil-type filters, (2) electrostatic filters, and (3) dry filters. The first type is little used today and need not be discussed here except to say that it can release droplets of oil into the HVAC system and for this reason is totally unsuited for library and archives applications. Electrostatic filters are effective when operating properly. However, they go out of adjustment easily and are then not only ineffective but also release ozone into the airstream. Since ozone hastens the oxidation and embrittlement of paper, this system, too, must be considered unsuitable for library applications. Dry-type filters use fiberglas or similar materials as filtering media and are available with filtering capacities up to more than 95 percent. Unless otherwise requested, however, engineers generally tend to specify low-rated filters often around 80 to 85 percent. Because they require more energy and thus larger motors and fans to push the air through them, high-rated filters are somewhat more expensive. If possible, however, the college library should require a minimum filtering capacity of 92 to 93 percent, based on the dust-spot test of the National Bureau of Standards. It is highly desirable to filter both the primary air (air coming into the system from the outside) and the recirculated air, which carries in it the dust, lint, dirt, and other particulate matter brought into the building on the clothing and shoes of users.

If it is necessary to settle for filters of less than the capacity recommended above, then the special-collections area, at the least, should be protected with filters of the highest feasible capacity.

Librarians are generally aware of the deteriorative effects of pollutant gases, such as sulfur dioxide, nitrous oxide, and others, but are less familiar with what can be done to combat these insidious components of the air. Unfortunately, although these gases can be removed from the airstream, effective remedies add significantly to the cost of the HVAC system. However, college libraries with long-established collections of valuable materials should include such systems in their planning.

At one time spray systems utilizing alkaline washes to neutralize the acid components of incoming air were used. These, however, were never effective, and because they created corrosion problems are not used today. There are, however, new systems using dry-filtering materials that have been shown to be effective in removing these pollutant gases. In some cases the architect may recommend a gaseous removal system, using activated charcoal. Charcoal, unfortunately, has some disadvantages, not the least of which is the tendency to "dump" the adsorbed materials under certain atmospheric conditions. It can also release fine particles of charcoal into the duct system. It is not recommended for library use for these reasons.

Fire-Protection Planning

Fire-protection engineering is a field of increasing specialization requiring the services of an expert. In addition, the fire-protection system for the college library must meet local fire codes. Finally, it should be noted that no two libraries have quite the same requirements. The long-established library with very valuable collections clearly stands to lose more, for example, than the newer library with less important materials. It should be observed, as well, that the incidence of arson fires has increased dramatically during the past decade. More than one library has had fires set by its own staff. This article does not attempt to make recommendations in this area but only to provide sufficient background information to enable the librarian to discuss the subject in some detail with the architect and other members of the planning team.

A fire-protection system may encompass one or more, usually several, of the following elements:

- Hand-held fire extinguishers.

- Standpipe systems with connected fire hose and fog nozzles--not stream nozzles.

- Sprinkler systems of several types using water as the extinguishing agent.

- Gaseous extinguishment systems, such as Halon 1301 or carbon dioxide.

- Dry-chemical extinguishment systems. ·

- Various early-warning alarm systems.

- Fire walls to contain a fire within a given area.

- Standard alarm systems.

Such elements of a fire-protection system as hand-held fire extinguishers and standpipe systems are usually mandated by local fire codes and will be included in the building plans automatically by the architect.

Selection of the appropriate extinguishment system is a more complex problem. Librarians have traditionally been reluctant to accept the standard sprinkler system because they feared water damage more than they feared fire damage. This is probably not a justified fear, at least in the present writer's opinion, since there is always substantial risk of an uncontained fire devastating large areas of the collection or even the entire building. Indeed, history reveals that many significant collections have been lost to fire over the years. A functioning sprinkler system, on the other hand, will extinguish a fire before it can do serious damage to the collections, while, given today's techniques for salvaging water-damaged documents, the recovery of those volumes that may be wet by water, becomes a much simpler task than formerly.

There are, moreover, several types of sprinkler systems that offer increased protection from any excessive water damage. These include "on-off" sprinkler heads that shut off automatically when the temperature drops below some critical point and dry-pipe systems in which water is not admitted to the lines until the temperature at the head reaches a predetermined point. In such a system the valves admitting water to the heads close automatically when a temperature drop indicates the fire is under control. Dry-pipe systems offer additional safety from water damage as contrasted with those systems in which water is always present, because of the reduced risk of leaking pipes.

In rare-book rooms, where some type of fire protection is essential, sprinkler systems are not advisable under any circumstances. However, two nonwater systems are available for consideration here: carbon dioxide and Halon 1301. Carbon dioxide has been occasionally used in libraries for many years. Unfortunately, this gas poses a substantial danger to personnel because of possible asphyxiation, and it should not be used in any area where this could be a problem. In any such situation Halon 1301 is preferred. Halon 1301, a proprietary product of the DuPont Company, is nontoxic and highly effective in extinguishing fires and thus suitable for the protection of special areas where water could be damaging: rare-book rooms and computer facilities, for example.

Those interested in additional information on the subject of fire protection in libraries should consult John Morris's book <u>Managing the Library Fire Risk</u>. [4]

Planning for Automation

Few college libraries today are without some form of automation, and any new building must certainly be expected to
accommodate additional automated facilities. Planning for
automation is thus an essential part of the process, as important as planning for telephone and electrical services, although made more difficult by the rapidly changing state of
the art. At the same time, the increasing miniaturization
of computer hardware, the concurrent reduction in heat loads
imposed by the equipment, and some simplification in cabling
requirements are making the planning task easier.

Because of the rapidity of new developments, any
specific recommendations made here would likely be obsolete
before publication, but some general suggestions can be offered.

Insofar as possible the librarian should provide, in
the written program, detailed information on the automated
system to be installed in the new building: the type of hardware, head loads, cabling requirements, space requirements,
and other data.

Provision for cabling throughout the building is essential. Today, college libraries may have only a few terminals, probably at the circulation desk. Tomorrow, as libraries automate more of their traditional services and develop new services made possible by the computer, many
additional terminals will be required. When the card catalog goes on-line its place must be taken by terminals which
are connected by cable to the computer. Faculty who were
once satisfied with a cubicle or study equipped only with a
desk, a chair, and a bookshelf will now demand a computer
terminal tied not only to the library computer but to a regional or national networking service to enable them to use
a diverse range of data-bases. Every library service point,
from circulation desk to reserved-book desk to periodical
desk, will need one or more terminals. Key personnel,
from the librarian down, will require intelligent terminals
in their offices or at their work stations, if they are to
work effectively.

Such an array of terminals has significant implications for the building design, since they must be linked by
cables to the computer or computers and, frequently, to an
external network. In most cases a standard underfloor duct

system carrying electrical cables, telephone cables, and computer cables will be adequate. In a few instances, or in some locations, floor trenches or some other cable-carrying system will be required.

With the reduction in size and increasing capacities of hardware, many libraries will decide to purchase their own small computers rather than continue to depend on large computers housed elsewhere on campus. This means that the building must include a computer or machine room designed to accommodate the expected hardware and connected by cable-carrying facilities to all locations where the need for terminals can be anticipated.

Although heat loads generated by today's computers are significantly less than formerly, some additional cooling capacity will be required in machine rooms. Similarly, some computer installations will require special electrical facilities including emergency and uninterrupted power sources. Each of these special requirements should be noted in the building program and necessary space provided even if it is not expected that such facilities will be put to immediate use. Initially, the future machine or computer room can be an extra storeroom, for example. Conduits and ducts can be left empty until needed, or the design can contemplate the use of cable trays above a hung ceiling rather than the more expensive duct system.

Flexibility and the future ease of installation of automated facilities require that provisions be made for these when the building is designed, not after it is completed.

The Design Process

Although the precise steps will vary somewhat, depending upon the architectural firm involved, the design process usually follows an established and logical pattern. It is to the librarian's advantage to know how the architect will proceed.

Under normal and preferred circumstances the written building program will have been prepared, the architect will have been selected (ideally with the help of the librarian and the library consultant), and the other members of the planning team identified.

The building program may be simply forwarded to the

architect with a covering letter, but it is preferable for this document to be presented to the architect at a formal meeting of the planning team. This provides an opportunity for the librarian to introduce the other members of the team, for initial discussion of the building and the basic features of the program, and for the architect to outline procedures and introduce staff members, and for general discussion of the project. At this meeting, or at a similar meeting held soon thereafter, the team will need to visit the proposed site and discuss matters related to the site and the proposed building.

At this first meeting it is important that the librarian (or the chair if this is not the librarian) establish certain ground rules. In such a project it is essential that adequate records of meetings be maintained. Although other members of the team can do this, usually these "project minutes" are prepared and distributed to the members of the planning team by the architect, who has responsibility for the design work.

The librarian will also wish to indicate the responsibilities of the consultant, making certain, for example, that the architect understands that copies of all drawings, minutes, project memoranda, and other pertinent material are to be forwarded to the consultant. The librarian should also establish the ground rules for the procedures to be followed in submitting critiques of drawings to the architect. Most frequently the librarian and the consultant will review the drawings separately, perhaps meet themselves (in person, or by telephone, or letter) to discuss their ideas. This would normally be followed by a meeting with the architect and other members of the team to discuss their comments in detail. It is always preferable for the consultant to present comments in writing. If the consultant finds it advisable in some circumstances to submit comments directly to the architect, this procedure should have the prior authorization of the librarian or the chairperson of the committee, and the librarian (or chair) should receive copies.

One other important aspect of the planning process can be noted at this point. The architect should be required to prepare--in most instances this is normal procedure but needs to be understood--what is usually termed a "Design Summary" for the new building. This document sets forth the basic design features of the building: overall size, general design, building materials to be used, fenestration pattern, criteria for the design of the lighting, air-conditioning and fire-protection systems, and other essential features of the building. While the architect cannot do this until the program has been read carefully and until the building has been discussed by the planning team, it is important that it be completed at a reasonably early stage in the planning.

Basic Steps in the Design Process

Most design work today goes through two stages. The first is what architects call "Design Development." The second is the "Working" or "Contract Drawing" stage. In the design-development stage the architect begins by interpreting the written program in a series of simple line drawings, usually, but not always, prepared at a scale of 1/16-inch to the foot. Such drawings are intended primarily to show the size and interrelationships of the various functional areas of the building. Ordinarily schematic drawings do not show doors, windows, or other building details. Depending on the architect, bookstacks may or may not be roughly sketched, simply to show that it is possible to install all of the required stacks in a given area.

These first drawings are no more than an initial response to the program. The librarian should critique them carefully, have the consultant critique them, and then present their joint findings to the architect and the other members of the planning team. It is not unusual for the architect to prepare four, five, or more sets of schematics, and the librarian should feel no embarrassment at returning the drawings until satisfied. Some few architects will express dismay at having to return to the drawing board more than once or twice, but the librarian should insist that the schematics represent the best initial solution to the program of which the architect is capable. This is not to suggest, however, that no more changes will be necessary or desirable. Frequently, indeed, larger and more detailed drawings will suggest other solutions and improvements.

The next stage in the design process is to enlarge the scale of the drawings and develop them in greater detail. In the usual college library project the next drawing will be drafted at a scale of 1/8-inch to the foot. In some instances the scale will be even larger: 1/4-inch to the foot. In these drawings the architect will begin to show building details: doors, windows, service desks, walls, and other features. Many additional questions will arise here, and it

is in this stage that the review process must be especially
critical. Mistakes and omissions not identified and resolved
at this stage are very likely to find their way into the working drawings, at which point it is difficult and costly to
rectify them.

A major reason for such critical review at this stage
is the frequent tendency of the architect or the architect's
draftsman to make unauthorized changes after some particular feature has been approved by the librarian. If these are
not seen and clarified, they are almost certain to carry
through into the working drawings and the final building.

At the conclusion of the design-development phase it
is normal for the architect to submit the drawings for institutional approval. Before approval a thorough review and
critique is essential. Such approval should be withheld until the necessary corrections are made, although there will
often be pressure for immediate approval. If this is given,
it should be contingent upon the correction of mistakes or
the making of changes at the first stage in the development
of the working drawings.

During the period when the architect is working on
the detailed architectural drawings (1/8-inch to the foot),
engineers will be working on the structural design, the
HVAC, the lighting, and the other engineering aspects of
the building. It is essential that these processes be coordinated with the architectural drawings. In some cases
such coordination is inadequate or nonexistent. This is the
architect's responsibility, and there is little the librarian
can do to ensure that it takes place except to insist on a
report of engineering progress at each meeting with the architect and on regular review of the engineering drawings.

When this close coordination of architectural and engineering work does not take place, strange things happen,
as in the case of the librarian who discovered, almost at
the completion of the working-drawing stage, that the engineering work had not kept pace with the architectural work
and as a consequence a large vertical air shaft had been run
through the center of the loan desk. There is no real excuse for such lack of coordination, but these mistakes will
happen unless the librarian and the consultant (if there is
one) check the drawings at every step of the way.

Once the design-development drawings have been

approved the architect begins the final drawings, sometimes
called Contract, Construction, or Working Drawings. These
will be used as bidding drawings, then by the successful con-
tractor as the drawings used to construct the building. In
most instances the architect will request approval of these
drawings before they are complete. The working drawings
should also be presented for review at several points in the
process.

In the design-development phase the librarian, unless
he or she insists, may see only the architectural drawings
or, at best, only parts of the associated engineering drawings. In the working-drawing stage, however, the architect
will normally make all drawings available for review: architectural, foundation and structural, electrical, HVAC,
plumbing, and all other drawings that will be part of the
final set. These drawings require the same critical review
and attention as earlier drawings.

A few architectural offices follow a somewhat different pattern. In these, the development of schematic drawings constitutes the first phase. The second phase, in which
the drawings are enlarged to the 1/8-inch scale, is termed
the preliminary-drawing stage. The final stage is the
working-drawing stage. More commonly, schematics and
preliminary drawings are combined into the design-
development phase, as described above.

Critiquing the Architect's Drawings

Except for the preparation of a good building-program statement, nothing is more important to the success of the library building than a thorough, detailed, critical review of
the drawings at each step in the process. It should never,
under any circumstances, be assumed that the architect has
understood correctly every detailed requirement of the program, or has incorporated every detail in the drawings. In
fact, every drawing will have some omissions, or mistakes,
or will have additions that are not wanted or needed. To
identify such mistakes the librarian must either learn to
read blueprints, must have a consultant to assist, or both.

As a general rule, architects leave the actual work
of preparing the drawings to a draftsman or a beginning architect. Since such staff members have usually not had the
benefits of discussion with the client or a detailed briefing

on the project, it is not surprising that mistakes occur.
The larger and more complex the building the more mistakes or omissions will be found in the drawings, but the
drawings of smaller buildings will also have their share of
mistakes.   This means that the drawings must be checked
with care and attention to every detail.   Those responsible
for such checking must be able to visualize the building in
three dimensions on the basis of two-dimension drawings.
The reviewer should try to "walk through the building" in
imagination, visualizing every operation and how each element of the building will function.   Such visualization is
generally difficult and comes only with practice.   For some
persons such visualization may be impossible.   Again, a
consultant is essential if the work of reviewing the drawings
is to be fully effective.

Very often the results of such critiques are communi-
cated to the architect at a meeting of the planning team, but
it is better to put comments in writing, not only to provide
a written record for the architect's use but also to provide
a checklist against which to test the next set of drawings.

Space does not permit any detailed analysis or review of omissions and mistakes frequently observed, but the
following are indicative and should be checked in every
drawing:

- Failure to provide adequate or specified space for a
  given function, thus leading to reduced book, reader,
  or staff capacity.

- Failure to lay out bookstacks on proper spacing.

- Omission of essential spaces, not emphasized in the
  program, e.g., janitors' closets.

- Incorrect dimensioning and design of service desks
  and furniture.

- Omission or inadequate designing of facilities for the
  physically handicapped.

- Poor placement of elevators, or their omission entirely.

- Interior doors swinging in the wrong direction.

It will be more difficult for the librarian to identify technical mistakes in the HVAC, lighting, and fire-protection systems.   A good consultant will be helpful here, but even a

consultant of long experience will rarely have the expertise
to detect some omissions and mistakes in the engineering
work.   If there is any question about any of these specialized areas, it is a wise precaution to press the architect
for a detailed discussion or analysis of how the systems
will function.   In some instances, as noted earlier in this
chapter, it may be advisable to have an independent engineering consultant give an opinion.

Conclusion

The planning and construction of a new library, from initial
recognition of the need to completion and occupancy of the
building, is an intricate and involved process requiring the
best efforts of all concerned.   The building can be wholly
successful only if everyone involved performs with intelligence and a spirit of cooperation.   Where personal likes and
dislikes and political considerations enter the planning process, the building suffers.

A library is not, despite the view once expressed by
a noted architect, "the simplest of all buildings on a college
campus to design. "   Indeed, it is precisely the opposite.   In
the necessary and sometimes complex interrelationship of
functional areas; in its specialized requirements for environmental controls; in the need for high-quality lighting in such
diverse functional areas as bookstacks, reading areas, and
staff work spaces; in its need for a design that provides
flexibility, as well as efficient and economical future expansion; in its need to anticipate and provide for technological
developments of the future--a library demands the best and
most creative design talent that can be found.

This article has attempted to provide some basic
understanding of the planning process and to speak briefly
to some of the general problems common to college library
buildings.   How successful a given library may be is the
result of the care and attention devoted to the project by the
planning team.   "In the end, " as one library consultant expressed it to the writer many years ago, "the price of a
good building is eternal vigilance. "   There is no other way.

Notes

[1]Robert H. Rohlf, "The Consultant and the Process," in The Library Building Consultant Role and Responsibility, ed. Ernest R. DeProspo, Jr. (New Brunswick, N. J.: Rutgers University, 1969), p. 68.
[2]Ibid., p. 69.
[3]David Weber, "Research Libraries in the Year 2030," College & Research Libraries News 40 (November 1979): 1.
[4]John Morris, Managing the Library Fire Risk, 2nd ed. (Berkeley: University of California Office of Insurance and Risk Management, 1979).

Selected Bibliography

American Library Association. Association of College and Research Libraries. "Standards for College Libraries"; approved as policy by the Board of Directors of the Association of College and Research Libraries on July 3, 1975.

American Library Association. Library Administration Division, Buildings and Equipment Section. Library Buildings: Innovation for Changing Needs. Proceedings of the Library Building Institute conducted at San Francisco, June 22-23, 1967. ALA 1972.

American Library Association. Library Administration Division, Buildings and Equipment Section. Library Furniture and Equipment. Proceedings of a three-day institute conducted at Coral Gables, Florida, June 14-16, 1962, in cooperation with the University of Miami. ALA 1963.

American Library Association. Library Administration Division, Buildings and Equipment Section. Problems in Planning Library Facilities: Consultants, Architects, Plans and Critiques. Proceedings of the Library Building Institute conducted at Chicago, Illinois, July 12-13, 1963. ALA 1964.

American Library Association. Library Administration Division, Buildings and Equipment Section. The Procurement of Library Furnishings: Specifications, Bid Documents, and Evaluation. Proceedings of the Library Equipment Institute conducted at New York, New York, July 7-9, 1966. ALA 1969.

Bailey, Russell J. "Mr. Architect, Listen," Library Journal 90 (December 1965): 5147-51.
Bennett, P. M. "Users Come First in Design: Physiological, Psychological and Sociological Factors," Wisconsin Library Bulletin 74 (March 1978): 51-58.
Cohen, Aaron, and Elaine Cohen. Designing and Space Planning for Libraries, A Behavioral Guide. New York and London: Bowker, 1979.
Ellsworth, Ralph E. Planning Manual for Academic Library Buildings. Metuchen, N.J.: Scarecrow, 1973.
Ellsworth, Ralph E. Planning the College and University Library Building. 2nd ed. Boulder, Colo.: Pruett, 1968.
Langmead, Stephen, and Margaret Beckman. New Library Design. Toronto: John Wiley and Sons Canada, 1970.
McClarren, Robert R., and Donald E. Thompson. "Architectural Checklist," Library Journal 91 (December 1966): 5832-37.
Mason, Ellsworth. "Guide to the Librarian's Responsibility in Achieving Quality in Lighting and Ventilation," Library Journal 92 (January 1967): 201-06.
Mason, Ellsworth. Mason on Library Buildings. Metuchen, N.J.: Scarecrow, 1980.
Mason, Ellsworth. "Writing a Building Program," Library Journal 91 (December 1966): 5838-44.
Metcalf, Keyes D. Planning Academic and Research Library Buildings. New York: McGraw-Hill, 1965.
Mills, Jesse C. "A Catalog of Misfortunes," Library Journal 92 (December 1967): 4341-43.
Pollett, Dorothy, and Peter C. Haskell, eds. Sign Systems for Libraries: New York and London: Bowker, 1979.
Poole, Frazer G., ed. "Library Furniture and Furnishings," Library Trends 13, no. 4 (April 1965).

CONTRIBUTORS

MARIAN BISHOP is Head of Cataloging at Albion College, Albion, Michigan.

MARTHA COUNIHAN, o. s. u. , is Archivist at the College of New Rochelle, New Rochelle, New York.

PETER DOLLARD is Director of the Library at Alma College, Alma, Michigan.

EVAN I. FARBER is Director of the Library at Earlham College, Richmond, Indiana.

JENIECE GUY is Assistant Director of the American Library Association's Office for Library Personnel Resources.

H. PALMER HALL, JR. , is Library Director of the Academic Library at St. Mary's University of San Antonio, San Antonio, Texas.

KATHLEEN HEIM is a member of the faculty at the University of Illinois Graduate School of Library Science (Urbana), where she teaches Government Publications.

WALTER P. HOGAN is a former small college librarian who has recently become Assistant Acquisitions Librarian at Wayne State University Library, Detroit, Michigan.

FRANCES L. HOPKINS is Coordinator of Reference Services, Paley Library, Temple University, Philadelphia, Pennsylvania. She was formerly at Franklin and Marshall College, Lancaster, Pennsylvania.

SUSAN LEE is Director of the Library at American International College, Springfield, Massachusetts.

CHARLES B. MAURER is Library Director at Denison University, Granville, Ohio.

WILLIAM MILLER has recently been appointed Assistant Head of Reference at Michigan State University, East Lansing, Michigan. He previously served as Reference Librarian at Albion College, Albion, Michigan.

MARILYN MOODY has recently become a government documents librarian at the University of Miami, Miami, Florida.

GEORGE CHARLES NEWMAN is Director of Shafer Library, Findlay College, Findlay, Ohio.

FRAZER G. POOLE, retired from the Library of Congress after serving eleven years as LC's Preservation Officer, is a consultant in the planning of national and academic libraries.

DENNIS REYNOLDS, formerly Reader Services Librarian at Knox College (Galesburg, Illinois), is presently employed at the Bibliographical Center for Research, Denver, Colorado.

D. STEPHEN ROCKWOOD is Periodical and Government Document Librarian at Albion College, Albion, Michigan.

DANA E. SMITH is Acting Undergraduate Librarian at the Undergraduate Library of the University of Illinois at Urbana-Champaign.